Jonathan Edwards and the Enlightenment

Knowing the Presence of God

Josh Moody

UNIVERSITY PRESS OF AMERICA,® INC.
Lanham • Boulder • New York • Toronto • Oxford

Copyright © 2005 by
University Press of America,® Inc.
4501 Forbes Boulevard
Suite 200
Lanham, Maryland 20706
UPA Acquisitions Department (301) 459-3366

PO Box 317
Oxford
OX2 9RU, UK

All rights reserved
Printed in the United States of America
British Library Cataloging in Publication Information Available

Library of Congress Control Number: 2004116505
ISBN 0-7618-3054-5 (clothbound : alk. ppr.)
ISBN 0-7618-3055-3 (paperback : alk. ppr.)

♾™ The paper used in this publication meets the minimum
requirements of American National Standard for Information
Sciences—Permanence of Paper for Printed Library Materials,
ANSI Z39.48—1992

In this age of light and inquiry.[1]

I make it my rule to lay hold of light and embrace it, wherever I see it, though held forth by a child or an enemy.[2]

There is not nor ever was nor will be any man in the world Enlightened but by Jesus.[3]

He was pouring in a flood of light upon mankind, which their eyes, as yet, were too feeble to bear.[4]

---

1. "Freedom of the Will," *Yale Works*, i, 437.
2. "Some Thoughts Concerning the Revival," *Yale Works*, iv, 292.
3. John 1:9, "Blank Bible," *MSS*, Beinecke.
4. Sereno E. Dwight, "Life of President Edwards," reprinted, "Memoirs of Jonathan Edwards," *Banner Works*, i, cxcvii.

Contents

Summary		vii
Introduction		1
Edwards and the Enlightenment		
1	True Salvation	17
	The Gospel Made Real	18
	The Real Gospel	29
2	True Experience	58
	The Sense of True Experience	61
	The Signs of True Experience	65
3	True Reality	94
	The Substance	97
	The Inherence of Perception	101
	Beauty	104
4	True Light	119
	Reason and Revelation	120
	The Light of Nature	124
	The Light of Revelation	131
Conclusion		155
	Edwards Past	155
	Edwards Present	157
	Final Word	162
Bibliography		169
Index		197

Summary

The thesis is concerned with Jonathan Edwards (1703–1758) of New England. It analyses him against the back drop of the burgeoning movement that came to be known as the 'Enlightenment.' In this perspective it is found that Edwards' epistemology, his theology and practice of 'knowing the presence of God,' is particularly important. Edwards is found to be someone who tackled the foremost intellectual and social movement of his day, the Enlightenment, at what he took to be its most crucial aspect, epistemology. The thesis is careful to set Edwards in historical context, and careful to analyse his philosophical and theological relevance. In this junction Edwards is discovered to be someone who actively responded to the most significant movement of his day and sheds enlightenment on our more contemporary assessments of this movement and its effects.

Introduction

"Various tried and proved rules of conduct had already discreetly offered him their services: disillusioned epicureanism, smiling tolerance, resignation, flat seriousness, stoicism—all the aids whereby a man may savour, minute by minute, like a connoisseur, the failure of a life. He took off his jacket and began to undo his necktie. He yawned again as he repeated to himself: 'it's true, it's really true: I have attained the age of reason.'"[1] With such a savour of cynicism, Sartre prefigures what has grown into a substantial stream of modern 'disillusionment' with the culture of the Age of Reason.[2] Many agree that at least the normative epistemological assumptions of our age are under going changes of 'stomach-churning proportions.'[3] While some feel that the ideals of the Enlightenment are on course, there are many who feel that the very core pursuit of the Enlightenment is mistaken, that the question 'Was ist Aufklärung?' itself is imprudent.[4] We are now, it is said, in a post-Enlightenment era. In frustration with sequential methodology's limits to expressions of our profoundest thoughts, some have tentatively begun to search for another way to frame our intellectual endeavours. This is no doubt in part fuelled by cross-cultural scholarly exchange.[5] As we come to admit the validity of non-western modes of thought, so we see weaknesses within our own rich vein of intellectual heritage.

However more is at stake than a mere widening of our means to express thought patterns. Rather it may be based on something akin to a denial of our ability to express truth in traditionally 'enlightened' certitude. Montesquieu could boldly declare that without laws "le monde ne subsisterait pas,"[6] for, "the divinity has its laws, the material world has its laws, the intelligences superior to man have their laws, the beasts have their laws, man has its laws."[7]

Who now would dare to put their name to such a claim, even with relation to the material world let alone to man? But, it was this assertion of the possibility of the extension of empirical analysis from scientific experimentation, strictly speaking, to the anthropological study of man that gave the Enlightenment its shape.[8] Why could not Newton's remarkable successes in the physical sciences via empiricism be translated to a similar success in the social sciences? This was the great dream of the Age of Reason. Locke gave an unwavering answer to the foundational problem of human knowledge: "Whence has it [the mind] all the materials of reason and knowledge? To this I answer, in one word, from *experience*."[9] Epistemological certainty ran into the later psychological declaration that "Everything in man can be reduced to sensation,"[10] and allowed many to expect that dream to be fulfilled.

Yet it is this link in the Enlightenment chain of reasoning that was and is now most in doubt.[11] Perhaps ironically, then, this weak link is that which has had the greatest effects on theology. For in the assertion that all knowledge must be empirical, knowledge of God has been forced into a different and separate realm. As a description of present reality, there can be little doubt that for many 'faith' means not the acceptance of what can be proved but the acceptance of what can not. It is close to the truth, at least, to summarise the broad sweep of our culture in this respect by remarking that, "all this is obvious today and everyone takes it for granted."[12]

EDWARDS AND THE ENLIGHTENMENT

It is in the context of the Enlightenment and our reassessment of it that Edwards is correctly analysed. Edwards, I will argue, was neither ignorant of the process of Enlightenment nor unwilling to interact with it but actively responded to it. A tight grasp of the nature of this 'response' will breathe much needed fresh vitality into the ever expanding organism of Edwards scholarship. This many-headed monster of learning is sometimes profound, often erudite, occasionally exceptional, and as a whole without direction. What is required is a new organising principle upon which the many good studies of Edwards can be hung. As I laboured with the mass of still unpublished Edwards manuscripts it became gradually apparent that not only was this needed, it was evident. The principle of Edwards' response to the Enlightenment will, however, have significance beyond the confines of historiography. It will provide a valuable case study to complement the developments in our understanding of the history of the Enlightenment. It will also be relevant to the contemporary philosophy and theology that in one way or another takes the Enlightenment as its starting point.

A New Principle for Edwards Scholarship

A near truism of Edwards scholarship is that he is in some way or other related to both Puritanism and the Enlightenment.[13] The questions, however, that are often left unasked and always left unanswered are: How? In what way? With what significance for Puritanism? With what significance for the Enlightenment? Around these unanswered questions circles the enigma of Edwards, intriguing because difficult to tie down. Edwards has captivated an extraordinarily varied expanse of scholarship and commentary. He has been analysed as a philosopher, a theologian, a preacher, a pastor, a social theorist, and any number of interdisciplinary minglings.[14] He has been known in work both as a Hell-fire preacher and an artist,[15] in thinking both as a Lockean philosopher and a medieval traditionalist,[16] in character both as a family man and a withdrawn intellectual.[17] While a chronological progression of the dominant arguments can be constructed, and the matters at debate are fairly constant, the picture of Edwards that emerges displays little focus.[18] The many works on Edwards seem to be caused more by a burgeoning fascination with the intricacies of his thought than by heated disagreement over essential issues.[19] The writings cover so much ground that there are now several works of secondary literature just to keep track of the secondary literature.[20] So much has Edwards' scholarship ballooned, that M.X. Lesser records that there have been eighteen hundred books and articles written about him, and this up to only as recently as 1979.[21] Henry F. May inadvertently expressed the atmosphere when he wrote that, "Edwards was *somehow* a great man, whether we admire him most as an artist, psychologist, preacher, theologian, or philosopher."[22]

In researching Edwards' relation to the Enlightenment the aim is not to multiply the celebration of Edwards as 'somehow' great. Nor is it primarily to establish the precise nature of Edwards' intellectual debt to the Enlightenment, whether it be best formed in relation to Locke, or to Berkeley, or to Malebranche, or to the Cambridge Platonists.[23] Each of these linkings have, or have had, eminent proponents.[24] Rather the aim is to explain why he is fascinating, why some think he was a great man. If the nature of Edwards' response to the Enlightenment can be discovered, then I believe we will find a kernel of insight that will provide the necessary explication. The approach adopted here is to draw from the whole body of Edwards' writings, published and unpublished, early and late, and relate the emergent picture of Edwards to his Puritan tradition and the intellectual climate of the age. Lengthy coalface manuscript research (itself not as common in Edwards studies as might be expected) is coupled with work on both Puritanism and the Enlightenment to produce new insight. Thereby it is discovered that an organising principle of interpretation lies in the enigma of Edwards' interaction with the most important cultural and intellectual movement of his time, the Enlightenment.

A Contribution to New Enlightenment Scholarship

Recent developments in our understanding of the Enlightenment help to make such a study possible. A view of the Enlightenment dominated by the thought of certain outstanding philosophers and intellectuals[25] has given way to a more fragmented, pluralist view, hesitant of sweeping generalisations about the so-called 'Age of Reason.'[26] The Enlightenment is increasingly seen not as a set of propositions commonly espoused in a set time period, but as a package of discussions or a "series of debates" which, to be sure, were originally resident in the eighteenth century and argued by certain thinkers but which may be characteristic of other times and people.[27] One can more readily see how Edwards dialogued with such an Enlightenment, than with an Enlightenment that is so defined that it would require drawing connections between Edwards and, say, Rousseau or Montesquieu. Various studies have shown how it may in fact be the peripheries of the Enlightened civilisations, such as the fringes of Europe and America, which were most at the forefront of Enlightenment.[28]

Far away, then, from the intellectual hot house of Paris, on the other side of the Atlantic, Jonathan Edwards was living in the small frontier town of Northampton.[29] Small and frontier the town certainly was, but isolated he was not. In our age of rapid telecommunication it is difficult to appreciate the lengths to which an eighteenth century leader would go to be in contact with the wider world. Such familiarity with world affairs was accomplished firstly though the postal service. It is known that Bengel in Wütternberg wrote about one thousand two hundred letters a year, while Francke had about five thousand correspondents, and was in constant contact with three to four hundred of them.[30] It is startling to realise that nearly all of the major philosophical figures of the day—Montaigne, Bacon, Hobbes, Descartes, Gassendi, Pascal, Leibniz, Malebranche, Locke, Newton, Bayle and others- "were in some form of contact. One can step into this circle almost anywhere and be led around its entirety."[31] Edwards himself was far from unaware of the thinking of these authors. He too was a correspondent, transatlantically with Scottish Christian leaders,[32] but for his early knowledge of the new science he had other sources of information. It was through these other sources by which information was disseminated around the globe that Edwards' first caught new ideas from European waters: not through the time-consuming labour of acquiring books for his own library, significant though that was for his store-house of knowledge,[33] but by way of his reading of learned journals. In this format new ideas were summarised and quickly passed on. "The History of the Works of the Learned," an English periodical that flourished from 1699–1712, the "Nouvelles de la République des Lettres," a journal under Pierre Bayle's editorship from 1684–1687 and that ran until 1718, and others made it possible to gather information on every kind of learned endeavour. It is difficult to know exactly when Edwards first read such journals; we know that Samuel Johnson had amassed copies of some of them by 1726 and that Cotton Mather was familiar with both "The History of the Works of the Learned" and the "Nouvelles de la République des Lettres." At any rate, by 1732 Edwards was referring to Journals in his 'Catalogue.' So it seems likely that by the age of twenty-five he had come across the ideas of all the afore-mentioned thinkers, with the possible exception of Leibniz.[34]

The significance of Edwards' integration with the intellectual cross currents of the Enlightenment is not compromised by the slippery nature of the term itself. 'The Enlightenment' is, of course, a historical construct and not a historical actuality, for the age was only formally designated the Enlightenment in the late nineteenth century, where it became "affixed to a cluster of ideas and attitudes, [and] hence to the writers who embraced and expounded them."[35] However, the term does have accurate historical reference to the age. The Enlightenment was indeed a period of time when the words 'light,' 'enlightened' and 'enlightenment' were used to signify the advance of truth and learning in what we have come to think of as enlightened ways.[36] A similar historical deconstruction as that which might be applied to the Enlightenment age may be carried out on any number of periods of history. What, it might be asked, were the Middle Ages to someone who lived in the middle of them? Or the Dark Ages to someone who was unfortunate enough to be darkened by them? Certainly, one must be careful in employing these academic shorthands, avoiding giving the impression that they have a qualitative and not merely descriptive content to their use. Still, unless they are found to be inherently misleading, these terms are a necessary part of discussion, if only for the sake of brevity. As regards the Enlightenment, there are no doubt misleading connotations given to that description of the period, but yet it seems to the present writer that that period may be helpfully grouped under some such label, and that 'Enlightenment' does indeed represent the self-consciousness of the intellectual thrust of the period. There are enough factors of commonality and linear development within the period to mean that the age as a whole may be thought of as bearing this, albeit developing, characteristic.

Neither is the significance of Edwards' integration compromised by the fact that Edwards did not outlive all the contributions to the chronology normally designated by the Enlightenment. Though by Edwards' death in 1758 the Enlightenment was still waiting for the real sceptical effects of Hume's thought to be felt and for the systematic expression of its philosophy that Kant produced, Edwards was able to respond to the issue at the heart of the Enlightenment 'series of debates.' Edwards was thoroughly acquainted with the Enlightenment, even though he was not versed with everything the Enlightenment thinkers said. For if the Enlightenment discussions had any common ground then it lay in a gravitation to, interpretation of, ability to master or comprehend, those two seventeenth century intellectual giants, Locke and Newton.[37] It was to their impetus that the English as well as the European Enlightenment owed its existence; they to a large extent set the intellectual agenda for the next hundred years. Edwards imbibed both these seminal thinkers and dynamically interacted with their thought. Of Locke Edwards famously remarked that he read him with far more pleasure, "than the most greedy miser finds in gathering up handfuls of silver and gold from some newly discovered treasure."[38] As the influence of Locke and Newton permeates every aspect of the Enlightenment, so it can be felt throughout the work of Edwards.[39]

There are, therefore, no theoretical reasons why Edwards cannot be related to the most crucial issues of the Enlightenment. Hence, it will come as little surprise to find that in practice as well New England, far though it was from Europe, was during and even before Edwards' life time inculcating basic Enlightenment principles. Distance itself was not a barrier to the spread of these new ideas; as is argued above, the miles were spanned by the prevalence of learned journals and the correspondence patterns of intellectuals at the time.[40] Enlightenment influence is not found so much in the presence of specific figures, of French style philosophes or Thomas Paine look alikes, but in the impregnation of the general culture with some Enlightenment assumptions. The education of the elite had become influenced by the Cambridge Platonists towards rationalism, and the churches by Latitudinarians towards heterodoxy, both of which in New England were preparation for and signs of a capitulation to an 'enlightened' type of reliance on reason.[41] It is necessary to beware drawing a straightforward time line from Latitudinarianism to heterodoxy [42]or from Platonism to rationalism, yet it may be that the Enlightenment's growth came as much from changing attitudes within as without the church.[43] A rationalist approach to theology and to the psyche was the thin end of the wedge of the Enlightenment.[44] Together they made sure that at the start of the eighteenth century New England was merrily imbibing the new light.

Recently it has been argued that Evangelicalism was more of a symptom of the Enlightenment than a reaction against it.[45] The interpretation is rooted in an understanding of the importance of the doctrine of assurance for the Evangelical movement and the relation of this doctrine to the empirical confidence of the age.[46] To the extent that this argument is evidence that those involved with religious awakenings on either side of the Atlantic were not all intellectual luddites, and were not all anti-Enlightenment, an understanding of Edwards' relation to the Enlightenment will support the work. His belief in and practice of revival was determinedly doctrinal not only experiential, reasonable and not only emotional, contemporary not only traditional. To the extent, however, that the argument sees Evangelicalism as created by the Enlightenment,[47] then the nature of Edwards' response to the Enlightenment will be seen not to be supportive of such a conclusion. He does not unconsciously mirror the Enlightenment but makes an active, conscious response to it. It is better to picture the Enlightenment as Edwards' springboard, than as Edwards' data source. Edwards does make substantial withdrawals from the Enlightenment bank, particularly the proto-Enlightenment of Locke and Newton, but only to invest in his own, essentially Biblical, view of reality.

A Consideration for Current Philosophy and Theology

There is perhaps no more important task facing contemporary philosophy and theology than a right understanding or re-evaluation of the Enlightenment heritage. As such, the nature of Edwards' response to the Enlightenment may be of no small importance. Studies of the Enlightenment on the historical/philosophical interface have concluded that an appreciation of the Enlightenment is of present value to the philosophical agenda.[48] Perhaps the most influential twentieth century theologian formed his restatement of the traditional Christian faith in the context of a critical reassessment of the Enlightenment.[49] For some the Enlightenment heritage of freedom from 'superstition' and exaltation of rational enquiry is to be embraced.[50] For others the Enlightenment heritage of authoritative claims to universal knowledge and 'metanarrative' is less than attractive.[51] It may be agreed that something in the Enlightenment poses a challenge to traditional Christianity, whether that challenge be framed as the evidentialist challenge or the challenge of historical criticism of the Bible.[52] Apologists of Christianity have responded to this challenge with an acceptance of the cogency and success of the challenge but an assertion of Christianity nonetheless on some sort of 'existentialist' grounds;[53] or with a denial of the success, at least the complete success, of the challenge and the formation of various arguments for Christianity in response;[54] or even with an acceptance of the success of the challenge and a resulting denial of objective truth to Christianity but a continuing assertion of the value of faith to modern society.[55] Recently, there has been an interesting and influential approach, asserting the validity of Christianity on its own grounds and denying the validity of the evidentialist challenge.[56]

Edwards differs from some modern responses to the Enlightenment in, as will be seen, significant ways. His assertion of Christianity is characteristic in holding to the objective as well as the subjective nature of Christianity. It is doctrinal and experiential, true as well as valuable. There is a balance, a certain poise at this juncture in his writings. While Edwards claims objectivity, it is not an objectivity that is mechanistic and rationalistic; he is careful to argue against the materialism of Hobbes and the rationalism of the Deists. While Edwards preaches for experience it is not an anti-intellectual or fanatical experience; he is careful to distinguish his position from the 'enthusiasts' of the Great Awakening period.

If there is a point of commonality with the patterns listed above, it is mainly with the last recorded.[57] Edwards identifies the issue of epistemology as of prime importance in responding to the Enlightenment. More important for him than historical criticism of the Bible (though he does defend the historicity of the Bible), than evidentialist apologetics (though he does engage in natural theology) is what he took to be at the root of these challenges. His aim in response to the Enlightenment is to form a certain spiritual epistemology. His aim is to know and make known the presence of God.

It is well said that Edwards, "was not a storehouse of Truth but a dynamic force that is not yet spent."[58] To our age he offers again his rejoinder to the Enlightenment, that was to hold together rational and spiritual, and so study, write and preach as to convince men and women that the God of the Bible was present. The communication of the presence of God in response to the Enlightenment is the axis around which Edwards' globe spins. Miss that and we miss everything.

A Contemporary Need

Edwards' response to the Enlightenment was far from being a solely cerebral affair. His work was directed at a practical contemporary need. For society was not only intellectually imbibing the 'new light;' there is also evidence that certain sections of it were partaking of a degree of moral looseness not before seen in the 'city on a hill.' There was less concern for Godliness, less concern with pure living; there was in fact a spiritual decline. Harvard is a case in point. There seems to have been a degree of moral looseness as well as doctrinal aberration in this flagship of New England.[59] While some might dismiss the Harvard activities as the misdemeanours of youth, yet men who could content themselves with such moral laxity were not cut of the same cloth as the Mathers, or Ames or Edwards himself. Perhaps it is no wonder that Whitefield found preachers that he judged were without personal knowledge of Christ.[60] Furthermore, even renowned Godly congregations were increasingly finding conversions hard to come by. Stoddard's 'harvests,' his sequences of mini-revivals, were famous, yet at the end of his life it is apparent that much of the fruit had turned to dust.[61] Even under Stoddard's remarkable ministry the new generation were being lost. The need, then, was for an awakening, and Edwards' burden was the same: his work was to revive the work of God and his endeavours to this end are the practical thrust of his response to the Enlightenment.

A common pitfall in Edwards' scholarship is to squeeze most of him into either the spiritualist or the rationalist box; as Joseph Haroutunian remarked, those critics that have been impressed by Edwards' spirituality "have done no justice to his intelligence, and those impressed by his intelligence have been impervious to his 'sense of divine things.'"[62] Even those who have acknowledged Edwards' contribution in both realms, have tended to divorce them within his work. Edwards is seen as rational when writing philosophy, spiritual when preaching and praying. Such a split personality Edwards is created who, it is assumed if not stated, would have been quite different if only he had the benefit of 'modernity.' He is condescendingly eulogised as one who could have been brilliant but sadly left "monuments so crumbled and overgrown;" what wonders he might have achieved, it is felt, if only he had "not been so tightly bound by theological dogma."[63] Edwards himself came across this attitude, writing that "some of these new writers" treat,

". . . these ancient and eminent divines, as in the highest degree ridiculous, and contrary to common sense . . . [but] . . . have allowed that they were honest well-meaning men . . . [and] . . . have allowed that they did pretty well for the day which they lived in, and considering the great disadvantages they labored under . . . living in the gloomy caves of superstition, [but still they] fondly embraced . . . monstrous opinions, worthy of the greatest contempt of gentlemen possessed of that noble and generous freedom of thought, which happily prevails in this age of light and inquiry."[64]

Some find it hard not to look on Edwards in the same way, and extract from him what is palatable for our age and happily ignore what is not: "Exegesis of Edwards has often been its antonym, eisegesis."[65] Edwards must not be divided along the lines of our division. He is rational when preaching[66] and spiritual when philosophising, yet spiritual in his sermons and rational in his philosophy. He has a 'holistic' response to the Enlightenment. And he most usefully interacts with the post-Enlightenment world on his own terms too. His goal is to awaken the work of God by communicating the presence of God; to show God to weary hearts and to weary minds.

This study will examine Edwards' response to the Enlightenment under four chapter sections: True Salvation, True Experience, True Reality, True Light.

NOTES

1. Jean-Paul Sartre, *The Age of Reason*, (New York, 1968), 342.
2. I am referring to Existentialism and Postmodernism. There was, of course, earlier dissatisfaction with the Enlightenment in the Romanticism of the Nineteenth century.

3. Don Cupitt, *The Time Being*, (London, 1992).

4. Kant's famous answer to this question appeared in the Berlin newspaper *Berlinische Monatsschrift* in 1783, and is reprinted in, Jean Mondot, ed., *Immanuel Kant, Qu'est-ce que les Lumières?* (Paris, 1991),71–86. Foucault believes the Enlightenment question itself is unwise: "What is modern Philosophy? . . . modern Philosophy is the Philosophy attempting to answer the question raised so *imprudently* two centuries ago: was ist Aufklärung?" (Michel Foucault, "Was Ist Aufklärung?" *The Foucault Reader*, ed. Paul Rabinow, [London, 1984], 32. My italics).

5. Lamin Sanneh, *Encountering the West: Christianity and the Global Cultural Process*, (London, 1993).

6. Pierre Chaunu, *La Civilisation de L'Europe des Lumieres*, (Paris, 1971), 288.

7. Montesquieu, *The Spirit of the Laws*, trans. and ed. Cohler, Miller, Stone, (Cambridge, 1989), 3.

8. A. Cobban, "The Enlightenment," *The New Cambridge Modern History*, vol.7, (Cambridge, 1957), 91–92.

9. John Locke, *An Essay Concerning Human Understanding*, bk.2, ch.1, (London, 1706), 51.

10. C.A.Helvetius, "De L'Esprit," discours 1, ch.1, *Oeuvres Completes*, vol.1, (1795), 135.

11 Dorinda Outram, *The Enlightenment*, (Cambridge, 1995), 63–79; A. Pagden describes the Enlightenment relationship with 'the other' partly as a search for empirical data for social science study, (A. Pagden, *European Encounters in the New World*, [London, 1993]); Pierre Chaunu argues that Enlightenment certitude is based in pre-Enlightenment belief in divine order, yet it was just this belief that was to be challenged, (Pierre Chaunu, *La Civilisation de L'Europe des Lumières*, [Paris, 1972], 289–291).

12. Don Cupitt, *The Sea of Faith*, (London, 1984), 19.

13. John Opie, ed., *Jonathan Edwards and the Enlightenment*, (Lexington, Mass., 1969). Stephen J. Stein, "Jonathan Edwards," *Encyclopedia of Religion*, vol.5, (New York, 1987), 34.

14. See, for the philosophy angle the seminal work by Perry Miller, *Jonathan Edwards*, (New York, 1949), the works of Wallace E. Anderson (particularly his introduction to *Yale Works*, vi), and Stephen H. Daniel, *The Philosophy of Jonathan Edwards*, (Bloomington, 1994); for theology, Conrad Cherry, *The Theology of Jonathan Edwards: A Reappraisal*, (New York, 1966) and Harry S. Stout, "The Puritans and Edwards," in, *Jonathan Edwards and The American Experience*, ed. Harry S. Stout and Nathan O. Hatch, (Boston, 1981); for Edwards as a preacher, Wilson H. Kimnach's introduction to *Yale Works*, x and xiv; for Edwards as a pastor see P.J. Tracy, *Jonathan Edwards, Pastor*, (New York, 1980); and as a social theorist see Alan Heimert, *Religion and the American Mind*, (Cambridge, Mass., 1966), Gerald R. McDermott, *One Holy and Happy Society*, (Pennsylvania, 1992). Many of these, of course, contain emphases of all four categories, and others beside; for other interdisciplinary minglings see, *Critical Essays on Jonathan Edwards*, ed. William J. Scheick, (Boston, 1980) and, *Jonathan Edwards and the American Experience*, ed. Harry S. Stout and Nathan O. Hatch, (Boston, 1981).

15. For the Hell-fire type see Leslie Stephens, "Jonathan Edwards," *Hours in an Old Library*, (London, 1876), 85–90 (reprinted, *Critical Essays on Jonathan Edwards*, ed. William J. Scheick, [Boston, Mass., 1980), or Oliver Wendell Holmes, "Jonathan Edwards," from, "Pages from an Old Volume of Life", *Complete Works*, vol.8, (Boston, 1889), or V.L. Parrington, "The Colonial Mind, 1620–1800," *Main Currents in American Thought*, vol.1, (New York, 1927), 148–152, 159–162; and as an artist see Edwin H. Cady, "The Artistry of Jonathan Edwards," *New England Quarterly*, (22 March 1949), 61–72, (reprinted, *Critical Essays on Jonathan Edwards*, ed. William J Scheick, [Boston, 1980]).

16. Perry Miller never went so far as to claim Edwards as specifically a 'Lockean Philosopher' and there is danger in creating a caricature of Miller (see Francis T. Butts, "The Myth of Perry Miller," *American Historical Review*, vol.87, no.3, (June 1982), 665–694), though he is normally imputed with having started the modern analysis of Edwards in relation to Locke. Some of his followers became more explicit, however. Morton White, for instance, calls Edwards a 'Lockean Philosopher' in his, *Science and Sentiment in America: From Jonathan Edwards to John Dewey*, (New York, 1972), 35, while John E. Smith gives a more sophisticated rendition of the Miller score with, *Jonathan Edwards: Puritan, Preacher, Philosopher*, (London, 1992), and for a new angle on Edwards the philosopher see Sang Hyun Lee, *The Philosophical Theology of Jonathan Edwards: The Idea of Habit and Edwards' Dynamic Vision of Reality*, (Princeton, 1988); for a general view of Edwards as more traditional see, Alfred Owen Aldridge, *Jonathan Edwards*, (New York, 1966), and, *Jonathan Edwards and the American Experience*, ed. Harry S. Stout and Nathan O. Hatch, (Boston, 1981) for a compilation with a desire to relocate Edwards in history. V.L. Parrington sees Edwards as an anachronism in his, *Main Currents of American Thought*, (3 vols., New York, 1927, 1930). For Edwards as specifically medieval, see Peter Gay, *A Loss of Mastery: Puritan Historians in Colonial America*, (Berkeley, 1966), and Vincent Tomas, "The Modernity of Jonathan Edwards," *New England Quarterly*, 25, (1952), 60–84.

17. For Edwards as a family man see George Perry Morris, "The Human Side of Edwards," *Congregationalist and Christian World*, vol. 88, (3 Oct. 1903), 454; the picture of Edwards as a withdrawn intellectual is still best drawn by Perry Miller: "The real life of Jonathan Edwards was the life of his mind," (*Jonathan Edwards*, [New York, 1949], xi).

18. W.S. Morris' view in his fine 1955 Ph.D., *The Young Jonathan Edwards*, (published, Brooklyn, N.Y., 1991), that debate around Edwards can be schematised as attempts to solve the "cluster of problems" about the relation of theology and philosophy in Edwards' thought, with the solutions themselves reducible to analysis under five overlapping chronological periods of criticism, while still helpful, has been overwritten by the more recent burgeoning of scholarly interest around Edwards. For a summary of the debate see Donald Webber, "The Figure of Jonathan Edwards," *American Quarterly*, 35, (1983), and Daniel B. Shea "Jonathan Edwards: The First Two Hundred Years," *Journal of American Studies*, 14, (1980), 181–197.

19. So the scholarly but disparate anthology, *Jonathan Edwards's Writings*, ed. Stephen J. Stein, (Bloomington, 1996).

20. See the reference works of Clarence H. Faust and H. Thomas, *Jonathan Edwards: Representative Selections*, (revised edition, New York, 1962); M.X. Lesser, *Jonathan Edwards: A Reference Guide*, (Boston Mass., 1981); Nancy Manspeaker, *Jonathan Edwards: Bibliographical Synopses*, (New York, 1981); and specifically for Ph.Ds. see Richard S. Sliwoski, "PhD's on Jonathan Edwards," *Early American Literature*, vol.14, (1979–80).

21. M.X. Lesser, *Jonathan Edwards: A Reference Guide*, (Boston, Mass. 1981).

22. Harry S. Stout and Nathan O. Hatch, ed., *Jonathan Edwards and the American Experience*, (Boston, 1981), 3. My italics.

23. The importance of understanding Edwards' intellectual inheritance is of course not denied. Helpful studies here are: William Sparks Morris *The Young Jonathan Edwards*, (Brooklyn, N.Y., 1991); Norman Fiering, *Jonathan Edwards' Moral Thought and its British Context*, (Williamsburg, Va., 1981); Richard Warch, *School of the Prophets: Yale College, 1701–1740*, (New Haven Conn., 1973); Samuel Elliot Morison, *Harvard College in the Seventeenth Century*, (Cambridge, Mass. 1936); Perry Miller, *The New England Mind*, (Harvard, 1954). For primary literature Edwards' 'catalogue' repays study (reprinted, Thomas H Johnson, "Jonathan Edwards' background of reading," *Colonial society of Massachusetts Publications*, xxviii, [1931], 193-222).

24. For the link to Locke see Perry Miller *Jonathan Edwards*, (New York, 1949); for Berkeley (and Malebranche) see David Levin, "Edwards, Franklin and Cotton Mather: A Meditation on Character and Reputation," in *Jonathan Edwards and the American Experience*, ed. Harry S. Stout and Nathan O. Hatch, (Boston, 1981); for Malebranche see Norman S. Fiering, *Jonathan Edwards' Thought and its British Context*, (Williamsburg, Va., 1981); and for the Cambridge Platonists see Daniel Walker Howe, "The Cambridge Platonists of Old England and the Cambridge Platonists of New England," *Church History*, vol.57, (1988), 470–486, and Emily Stipes Watts, *Jonathan Edwards and the Cambridge Platonists*, (Ph.D., University of Illinois, 1963).

25. Older interpretations are found in Ernst Cassirer, *The Philosophy of the Enlightenment*, (Princeton, 1951); Peter Gay, *The Enlightenment*, 2 vols., (New York, 1966, 1969). Gay recognised a broader Enlightenment but chose to concentrate on the great thinkers.

26. Barth's warning against seeing the Enlightenment in too cyclops fashion as exclusively rational needs to be heeded; there was mystery as well as rationality in the Age of Reason, (Karl Barth, *Protestant Theology in the Nineteenth Century: Its Background and History*, [London, 1972], 36, 37).

27. Robert Darnton, *Mesmerism and the End of the Enlightenment in France*, (Cambridge, Mass., 1968); Alfred Owen Aldridge, *The Ibero-American Enlightenment*, (Illinois, 1971); Franco Venturini, *Utopia and Reform in the Enlightenment*, (Cambridge, 1971), 2; Henry F. May, *The Enlightenment in America*, (New York, 1976); Margaret C. Jacob, *The Radical Enlightenment*, (London, 1981); Dorinda Outram, *The Enlightenment*, (Cambridge, 1995), 3.

28. Bernard Plongeron, "Recherches sur L'Aufklärung Catholique en Europe Occidentale," *Revue d'Histoire Moderne et Contemporaine*, vol.16, (1969), 555–605;

Franco Venturini, *Utopia and Reform in the Enlightenment*, (Cambridge, 1971), 133; Alfred Owen Aldridge, *The Ibero-American Enlightenment*, (Illinois, 1971); Henry F. May, *The Enlightenment in America*, (New York, 1976). Boorstin denied the existence of an American Enlightenment on the grounds of a disinclination to a homogeneous Enlightenment, (Daniel J. Boorstin, "The Myth of An American Enlightenment," *America and the Image of Europe*, [New York, 1960], 65–78). On the broader issue of homogeneity he has been heard, on the specific matter of the American Enlightenment more recent research has overtaken him.

29. Sereno E. Dwight, "Life of President Edwards," (New York, 1829), "Memoirs of Jonathan Edwards," *Banner Works*, i, xxxvii.

30. W.R. Ward, *The Protestant Evangelical Awakening*, (Cambridge, 1992), 2.

31. Norman Fiering, *Jonathan Edwards's Moral Thought and its British Context*, (Williamsburg, Va., 1981), 15.

32. See for example the "letter from Mr. Gillespie, *Carnock*, Nov. 14, 1746" and Edwards' reply of Sept. 4, 1747; also Edwards letters "To the Rev. Mr. M'Culock, of Cambuslang" Jan. 21, 1747 and Edwards' reply to a letter from the same on Sept. 23, 1747, (Sereno E. Dwight, "The Life of President Edwards," [New York, 1829], "Memoirs of Jonathan Edwards," *Banner Works*, i, lxxxiii–xcii).

33. Edwards comments on the new possibilities of book learning, "Those who have not an education in these days may get much by books, which are so common . . ." (no.140, "The 'Miscellanies,' a-500," *Yale Works*, xiii, 297). See also, David Hall, "The Uses of Literacy in New England, 1600–1850," *Printing and Society in Early America*, ed., William L. Joyce, 1–47; G.T. Tanselle, "Some Statistics on American Printing, 1764–1783," *The Press and the American Revolution*, ed. B. Bailyn, (Boston, 1981), 315–364.

34. Norman Fiering, *Jonathan Edwards's Moral Thought and its British Context*, (Williamsburg, Va., 1981), 16–18.

35. John W. Yolton, ed., *The Blackwell Companion to the Enlightenment*, (Oxford, 1995), 1.

36. Varying terminology for the Enlightenment in different countries is not a barrier, (Im Hof, *The Enlightenment*, [Oxford, 1994], 3–4).

37. Dorinda Outram, *The Enlightenment*, (Cambridge, 1995), 40, 56, 120–121.

38. Samuel Hopkins, *The Life of Jonathan Edwards*, (Boston, 1765); reprinted, *Jonathan Edwards*, ed. David Levin, (New York, 1969). The evidence of Edwards' familiarity with Locke in his student years pre-1722 may not be as conclusive as Hopkins suggested, and Miller and others assumed, but Edwards was still clearly influenced by Locke, (Wallace E. Anderson, "Editor's Introduction," *Yale Works*, vi, 17–26).

39. When it is said that Edwards was involved with science and philosophy a right understanding of what this implies needs to be carefully nuanced with an appreciation of the ways these words were used in the eighteenth century. 'Science' was not the discipline of professional empirical analysis that a modern would expect but was used to indicate knowledge; 'natural philosophy' was the term which most closely approximated to our understanding of science, (Sydney Ross, "Scientist: The Story of a Word," *Annals of Science*, vol.18, (1962), 65–86; Geoffrey Cantor, "The Eighteenth

Century Problem," *History of Science*, vol.20, [1982], 44–63; Simon Schaffer, "Natural Philosophy," *The Ferment of Knowledge*, ed., G.S.Rousseau and Roy Porter, [Cambridge, 1980]). Edwards did engage in 'philosophical' thought, both of the natural and more metaphysical sort, but he can only strictly be said to be a philosophical thinker in the Puritan sense of the word. It was never his aim to construct a system of thinking to supplant plain Biblical understanding, but rather to search into the lengths and breadths of human knowledge, into 'philosophy,' confident that therein would be found a description of the activities of God, already asserted in the Bible. Such was the normal certainty of Puritan thought; as Chauncy argued against Dell in 1655, the perfect doctrine contained in Scripture "comprehends the doctrine of God's works, which is called *philosophy*," (Perry Miller, *New England Mind*, [Harvard, 1954], 85). So also would Edwards' 'Ramist' training have suggested to him. Ramus, the founder of a new system of academic curriculum which was reworked by Richardson and Ames into 'technologia' (the "official philosophy of the New England Puritans"), had re-emphasised the Aristotelian definition of art as the practical outworking of science. In this strict sense, though Puritans also referred to art as the sum of knowledge, nature was 'science' for us, it was something to be known, but for God, it was 'art,' something that He did, (Flower and Murphy, *A History of Philosophy in America*, [New York, 1977], 21): "All the arts are nothing else but the beams and rays of the wisdom of the *first Being* in the Creatures, shining and reflecting hence, upon the glass of man's understanding," (Perry Miller, *The New England Mind*, [Harvard, 1954], 180). This was not only true for natural philosophy, but also for the philosophy of the Scholastics and of the pagans, of those eminent Greek philosophers. The Puritan belief in 'common grace' allowed an inherent flexibility to their approach to teaching on secondary matters from pagans and non-Christian sources, knowing that the ultimate source of all good is God alone. For within the Puritan framework God is by definition the gold standard of both morality and the gospel. This was the 'philosophy' that the Puritans were interested in, the whole 'encyclopedia' of the revelation of God, (Flower and Murphy, *A History of Philosophy in America*, [New York, 1977], 20; Norman Fiering, *Moral Philosophy At Seventeenth Century Harvard*, [Carolina, 1981]; Perry Miller, *The New England Mind*, [Harvard, 1954], 90, 98).

40. England and America also had particularly close communication, (W.R. Ward *The Protestant Evangelical Awakening*, [Cambridge, 1992], 33.)

41. See Norman S. Fiering, "The First American Enlightenment: Tillotson, Leverett, and Philosophical Anglicanism," *New England Quarterly*, vol. 54, (Sept. 1981), 307–344; "Will and Intellect in the New England Mind," *William and Mary Quarterly*, 3rd series, xxix, (1972), 515–558; *Moral Philosophy at Seventeenth Century Harvard: a Discipline in Transition*, (Chapel Hill, 1981); S. E. Morison, *Harvard College in the Seventeenth Century*, (Cambridge, Mass., 1936), 554; R.W. Warch, *School of the Prophets: Yale College, 1701–1740*, (New Haven, Conn., 1973),18); David Walker Howe, "The Cambridge Platonists of Old England and the Cambridge Platonists of New England," *Church History*, 57, (1988), 407–486; John Tillotson, *Works*, vol. 2, (London, 1752), 302.

42. There has been something of a reaction against what some have felt is an overtly 'whiggish' reading of Latitudinarianism. For a time Leslie Stephen and Gerald R. Cragg

dominated the interpretative structure, framing Latitudinarians as a staging post on the way to full blown Deism, Arianism, and Atheism, (Leslie Stephen, *English Thought in the Eighteenth Century*, [London, 1876]; G.R.Cragg, *From Puritanism to the Age of Reason*, [Cambridge, 1950]). This hermeneutic was first seriously questioned in H. R. McAdoo, *The Spirit of Anglicanism*, (London, 1965), and more recently in W.M. Spellman, *The Latitudinarians and The Church of England, 1660–1700*, (Athens, Ga., 1993). However, there have been other recent works that, while affirming the theological orthodoxy of the Latitudinarians, see this orthodoxy as invested with an inherent heterodox bacteria that was the germ of later 'free thinking' heterodoxy, (Isabel Rivers, *Reason, Grace, and Sentiment A Study of the Language of Religion and Ethics in England, 1600–1780. Volume 1: Whichcote to Wesley*, [New York, 1992]; Martin I. J. Griffin, Jr., "Latitudinarianism in the Seventeenth-Century Church of England," *Brill's Studies in Intellectual History*, ed. Lila Freeman, vol.32, [Leiden, 1992]). What seems undeniable in McAdoo and Spellman's revisionist critique, is the underlying assertion of the methodological principle of, what might be called, 'non sequitur.' In other words we can not neatly equate a time line with a line of causation; if something is followed by something else it does not, of course, mean that it caused that something else. But one wonders whether Cragg and Stephen really made such an obvious error. Rather the debate seems more fuelled by whether the Latitudinarians are to be *valued* in themselves, or denigrated to the position of causes of which Deism is the effect. It may be asserted that they are to be valued on their own terms, but yet that their particular handling of reason laid themselves and their followers open to heterodoxy.

43. "Put briefly, unbelief was not something that 'happened to' religion. On the contrary, religion caused unbelief," (James Turner, *Without God, Without Creed: The Origins of Unbelief in America*, [Baltimore, 1985], xiii).

44. For Barth it was not biblical criticism but doctrines concerning the will that marked the start of the Enlightenment, (Karl Barth, *Church Dogmatics*, vol.4.1, (Edinburgh, 1956), 479).

45. D. W. Bebbington, *Evangelicalism in Modern Britain: A History From the 1730s to the 1980s*, (London, 1989), 43, 57.

46. A contrary view of assurance is found in, Joel R. Beeke, *Assurance of Faith: Calvin, English Puritanism, and the Dutch Second Reformation*, (New York, 1991).

47. "The Evangelical version of Protestantism was created by the Enlightenment," (D. W. Bebbington *Evangelicalism in Modern Britain: A History From the 1730s to the 1980s*, [London, 1989], 71).

48. Theodor Adorno and Max Horkheimer, *Dialectic of Enlightenment*, (New York, 1971); Jürgen Habermas, *The Structural Transformation of the Public Sphere: An Enquiry into a Category of Bourgeois Society*, (Cambridge, Mass., 1989); Michel Foucault, "What is Enlightenment?" *The Foucault Reader*, ed., Paul Rabinow, (New York, 1984), 32–50.

49. Karl Barth, *Church Dogmatics*, 4, (Edinburgh, 1956–1958); *Protestant Theology in the Nineteenth Century*, (London, 1972).

50. Isaiah Berlin, *The Age of Enlightenment*, (Oxford, 1979), 29.

51. Francois Lyotard, *The Postmodern Condition: A Report on Knowledge*, trans. Geoff Bennington and Brian Massumi, (Manchester, 1984); Richard Rorty, *Philosophy*

and the Mirror of Nature, (Oxford, 1980). Postmodernism is difficult to define almost by definition, (Daniel W. Hardy, *God's Way With the World*, [Edinburgh, 1996], 259), and is an "immense challenge" to the church, (Richard H. Roberts, "A Postmodern Church?" *Essentials of Christian Community*, ed. David F. Ford, [Edinburgh, 1996], 195).

52. Brian Hebblethwaite, *The Christian Hope*, (Basingstoke, 1984), 93–108.

53. Rudolf Bultmann, *Theology of the New Testament*, vol.2, (London, 1955), 250.

54. Paul Tillich, *Systematic Theology*, vols. 1–2, (London, 1951–57).

55. Don Cupitt, *The Sea of Faith*, (London, 1984); Don Cupitt, *The Time Being*, (London, 1992). Cupitt is countered in, Brian Hebblethwaite, *A Defence of Objective Theism*, (Cambridge, 1988); *Ethics and Religion in a Pluralistic Age*, (Edinburgh), 117–136.

56. Alvin Plantinga, "Is Belief in God Properly Basic?" *Nous*, xv, (1981). Since this initial article many works have followed.

57. See Chapter "True Experience" for further discussion.

58. Editorial comment, *Congregationalist and Christian World*, vol.88, (3 Oct. 1903), 454.

59. S. E. Morison, *Harvard College in the Seventeenth Century*, (Cambridge, Mass., 1936), 456–463. Harvard set the tone for New England, (Perry Miller, *The New England Mind*, [Harvard, 1954], 75–76). For doctrine see footnote 41.

60. Joseph Tracy, *The Great Awakening*, (Edinburgh, 1989), 95.

61. *Yale Works*, iv, 146; Sereno E. Dwight, "Memoirs of Jonathan Edwards," *Banner Works*, i, xxxvii–xxxviii.

62. Alfred Owen Aldridge, *Jonathan Edwards*, (New York, 1966), 150.

63. Thomas H. Johnson, "Jonathan Edwards' Background of Reading," *The Publications of the Colonial Society of Massachusetts*, xxviii, (1931), 193–222.

64. *Yale Works*, i, 437.

65. Daniel B. Shea, "Jonathan Edwards: the First Two Hundred Years," *Journal of American Studies*, vol.14, (1980), 181–197.

66. The 'proof' section of the traditional triadic Puritan sermon gave Edwards plenty of scope to reason, (Horton Davies, *The Worship of the American Puritans, 1629–1730*, [New York, 1990], 82).

Chapter One

True Salvation

Edwards' true salvation was proposed as an antidote to the soteriological heterodoxies that were germinating within Arminianism[1] and Deism.[2] When Edwards preached against these two archetypal Puritan foes it was not their doctrinal aberrations with which he was primarily concerned, but the spores of Enlightenment danger that he believed they carried.[3] Edwards' target was not Arminius and the Remonstrance of 1610, nor was it the intricacies of Deistic philosophy. Rather, under both these labels Edwards was aiming at what he took to be the humanisation, the rationalisation, the naturalisation of the gospel.[4] These were the soteriological symptoms of Enlightenment influence with which he was concerned. The substance of Edwards' remedy was a radically God-given gospel, in which justification is by faith alone and it is only a supernatural faith that saves.[5] In other words, the grace of God is the heart of the gospel. Broadly speaking, this understanding of the gospel is traditional, traditionally Puritan and Reformed, traditionally covenantal, and with perhaps minor variations has become traditionally reformed evangelical.[6] What was not normal or traditional about the gospel that Edwards preached was its effectiveness. Few sermons have had such influence as his, or seen such results. It is, then, for some a matter of curiosity, for others a matter of no mere intellectual interest, how it was that Edwards propagated the gospel. What was the message he preached, and how did he preach it? This Chapter will look at his work in relation to mission and revival. Undergirding all is the theme of Edwards the evangelist. And the crucial issue that must be grasped is how the gospel which had been for many true but distant, a theory, became true and present, real.

THE GOSPEL MADE REAL

Historians do not find it easy to explain religious revivals.[7] There is something about a revival that does not quite fit into the neat hermeneutical packages of modern historiography. It could be argued, in fact, that revivals are inevitably ill-fitted to the accepted ground rules of historical debate in the secular academy. For if it must be assumed that, whether one is theist or antitheist by presupposition, discussion of the transcendent is out of court, it may be hard to give appropriate consideration to revival which by its nature is an appeal to such a transcendent. Useful as Freudian, Marxist and Weberian analyses have proved, when employed to interpret revival a somewhat insipid taste has been engendered, as if an essential ingredient were missing.[8] While revivals can be squeezed into the various modern interpretative grids there are usually enough strands that hang out of the mesh to lead to a certain frustration. That most famous of all revivals in the English speaking world, the Great Awakening, seems to exemplify these interpretative complexities.[9]

A common approach has been to leave explanation on one side and construct analysis in terms of effect. So, Parrington described the Great Awakening as having the effect of breaking up the last vestiges of the Puritan order to make way for the rationalism that was to be the future of the American mind.[10] Niebuhr argued that the millennialism in the Great Awakening brought into being a hunger for progress that framed American idealism.[11] Heimert similarly has seen millennialism as enshrining an idealistic idol in the American character, famously arguing the reverse of Parrington, that it was the Awakeners who were progressive and the enemies of the Awakening who were anachronistic.[12] Miller saw the Great Awakening through the lens of his interpretation of Jonathan Edwards, where he claimed to find the signs of a change from a scholastic to a more democratic conception of authority.[13] These interpretations have in common a kind of 'booster rocket' interpretation of the revival, seeing it as a phenomenon that kick started modernity.[14] Be that as it may, they serve little to offer explanation. Another approach, in the search for insight into cause as well as effect, has been an attempt to find explanatory interpretation by implication in description. So in the 'kick start' tradition, Bushman also saw the cause of the revival as a psychological outburst of unrequited guilt stemming from increased prosperity.[15] Gaustad, in a classic study of the Great Awakening, argued against socio-economic explanations of the revival that limited it by area or class, describing it as indeed the 'great and general awakening' that contemporaries called it, though not merely a religious awakening but a movement of the whole culture.[16] Stout sees the awakening as formed by the supreme acting ability of Whitefield, his biography implying that the revival was propelled by Whitefield's dramatising of the gospel.[17] It has even been suggested that the search for explanation itself is mistaken, for the Great Awakening was neither great nor general, indeed the very term 'Great Awakening' should be abandoned because it "falsely homogenises the heterogeneous," it being actually descriptive of widely varying "local events."[18] Ward, on the other hand, sees the awakening as a truly international revival. It may be concluded from his work that the afore-mentioned position is exaggerated.[19] In short, while it could be said that there are illuminating strands of interpretative analysis of effect and description, there is little that amounts to satisfying explanation; it is still true, it seems, that, "what caused this remarkable movement . . . remains one of the most perplexing problems of American History."[20]

In contrast to these interpretations it is suggested that it would be more instructive to see the revival through the eyes of its contemporaries. An approach akin to this is gaining respect in the sociological study of religion.[21] There have, after all, been some for whom the inadequacy of a Freudian paradigm has long been apparent, as the works of James and Jung bear witness,[22] as also does the wry comment that "many modern scholars have no idea what it feels like to perceive holiness."[23] To some extent, every history seeks to be contextual, but the approach being denoted here is to endeavour to be empathetic, to see events as the participants said they saw them rather than as we think they really saw them.[24] So for the Great Awakening, it seems clear, the question that prompted the interpretations of both the leaders and antagonists of the revival was the question of theological origin, whether 'it was of God or not.'[25] If there is, then, to be a remodelling of a contemporary explanation of the Great Awakening the best approach to interpretation will not be in terms of socio-economics, or the dramatic revivalism of its leaders, or the psychological make up of the awakened, but in terms of theology. To be true to the historical context of revival it is necessary to interact with a theological interpretation. To do less is to be at the least patronising and at the worst prejudiced, because an attempt at interpretation without recourse to such a mentality is to fail to take seriously, or to be tolerant of, such a different ideology from that of secular society.

Seeing revival with Edwards' eyes is, indeed, to have a theological vision of the Great Awakening.[26] In fact, revival takes a central place in Edwards' theology. Before Edwards it was unusual so to emphasise revival.[27] More recently revival has fallen on hard times. At the risk of simplification, it seems that it is either regarded as an inexplicable, if welcome, blip in the normal pattern of evangelism, almost as an overheating of the engine of salvation; or as the expected and normal pattern that is evangelism. In both cases revival is peripheral to the core theology. Within the former, more reformed, evangelical tradition it is not unusual to find systematic theologies that have no discussion of revival,[28] and among the latter, more Arminian, evangelicals the concepts of evangelism and revival can become indistinguishable.[29] For Edwards, revival was never so sidelined; it was the primary means by which God carried on his plan of salvation. Edwards had a theology of revival and not just an experience of revival, and his theology told him that revival was integral to God's salvation purpose.

Historically it may be that the results of the Second Great Awakening and Finney's revivals were the most significant factors in causing this divergence of the inheritance of Edwards' theology of revival,[30] but there is also a theoretical dislocation that stems from a misappropriation of Edwards' revival writings. Surprisingly, the essence of Edwards' theology of revival is not found in his works explicitly given to analysing the revival, important as these are to his understanding of spiritual experience,[31] but in his "A History of the Work of Redemption."[32] Here there is some analysis of the experience of revival, but more importantly he describes revival in a way that provides an interpretation of its role. In the process of the work of redemption revival is described as the fuel of God's evangelistic engine. Such a message received great popular acclaim,[33] but it was one which was never easy to congeal and induct into evangelical theology. The work has often puzzled scholars, for Edwards saw it as written in an entirely new method,[34] while for many moderns it seems entirely traditional in the theological vision it gives to history.[35] However, what is new about this series of sermons is the idea of progress that is embedded in its heart, in much the same way that there is novelty in Robertson's "The Progress of Society in Europe."[36] Certainly its history is theological, but that alone, if polemics are to be avoided, can not be sufficient to label it as traditional. It is new in that there is a theology of development to its history. Edwards argues that the "work of redemption" is not merely "by repeating or renewing the same effect" but by many "successive works and dispensations of God, all tending to one great end and effect," it is "like an house or temple that is building," step by step until "all is finished."[37] It is revival that is the key to this development. Revival is central to Edwards' theological vision as it is the progressive force used by God to advance salvation.

Such a progressive view of revival might seem to suggest that novelty for Edwards, whether in experience or theology, was a cause of revival.[38] Indeed, Edwards has time and time again been interpreted as successful because he was ahead of his time, a proto-modern. However, it does seem fairly clear that true doctrinal novelty was anathema to Edwards, and though some of those who argue for originality as the cause of Edwards' effectiveness may believe that he introduced this kind of novelty, there are enough who argue on the other side that Edwards was entirely traditional, to make it highly probable that even if there were minor Edwardean doctrinal innovations, they were not intended as such.[39] Edwards, it must be remembered, was a Bible man, and thus saw any novel interpretations that he may or may not have had as entirely traditional.[40] Such an understanding of novelty is what Reformed theology is all about.[41]

In any case 'progress' is not the dominant interpretative concept that Edwards uses for the cause of revival but for its effects; the cause of revival is rather conceptualised as 'reality.' Progress, in terms of new converts, greater holiness and glory to God, was an effect of revival; the cause of revival was a renewed experience of the presence of God, an experience of God made real. For Edwards, therefore, an 'awakened' experience was the heart of revival, not because that experience equated with the progress of salvation, but because salvation was most likely to occur when the experience of God was most manifest. So it is Edwards' doctrine that, "If ever those that are in a special manner far from conversion are converted, 'tis most likely to be when X[Christ] is extraordinarily present."[42]

Some have argued that Edwards was disillusioned by the effects of the Awakening, by the numbers who seemed to fall away, but while such disappointment in some measure is likely to be true, it is plain in this sermon that from the beginning Edwards made this dislocation between the experience of revival and the progress of salvation, the experience of genuine regeneration or salvation.[43] To be awakened was not the same as to be saved, and the results of awakening might be positive or negative in the life of an individual or Church. Indeed, if someone is not converted when Christ is so present they are likely never to be converted, but rather hardened. He pleads with his hearers, therefore, to be saved, because they have been awakened. See, Edwards urges, "now how X[Christ] is extraordinarily present. what tokens there are. dont you see how X[Christ] is come down. what tokens there are."[44] The 1735 awakening and the Great Awakening both resulted in large numbers of conversions, and Edwards expected awakenings to be 'most likely' to produce regeneration, and thus the progress of salvation, but awakening and salvation were not the same phenomenon. A group could be fully awakened and yet many in that group not be saved, it is by no means everyone in whom, "awakenings seem to have a saving issue."[45]

Because Edwards distanced the experience of revival from the certainty of salvation he was able to feel confident in identifying revival and yet feel that revival was unpredictable. He willingly described particular times as an "extraordinary season,"[46] as "awakenings;"[47] such times as these are "times when God be nearer," not a time of necessary salvation but a time when God is more likely to be merciful, "like the year of Jubilee."[48] Of course, such an experience was something that needed to be tested, as Edwards strenuously sought to do,[49] but revival for Edwards could be at the time known. Still this did not entail a systematic pattern to revival, for as the spiritual temperature was measured by the thermometer of 'extraordinariness' revival could not be ordinary or normal. Edwards put revival at the heart of his theology of God's redemptive purpose but it was not normative in the sense of being predictable. It could not be expected in the course of events or be arranged. When awakening did come the method, the outward form of gospel preaching, was no different but the effect was incredibly greater than before: "The arguments are the same that they have heard hundreds of times; but the force of the arguments, and their conviction by 'em is altogether new."[50] This newness is not new doctrine or new methods, but a new understanding of the old: "Things now look exceeding plain to 'em, and they wonder they did not see 'em before."[51]

In regaining a view of revival as understood by Edwards at the time of the Great Awakening, it is possible to find grist to the mill of scholarly interpretation. First, historical analysis would benefit from the increased degree of empathy for the essentially theological nature of the revival debate in this period. Secondly, Edwards' view that revival was marked by the gospel becoming real, the presence of God becoming known, in the experience of individuals and communities, makes it plain that he recognised the psychological element of revival. It was not doctrine but experience of doctrine, a psychological 'owning' of teaching, that caused the revival. In other words, his theological interpretation need not exclude the psychological, nor vice versa.

The Return to Reality: Preaching

How, though, was revival, this reality, the experience of the presence of God appropriated? In one sense, such a question seems unwise. Not only because of Edwards' Calvinistic theological framework but also because, as argued above, he did not introduce new doctrines or methods *per se* into his revivals, rather self-consciously seeking to re-establish the old. So his famous "Justification by Faith" sermon, which, if we are to take Edwards' word for it, was the harbinger of the 1735 awakening, was a deliberate re-iteration of the historic reformed understanding of justification as against the perceived Arminian novelty.[52] However, to see Edwards as entirely traditional at this point, as only using established preaching methods, is to make a serious mistake. For Edwards is novel in his application of his own epistemology of spiritual experience to his revival preaching. It is his principle that intellectual faith alone is insufficient, that conviction of sin always precedes true saving faith, and that this is manifested in an experience of God's reality, which elsewhere he calls the sense of the heart. Edwards understood that humans needed to be awakened to a consciousness of their need before they were converted, and that this was possible in the unregenerate due to human conscience.[53] Such an understanding of preaching was by no means commonly accepted, "I know it has long been fashionable to despise a very earnest and pathetical way of preaching; and they only have been valued as preachers, that have shown the greatest extent of learning, and strength of reason, and correctness of method and language."[54] His aim, rather, was to preach so that people, "in some measure feel the reality and weight of eternal things."[55]

In Edwards' unpublished sermons, there are many examples of Edwards practising the preaching of spiritual reality. The most insightful of these is a group of thirteen sermons preached on the parable of the sower, with a core series of six that might be entitled the "Sower Series," which combine a unique combination of both practice and explanation of the preaching of spiritual reality.[56] The "Sower Series" was preached first in November 1740, during the build-up to the Great Awakening, and then again in April–May 1756, probably to the English congregation at Stockbridge.[57] They are marked by a profound analysis of that which may hinder human hearts from being 'good ground.' Few passages did Edwards preach so often upon. He returns to the Sower over and over again to gradually establish what it is that causes an awakening experience of the reality of spiritual things, of the reality of hell, of God, of salvation by faith alone, to be experienced and what it is that causes these things to result in genuine salvation or to prove worthless and result in damnation. It is in such descriptions that Edwards is most powerful as a preacher. He aims to read the very heart as he speaks, attempting to describe the intimate workings of the human psyche in relation to God. All of the series is a sustained call for revival, it begins with news of a great work of God from a distant shore, ends with the acknowledgement that some promising growth can be choked by the worries of this life, and through it all urges for preparation of heart through prayer and a removal of worldliness. Indeed it is worldliness that appears as the besetting sin, not of Northampton alone, but of all who refuse to hearken to the word of God. So it is that Edwards shows his aim to bring the transcendent into the immanent, through removing distant Deistical notions of God, encouraged by a too great love of possessions, by heart preparation to experience reality in the presence of God.

Sermons one and two, originally preached on the same day,[58] are intended to make spiritual breakthrough. It is true, he argues in the first sermon, that the preacher is to be a faithful sower and "leave the event with God" yet of "late years" this preacher's hearers have not been like soil but "frozen ground" from which the word has "rebounded as from a rock."[59] The people need to fulfil their role, to be prepared to hear. Preparation is prayer and a "behaviour answerable," which for Northampton means removing "our pride our affecting to adorn our selves with Gay clothing & keeping up two parties as we have done in this Town year after year."[60] The special preparation

Northampton needs is to stop squabbling and be at peace. If this is done, which though difficult is possible "we may have the blessing of G[od] with us" which is the experience of "the Presence of G[od]."[61] The second sermon is an epistemology of satanic influence. Satan has some "invisible influence" that hinders impressions being made however powerful the preaching. Even in the midst of the most solemn assembly many have some object brought into their view that keeps them from concentrating, so that they, "are at that very Instance spending their time in wallowing in the mire of some Lust." In his most frightening mood, Edwards applied the doctrine to the unregenerate children present, "in the week the devil is with you here at meeting & the devil is with you at home when you lie down on your beds . . . he catches away the word & persuades you to sin for that End that he may bring your soul to hell when you die."[62]

Having thus made some impression Edwards next seeks to show what kind of impression he wants. It is not (sermon three) of a heart which is still like a rock but with just a "thin covering of earth;"[63] nor (sermon four) is it a sudden conversion, which is "very often false;"[64] nor (sermon five) is it that which is only "superficial impressions."[65] Even when it is the right kind of impression, it still may be (sermon six) "choked" by the thorns of worldliness, the same thorns that hindered the original impression.[66] What, then, is the result that he does want? First, he wants hearts that are not hard as rocks, but softened. By this he means those whose joy primarily stems not from what they get from God but from a love for God. Hypocrites, that is those who are self-deceived in their confession either deliberately or subconsciously,[67] are those who have "a kind of love to X[Christ] but 'tis only as they conceive of him as making much of them." A "true saint," that is regenerate, is one who "Rejoices in the Glo[rious] things of the Gospel as Glorious in thems[elves]," whereas, "the Joy of the stony Ground hearers is Joy in hims[elf] and not Joy in G[od]."[68] Secondly, such a true love for God is preceded by conviction of sin. It is rare, though not impossible, for there to be a quick conversion because there must be such conviction before conversion. This is a general rule that holds except in "Times of Extraordinary Pouring out of the Sp[irit]" which "are Exempt." It is God's way to make use of the means of grace, so it is God's "more usual manner to make use of this means . . . Earnest seeking salvation." Actual conversion is not a process, but at God's command as in the beginning "God said let there be light and there was light in a moment," but still the heart needs to be prepared for conversion by conviction of sin, which normally arises from an extended period of seeking.[69] Thirdly, Edwards looks for deep roots, not superficial impressions. Those impressions that are merely superficial are found out by the trial of suffering and the trial of prosperity, they die for "want of rooting." Those with deep roots are marked by a "thorough conviction of the understanding" and "a change of nature" which are more than mere superficial emotions.[70] Finally, Edwards sees that the reason why impressions do not last is because the ground was insufficiently prepared for the seed. Thorns of worldliness, that is in Edwards understanding not desire for wealth but a priority desire for this world rather than the next, grow because the "ground of the heart" has not been ploughed "1. By being convinced of sin . . . 2. By being convinced of the vanity of the world," in which together "consists the Great duty of self-denial."[71]

Spiritual reality is, then, that which Edwards seeks to impart to his hearers. It is, in fact, the lack of such reality that causes people to take no notice of the danger of hell. Edwards argues in an unusually powerful sermon that, "The reason why men no more regard warnings of future punishment, is because it dont seem real to them."[72] Taking his text from Genesis 19:14, where Lot warns his sons-in-law of the coming judgement to Sodom, "But he seemed as one that mocked unto his sons-in-law," Edwards attempts to establish what it is for something to seem real to one, why spiritual things do not seem real, and then finally so to describe punishment as to make it seem real. He argues that there are "these two things in realizing a thing," that is "believing the truth of it," and "having a sensible idea or apprehension of it."[73] The cognitive, believing, side to something seeming real needs to be not merely by education or example of others who believe it; this is only believing "as the Papists do transubstantiation and purgatory: because so their fathers believed, and so the church believes." Really to believe something it needs not to be just from "universal custom" but from "evidence shown to their minds." To explain the subjective side to this second element, that is the 'sensible idea,' Edwards compares the difference in impression that we have from seeing a man to the impression we have when we are told of him or see his picture. It is the former that he describes as the "plain and sensible idea," so some form of immediate apprehension is that with which he is concerned.[74] For something to seem real it needs to be directly perceived. Of the three hindrances Edwards believes inhibit perception of the spiritual, it is the diverting habit of only taking the physical as real that most concerns him, for when he goes on to show that future punishment is indeed real, having given evidence to encourage reasonable belief, he concludes the sermon with the terrifying proposition: "that you may have a more lively sensible apprehension of this punishment, I'll endeavour in some measure to describe it to you."[75] The description that he gives is an attempt to make the spiritual come alive to those who are bound by habit to the realm of the physical. As one of the preeminent examples of Edwards preaching of spiritual reality it is worth quoting at length.

The devil thirsts for the blood of souls . . . as soon as ever the man is dead, God restrains him no more, but then these hell hounds fly upon their prey, these roaring lions dare then lay hold as it were with open mouths . . . then the soul is immediately hurried down to hell, a certain place of misery . . . In that place God has some way of dreadfully expressing his wrath . . . We don't know exactly how it is, but we know it is compared to fire . . . The wicked soul will be tormented by devils. . . .[76] There will be [no] help to be had. We are taught that there won't be allowed one drop of water to cool their tongue. . . . They won't be able to help themselves. They wont find any friend that will be able or willing to help 'em. They wont have any God to go and cry to . . . God will cast them out of his presence . . . They will know that it will be so forever . . . Therefore I shall close the Use with an exhortation not to disregard the threatenings of future punishment, but to realize it to your self; and take care now in this only opportunity to escape this punishment, and let nothing, no worldly business or pursuit, divert you from this great concern.[77]

With such emotive language Edwards sought to bring the spiritual into the realm of sense, by an understanding of both thinking and feeling, that was the sense of the heart.[78] Some may take this kind of preaching to be theological terrorism. It is to be remembered, though, that Edwards believed in the utterly awesome reality of hell. As such his words may be excused on the lines of legitimate warning. Sinners may not be able fully to understand the fate that awaits them, but even so it is imperative that they feel its danger to an appropriate degree.[79] There is no doubt a medieval tinge to the description of hell, which more modern theologians may believe to be an illegitimate inference from Scripture. Yet the physicality of his description of hell underlines his general desire to release his hearers from a preoccupation with this physical world so that they can see the reality of the spiritual: he urges his hearers to "realize" this description to themselves.[80] It was not only fear that people felt when so awakened, but love and joy and the whole range of human responses to the experience of God.[81] Such experience was the heart of the revival: "Men and women of all ages and descriptions felt themselves to be in the presence of God."[82] It was this that characterised Edwards' preaching, he was "a preacher . . . looking and speaking as in the presence of God."[83]

The Return to Reality: Praying

One debate that rages over revivals is that which centres on the comparison of the Great Awakening, a 'revival,' with what is sometimes called the 'revivalism' of Finney.[84] Edwards certainly had a different theology of revival to Finney. As revival was in the hand of the sovereign dispensation of God, there was no method that would guarantee revival.[85] But there were methods which

Edwards encouraged his congregation to pursue in order that revival might come. Principally that of prayer, and the associated ways of seeking blessing from God, fasting and repentance from sins. Some great nonsense is spoken about Edwards and prayer. It has even been said that Edwards, "explicitly denied the efficacy of petitionary prayer to bring about external change in the world."[86] Some histories of Edwards' 'international concert of prayer' may inadvertently suggest that it was a theological innovation against the puritan simple 'waiting' upon God,[87] and that previous to this Edwards had, like other puritans, so believed in the sovereignty of God that praying for blessing was not part of their piety. To the contrary, Edwards, and other Puritans before him, prayed not in spite of but because they believed in a sovereign God. What was the point, a Puritan would say, of praying to a God who was not sovereign? Certainly a fatalistic interpretation of predestinarian theology would tend to mitigate against a piety of prayer, but a predestinarian theology can incorporate prayer because prayer, like preaching, can be seen as a means of grace. Prayer need not be a denial of God's electing sovereignty because prayer can be the means that God has ordained for his people to be blessed by him.

Such is Edwards' view of prayer. He teaches that prayer is God's sovereignly ordained means to blessing. In an undated sermon on the text of Jacob's wrestling with God, he argues that "The way to obtain blessing of God is not to let God go except he bless us." They are to seek blessing with all their might, they "must do something to answer his [Jacob's] wrestling." But a 'violent seeking' is not contrary to the sovereignty of God, for God is not sought so that he be made willing, rather "God is willing to bless his people which is why he stirs [th]em up to wrestle for it." In other words, if one is seeking God in prayer it is a sign that God will answer the prayer in some way or other, for it is God who causes the prayer, and his design must answer some end. What, though, is it that makes prayer the means to God's end? Edwards' answer is that prayer's distinguishing significance as a means is the effect that it has on the person who prays not the effect that it has on God. Prayer as seeking for blessing puts the seeker in a "suitable disposition" to receive the blessing. The person becomes aware of sin, aware of God as the author of the blessing, humble and thankful. The sermon concludes with a confident assertion of the effectiveness of prayer, in this instance prayer for conversion, when it is accompanied by this suitable disposition: "God is Ready enough to bestow the blessing upon you if you would but seek it with suitable earnestness & resolution."[88]

It is within this theological framework that Edwards believed it appropriate to pray for revival. History records that before the Great Awakening came to Northampton Edwards counselled his people to seek a similar awakening blessing to that which they had had recounted to them from other places, and to pray for the Spirit to be 'poured out.' First in a sermon in August 1740, Edwards uses the example of the way that God was working elsewhere through George Whitefield to stir up the young people to seek a similar awakening: "on this occasion I will tell you what account the Rev. Mr. Whitefield has given me in a letter that I received from him this week past. The minister that you have doubtless heard of that has had such great effect in many Places. I will read a passage of his Letter that he sent me [letter not recorded]. Let such a wonderfull w[ork] of G[od] on Chil[dren] in other places stir you up Earnestly to seek G[od] that you may partake of the same blessing."[89] Then in November 1740, as it seems on the eve of the Great Awakening coming to Northampton,[90] Edwards preaches at a "Fast for the pouring out of the Spirit," with the doctrine that, "Of the more excellent nature any blessing is that we stand in need of the more ready God is to bestow it in answer to prayer." Evidently Northampton had slipped into a dire spiritual state after the 1735 revival. A "Great part of you Professed to have been converted a few years ago," but since then there has been a spiritual famine,[91] "here we have been in groaning circumstances in our souls in pinching want of supplies year after year." What most worries Edwards is that there has been no "concern," no active seeking for revival in the town at this dire state of affairs. The people had been very active "about a market for our Cattle" and "we have bestirred our selves about our Inner Commons," but the one thing that has caused no action is the spiritual demise: "we have not stirred up our selves to Lay hold on G[od]." It is prayer seeking for the blessing of revival that Edwards desires, for the second "use" that he derives from his doctrine is, "to Exhort Gods People in this Town Earnestly to cry to G[od] for the Renewed Pouring out of his Holy Sp[irit] upon us." Indeed, with the confidence that comes from his theology of prayer, he teaches that if they really seek and not only in pretence, then "I am bold to say that G[od] is now offering this blessing of his holy sp[irit] to this Town & I am bold to say we may have it only for asking."[92] Such is the significance of prayer for revival for Edwards.

However, the prayer that Edwards sought to encourage was not only for the blessing of revival. As a part of his regular ministry he was beseeched with prayer requests to be brought before the congregation to intercede on behalf of individuals and families in the church. One of the most moving parts of Edwards' Manuscripts is the notebook that he entitled "Q", not for the theological questions that the book contains (enlightening as they are), but for the note paper that he chose to write those questions upon. Here is recorded for posterity sheet upon sheet of prayer requests from ordinary members of his congregation.[93] The handwriting is often bad, the grammar worse, but the sentiments expressed reveal a community of mutual concern, and of belief in the power of prayer. A certain "Ebenezer miller and his Children desire the prayers of gods poopel for his wife and their mother that is bereved of her understanding that god would restore her understanding to her again if it be his will if outher wayes fit them for his holy will;" and "Benjamin Bartlett Desires the Prayers of the Congregation for his youngest child that is Dangerously sick that god will be Pleased to Direct to & Bless means for its restoration if it be his will;" one week we hear of "Daniel Strong" needing prayers as having "the Bladey flewe," a little later that "the widow Sarah Clark & Caleb Desire prayers that God would sanctifie his Holy awful Hand in taking away their Relative Daniel Strong by Death" so that it "might work finaly for their spiritual and saving good." Northampton was a real world, and sometimes a sad world. Prayers were met with joy and tragedy, but whichever the people plainly believed in the power of prayer to effect reality, physical and spiritual.[94]

THE REAL GOSPEL

Edwards, though, was not concerned with 'spiritual reality' in a vague or mystical sense. Mysticism could be something of a danger for Puritanism influenced by neo-platonism.[95] An emphasis on experiencing the presence of God had led to surprising places in the past. The seventeenth-century English mystic Everard, for instance, sounds genuinely Edwardean when he asserts that God, "is the Motion and being of everything."[96] But for Edwards experience and doctrine were united, for a "minister of the gospel" must be "both a burning and a shining light."[97] When these two combine subjectivism is sidestepped for there is a mutual testimony to each other's truth, "it shows that each is genuine . . . and that both are divine."[98] The gospel doctrine that he preached was by and large the traditionally reformed doctrine of *sola scriptura, sola gratia, sola fides, soli deo gloria*. "Justification by Faith Alone"[99] might be seen as a defence of the middle two slogans, "God Glorified in Man's Dependence"[100] could be seen as a defence of the last, and the first slogan was the assumption of the careful exegesis of all of Edwards' sermons. Whatever the novelty of his arguments for these doctrines, the emphasis on union with Christ in the former sermon[101] and the use of Lockean terminology in the latter,[102] the position that they are defending is traditional, or rather Biblical as Edwards would insist. So his grandson wrote of him that, "It was the glory of this great man, that he had no love for innovation . . . To the Scriptures he yielded the most profound reverence and the most implicit confidence."[103]

Edwards' doctrine, however, has been seen to contain novel emphases. The secondary literature has focused on his covenantal or federal theology, or rather the seeming lack thereof.[104] It was Miller who first argued that Edwards "threw over the whole covenant scheme,"[105] bringing Puritanism back to the pure God of Calvinism, which for Miller was a God entirely arbitrary in the work of salvation. In a milder form the figure of Edwards the anti-covenantal theologian remains assumed in some general works,[106] though it runs counter to the most intricate studies of Edwards' covenant theology, and is based on at best an imbalanced understanding of the concept of federal theology.[107] Edwards, to be frank, uses the language of the covenant everywhere. There is an individual covenant. He explains that "all visible X[Chris]tians do enter into these Covenant Engagements wherein they engage to give up their hearts to J[esus] X[Christ]."[108] He holds to "the Cov[enant] of works as well as the Cov[enant] of Grace."[109] There is a church covenant, to which Edwards turns when trying to maintain the momentum of the Great Awakening in Northampton: "In the month of March [1742], I led the people into a solemn public renewal of their covenant with God," a written promise of repentance to God "on a day of fasting and prayer for the continuance and increase of the gracious presence of God."[110] Scholars now recognise that Edwards also held to a national covenant.[111] The covenant is not only for the more erudite world of Northampton but is basic to his fundamental understanding of the gospel. So even when he is constructing a testimony to be given of the essentials of the faith, spoken by the most uneducated, the covenant is still the organising principle that it was for earlier Puritans. In Edwards' hand and under his tutoring there is recorded the "Profession of Faith" of two Stockbridge Indians, Cornelius and Mary Munniwaumimmich. They described their conversion as when they, "entered into a Covenant of Life with Him" and committed henceforth "to comply with my part in the covenant."[112] To that even John Preston would have added his 'Amen.'[113]

The Return to Reality: Faith

What, then, makes such an anti-covenant view of Edwards attractive? For one thing it does suggest an appealingly compact interpretation of Edwards' success, seeing his effect as based in new doctrine rather than a renewal of old doctrine. Furthermore, it does form a framework for the apparent Edwardean stress on the sovereignty of God, seeing its starkness in the removal of the covenant. But its enduring attraction, in the face of work on primary materials to the contrary, seems to stem from a confusion of Edwards' complex notion of faith.

Along with the covenant, a trinity of debates circle around the disputed question of Edwards' novelty, all rooted in this faith. The debates interweave: the covenant is tied to preparation for salvation, which in turn is bound to the nature of the church. The linking factor is faith, the promise of salvation to those who believe (the covenant debate), the way of salvation to those who want to believe (the preparation debate), and the means of salvation to those who do not believe (the church debate). Some things about faith are clear: it is not merely 'notional' but also 'experimental,'[114] it is not salvation's condition but salvation's means.[115] However, both these elements are blurred by Edwards' belief in sinners' 'preparation' for salvation, and the fog that surrounds the nature of the church called the 'Communion Controversy,' the Eucharist argument. Edwards seems to be preaching a gospel where sinners are encouraged to seek salvation not accept salvation, and where the Church is a communion of saints not sinners, that is of the saved not of the seeking.[116] The potential in a society of nominal Christianity for explosive division is obvious, and history records the tale of such division. But there was also potential for explosive growth, as history also records.

The element of 'seeking' was one area where the emphasis accorded by Edwards was unusual. Gerstner carefully argues that the otherwise traditional evangelistic message of Edwards was set apart from other Calvinistic theologians by two matters, of which the 'seeking' method of evangelism was the more important.[117] Edwards holds that sinners while not willing to be saved have an ability to be prepared for salvation. There is not just a physical ability that makes a sinner as capable to hear the gospel as to hear a play, but there is also a moral ability, the conscience, which enables the sinner to feel her sin. This use of conscience stems from his Stoddard-like understanding of the effects of the fall.[118] For Edwards, all that was withdrawn from humanity after the fall was original holiness, and it was this lack that effected reason, though reason itself remained the same: "tho after the Fall he had Reason & Mind left yet that without Holiness does man no Good." [119] He is not denying the doctrine of total depravity, "all the faculties of the soul" were "darkened," but for this darkening all that was needed was the removal of God's Holy Spirit, for once this is removed man's "self love . . . will have all the Effects that Lust can have when once God sp[irit] is gone & ceases to . . . guide these Principles."[120] Therefore sinners were able to obey the law even though they were not, and but by grace could not, be willing to obey. This meant that Edwards' counsel to sinners to seek salvation is not counsel to salvation by works but counsel to realise that salvation cannot be gained by works. He encourages the seeking of salvation because, "God is ready enough to bestow the blessing upon you if you would but seek it with suitable earnestness & resolution;" it is the work of such earnest seeking not to make God willing to give it, but to put the person in a suitable disposition to receive it.[121] By encouraging preparation for salvation, Edwards, then, is not looking for faith that is mental assent to the doctrines of the gospel; nor is he looking for faith that is simple human trust, a wilful personal choice of the gospel. He is looking for something that has no natural residence in the human psyche at all, and it was the work of preparation to wean the human soul off such natural faith.

It is in response to Stoddard's understanding of preparation and its role in conversion that Edwards sought to establish his own doctrine. The Miscellanies record Edwards' developing thought on preparation under the notes entitled, 'Conversion,' 'Preparation,' and 'Humiliation.' Where Edwards gradually differs from Stoddard is not in believing that preparation is non-Biblical, but in holding that such preparation is gracious and not natural.[122] First he argues that the essential element of faith is the "disposition" to believe, even if the act of faith has not been realised, for otherwise what would happen if someone died while not in the actual exercise of faith? How else were the ancient Jews saved, who could not themselves 'believe on Christ?'[123] Secondly, he shows that as in human psychology, "There must be the principle before there can be the action," so there must be "a principle of holiness before holiness is in exercise." This principle of holiness can be from nothing but Grace, so that "sanctification must be in the soul before one of them [conviction, faith] is in the mind," which means that Edwards' theology of preparation is that Grace must come before faith.[124] By the end of 1727, he has formulated his permanent position on preparation, which is that while preparation is the normal pattern of God's work of conversion, for it suitably prepares the soul, it is not a rigid method, and that preparation itself is not natural but a work of Grace.[125]

The significance of these distinctions may be hard to grasp. There does seem to be something of the hair-splitting, logic-chopping, angel-counting scholastic theology to them. In fact, though, the result of these distinctions is crucial, and crucial to Edwards' doctrine of faith. By asserting pattern as against method, Edwards freed grace to be operative in a variety of ways to a variety of personalities, yet all according to the gospel analogy.[126] Edwards does not believe in 'steps to salvation' in any determinative fashion, but rather a pattern that is descriptive of God's normal way of acting.[127] In insisting on the graciousness of preparation, he inserted a bulwark against Arminian salvation by works. One could not prepare one's self. While in one sense it could be said that the operation of grace in preparation meant that the elect were saved before conversion,[128] they were certainly not converted before conversion, and therefore the field of preparation was the unregenerate heart. It was the work of God to make use of unregenerate conscience, not the work of man, the preacher or the hearer, to endeavour to work out salvation. Faith and the prepared disposition to faith were supernatural. Miller and others have argued that the apparent tendencies to salvation by works that crept into the practice of some New England puritans at this time stemmed from covenant theology, and Edwards released grace by removing the chains of the covenant.[129] It seems, though, that it was not covenant theology in principle that may have smoothed the path to salvation by works in preaching and practice, but a certain understanding of the particular doctrine of 'preparation.'[130] If preparation was not an act of Grace then it was a human act, a work of salvation. Edwards did not respond by removing preparation from his theology, but by making it gracious; as it has been said of another, earlier, Protestant, he sought to "rescue salvation by grace from . . . a system he believed promoted works-righteousness at the expense of God's glory."[131]

Many modern evangelicals have wished to distance themselves from any notion of 'preparation for salvation,'[132] seeing it as both denying the balance of God's sovereignty and human responsibility that they see in the New Testament, and as tending to a denial of the practice of the offering of the gospel as immediately available. Edwards' sermons often end with a call to 'seek salvation' not with a call to come to Christ, and here evangelicals squirm. Did not Christ himself say, 'come to me all you who are heavy laden and I will give you rest'? Edwards, it is my belief, did also see an insufficient quality to preparation theology, but only when it was held to be in the power of the person to be prepared. Gracious preparation he supported.

A redefinition of preparation, though, was not enough for Arminianism to be uprooted from the Puritan soil. There must not just be a change in the theory of grace there must also be a change in the institution of grace, in the means of grace as commonly practised in the church.

The communion controversy, therefore, provides another angle of insight on Edwards' understanding of faith. While the controversy was no doubt to a large extent enflamed by social changes and family quarrels surrounding Edwards,[133] it was not sparked off by them, for Edwards, in limiting communion only to those who could make a profession of the experience of grace, was turning the ecclesiological clock of the Half-Way Covenant back from the Cambridge Platform of 1648 against the formidable example of his grandfather Stoddard.[134] A doctrinal debate was at the heart of the struggle.[135] The theological essence of the communion controversy was a debate over the nature of the Church, whether it was to be, as Edwards believed, the communion of the saints or, as his opponents held, the meeting house of the community. The issue was not, as was and is commonly misunderstood,[136] whether Edwards was to be allowed to form a 'pure' church, that is a church of certain saints, but rather a church of 'visible saints,' which, in Edwards' interpretation, meant those who could give credible profession to having experienced regeneration.[137] The term 'visible saints' was common to congregationalism, and was a technical term employed to give a language of definition to the concept of a gathered Church. By appealing to such traditional Congregationalist terminology, Edwards attempted to show that his doctrine of the church was within the central stream of congregationalism rightly understood, and that nothing could be farther from his intention than to claim that he had the ability certainly to discern the elect from the reprobate.[138] For him, a profession of the experience of grace was necessary only as someone is "best able to determine what He finds in his own Heart." So there is a tentative nature to the form of the words that he suggested as a personal testimony to grace: "I hope I do truly find a Heart to give up my self wholly to God according to the tenour of the Covenant of Grace which was Seal'd in my Baptism and to walk in a way of obedience to all the commandments of God which the Covenant of Grace requires as long as I live."[139]

Historians have found it no easy matter to interpret the controversy. The conventional view stems from Dwight who saw Stoddardeanism as necessarily productive of Arminianism and then liberalism, which slide into heterodoxy Edwards sought to counteract.[140] Recently others have dissented, seeing that Stoddard and the Stoddardeans have been blackened by later Congregationalists as proto-liberals when in fact their motives and indeed practice were entirely reformed and evangelical.[141] Building upon these revisionists, Hall has advanced the thesis that the reason for Edwards' dismissal was that his doctrine of the church ran aground on the emotionally charged rock of popular religion and family loyalties.[142] At the risk of sounding prevaricating, it seems that none of these interpretations are necessarily contradictory, for the lynch pin of each argument may really be concerned with a different element in the controversy. Hall himself does not doubt that Edwards *believed* that Arminianism was the foe, he merely thinks that the evidence shows that Edwards was wrong so to believe.[143] But, of course, for the various interpretations that stem from Dwight's, that reading of the evidence is to be expected. The problem was not that Stoddard and others like him thought themselves to be Arminian; they clearly did not, and they certainly preached a recognisably reformed gospel. It is latent Arminianism that the older interpretation was concerned with, that a certain understanding of the church could unknowingly lead to a different view of saving faith. Edwards himself did not think that his predecessor was a proto-Arminian, but was rather proud to stand in his shoes.[144] His concern was that Stoddard had been unwise in innovating doctrinally for practical evangelistic purposes. To gain scholarly appreciation for Edwards' view point, it is essential to realise the perceived effects of a Stoddardeanism that allowed an individual to be admitted to communion when she or he only lived a life of outward morality and gave mental assent to the tenets of the gospel.[145] Such a practice, according to Edwards and Dwight, was bound to give false assurance by accepting the introduction of the self-confessed unregenerate into full church membership, and so confuse the difference between common and saving faith. However, Hall's analysis is at its strongest in the reasons he advances for the extraordinary fact, as it has seemed to many, of Edwards' dismissal. It was not the weakness of the congregational system that deprived Edwards of his ministerial power; he had often expressed approval for the checks and balances on the authority of individual congregations initiated under Stoddard and retained under his own ministry.[146] The furore that rapidly developed as Edwards' opinions became known was due to the threat that he posed to the historical linking of Church and family. Edwards was motivated by a doctrinal fear of Arminianism, but his undoing was the irrational fear of a tribe.

So it is, to say the least, interesting that Edwards himself did not see the actual controversy as centred upon his doctrine of communion but on the results of that doctrine upon baptism. He confessed in one letter that, "The greatest difficulty of all relating to my principles is here, respecting baptism. I am not sure but that my people, in length of time, and with great difficulty, might be brought to yield the point as to the qualifications for the Lord's supper (though that is very uncertain); but with respect to the other sacrament there is scarce any hope of it. And this will be very likely to overthrow me, not only with regard to my usefulness in the work of the ministry here, but everywhere."[147] His policy of restricting communion also restricted baptism, and it was this corollary that was most dangerous, as well as being most significant. In fact, it could be argued, that in tackling baptism Edwards was grasping the nettle of the true relation of church to society, and so tackling what some see as having become the single most debilitating factor in the witness of the Reformed churches, the spectre of State churches compromised on their historic gospel, full of 'Christened' members who know nothing of real Christianity.[148] Indeed, though Edwards never wavered from his paedobaptist inheritance throughout his ministry, there is a glimmer of evidence that on the nature of baptism, as the nature of the church, Edwards too had his doubts. In the midst of a series of discussions of baptism, Edwards remarked, "These things about Baptism doubtful."[149] It is no wonder that the separatists hoped that Edwards would join them, for he was proposing a separation of church and society, if not a separation of Church and State. His argument with them was over the certainty of knowing another's salvation; on the necessity of separating church from society they were one.[150] The controversy that Edwards had found himself embroiled in was a controversy not centred on the nature of communion, but on the separation of society from the church. For Edwards, the doctrinal crux was the issue of faith, whether, to enter the visible church, persons, "must profess saving faith, or whether a profession of common faith were not sufficient."[151] If common faith were enough, then the church would become full of the merely moral not the truly regenerate, and, Edwards believed, the Arminian understanding of faith would prevail.

That the problem of true faith was no small matter of concern to Edwards is further evidenced by the two extensive notebooks that he filled with "Observations Concerning Faith."[152] They are a somewhat tantalising read, with little by way of structure to aid understanding, other than a revolving, repetitive concern for the same question. But by means of these revolutions Edwards does gradually build to a crescendo of conclusions, and the pinnacle that he reaches gives the reader a mountain top view of his real gospel. It was no easy assent for Edwards, as his redundant reworkings of previous definitions of faith show. He struggles for a summary definition of saving faith over many of the pages of the "Observations." It is the lack of an appropriate verbal capacity in the English language for the idea that he has in mind that he sees as causing the difficulty, "that we have no word that . . . adequately expresses the whole act of or closing of [sic] the soul or heart." It is again, as with his analyses of spiritual experience more generally,[153] the problem of describing a 'whole soul' response that leaves him floundering in a verbal quagmire. He uses many of the familiar Edwardean phrases in his attempts at satisfying description, 'sense,' 'excellency,' 'reality,' 'whole soul' and as in "Justification by Faith Alone" he is ready to speak of true faith as a "kind of union." The project as a whole is sufficiently important for Edwards to speak of a planned "Treatise of Faith," and he even makes a 'treatise plan' that covers several pages as the "METHOD OF THE DISSERTATION."

The most interesting element of Edwards' remarks are where he discusses the relation of faith and assurance. This has become something of a 'cause célèbre' of comparative studies of the doctrines of the Reformers and the Puritans. The debate centres on the question of whether the Puritans unwittingly disagreed with Calvin's doctrine of assurance.[154] For Edwards, though the hope of assurance was not the same as true faith, yet true faith would produce it, "The hope dont enter into the Essential nature of Faith yet 'tis Essential to it," for the "next Immediate fruit of true faith" is the soul being "Enlightened with a sense of the merciful nature of God" so that "he cant but hope that that declared mercy will be exercised towards him." He continues later to argue that "To believe is to have a sense and a Realizing belief of what the Gospel Reveals of the mediation of X[Christ] and Particularly as it concerns our selves." It is this 'particular' to the individual certainty that Edwards emphasises, "& particularly how it may be with Respect to us in particular."[155] However, though assurance seems to follow true faith, the act of true faith itself is without assurance: faith "Gives Ease tho it be not yet Certain that he shall be saved," faith is a trusting in Christ "tho it bent trusting in him that he will save us." It is certain that the "application of Faith may be without the Application of Assurance," for "The one [faith] necessary the other [assurance] Comfortable." When acting upon this theory, Edwards was willing to offer assurance to individuals, for which he was criticised, but the assurance he offered was on the basis of the application of scriptural principles not the judgement of individuals. He wishes it to "be noted that what I have undertaken to judge of has rather been qualifications and declared experiences, than persons."[156] Edwards was willing to offer assurance of salvation because he believed that assurance was the immediate result of true faith, even if it was not the necessary result.

It is often so with Edwards that the profound theology in his notebooks is matched by clarity of expression of that theology in his sermons, and this is the case for his concept of faith. Edwards' sermons on 1 John 5 are especially germane. He applies the theological weight of his notebooks, of his seeking 'methodology,' of his growing understanding of the nature of the church, to preach that "Saving faith differs from all common faith in its nature, kind and essence."[157] There is nothing, then, within the human nature that can believe as it is necessary to believe, faith is entirely super-natural. The faith spoken of is a "supernatural thing." This he argues against what he sees as a common belief at the time that there is "no effectual diff[erence]" between common faith and saving faith. True faith is that which receives the truth, "not only with the assent of the mind but with the consent of the Heart." To give Scriptural support to what might seem an unwarranted extrapolation from a simple Biblical faith, he refers to 2 Thessalonians 2:10, that they perished "because they received not the love of the truth that they might be saved." True faith is a 'will faith' therefore, and it is this that distinguishes it from that faith of Deists, "But if it be not seated in the will, it is no more a holy faith, than the Faith of deists." Supernatural faith is that which distinguishes true Christianity from Deism.

It is also that which distinguishes it from the do-good Arminian polity of a social church.[158] This and another sermon on the same passage with a similar doctrine, were both drawn from the furnace of the communion controversy in July 1750. One of the two is written on the underside of a sheet marked "proposals to publish by subscription" Edwards' response to the communion controversy.[159] The communion controversy prompted Edwards to preach on true, supernatural, faith. So with the same textual platform but at an earlier and more peaceful time, Edwards' doctrine is the more prosaic, "with the saints, some graces are more sensible in them than some others," and there is no attempt to distinguish true faith.[160] As far as Edwards was concerned the communion controversy was really a controversy of faith.

A right distinction of justification by faith from the intrusions of Arminians and Deists had been a concern of Edwards since he began to formulate a mature theological doctrine. The subject of Edwards' "M.A. Quaestio" was, appropriately enough, "A Sinner is Not Justified in the Sight of God Except

Through the Righteousness of Christ Obtained by Faith." While this exam piece has the expected formulaic structure to it, it is by no means sterile and packs the typical Edwards punch. There are the characteristic doctrines and phrases and, most significantly, the familiar enemies and the familiar response. The enemies Edwards calls the "neonomians." They are those who treat the promise of the Covenant of grace as if it were the same as the promise of the "first covenant" of works, entailing that "imperfect obedience" under the gospel would be enough to give justification to the sinner. As imperfect obedience is inadequate to deal with the infinite punishment that sin deserves, so the same can be said for neonomianism as for "all good works, namely that they are infinitely inadequate for sin . . . " 'Neonomianism' or 'new-law-ism' seems most likely to be a kind of 'good works' theological party. The Enlightenment influence within Arminianism and Deism was leading towards a rationalisation of the gospel, a salvation not by grace but by law. Edwards' response is to restate "the righteousness of Christ obtained by faith," which is "assuredly central, both always for the first Christians and for those more recent who everywhere profess the purity of Reformed Christianity."[161]

We are now in a position to see what it was that caused Edwards to seem to be rejecting covenantal theology. First, it may be that historians have confused Edwards' rejection of Stoddardeanism and the Half-Way Covenant with a rejection of federal theology in general. These are quite different matters for, though a theology effects an ecclesiology, two essentially identical theologies may be seen to necessitate different ecclesiologies. Yet, in this potential blurring of boundaries there is a clue: Edwards' covenant was not an institutional covenant. The covenant that he desired was one that found its relation in a person's 'profession of godliness,' of personal faith in Christ. He did reject a notion of the covenant that entailed the possibility of organising grace, of 'attending on the means,' of baptism and communion as well as preaching, until faith was regenerated. His covenant was a covenant of promise of salvation to those who believe, not a promise of possible salvation to those who may believe, or whose fathers believed. Faith is a supernatural gift of God that cannot be manufactured. Secondly, Edwards' theological enemies may distort understanding of his message. When preached positively, Edwards' real gospel was a gospel of justification by faith alone, where that faith was a supernatural faith. As expressed negatively, however, it was preached against 'neonomian' Arminianism. It is mostly in its negative expression that it forms the doctrinal thread that links Edwards' understanding of the church, preparation, and the covenant. His concern to counter the Enlightenment trends of contemporary Arminianism and Deism led him so to stress the supernaturality of faith, that the emphasis in his discussions of saving faith rests upon salvation by the 'will of God' sometimes to the detriment of what he clearly also believes, that salvation is 'according to the promise of life which is in Christ Jesus.'[162] Later commentators have noticed this disjunction and posited a doctrinal shift. But a Puritan understanding of the promise of life to those who believe, a federal theology, there clearly was in Edwards.

Edwards' understanding of faith could by no means be a theoretical faith. It was not notional but experimental, not merely intellectual but an 'active union' with Christ. Despite the caricatures, it was not a faith that waited for the lightning bolt from heaven, but trusted on the basis of what God had promised, "G[od] having bound Hims[elf] to them by his Covenant so to do." False, Deistical, faith "brings down the notion of saving Relig[ion] leaves out the Life & soul of it every thing that is sp[iritual] & supernatural."[163] Real gospel faith, on the other hand, was a faith that was spiritually alive and produced spiritual life.

The Return to Reality: Practice

Reality rarely stops at theory. The notion that Edwards had of spiritual reality effected the kind of ministry that he pursued and the results of that ministry. Edwards' arch-rival for the life and soul of New England Christianity, Chauncy, had a very different ministry.[164] He became increasingly heterodox and ended in Unitarianism.[165] It would be expected that his understanding of the gospel, his theory or principle that governed his practice, would be likewise very different. On the contrary, however, Chauncy seems to have begun in orthodoxy,[166] and not dry orthodoxy either, but 'experimentally' being able to preach distinctions between the regenerate and the unregenerate, and at the Great Awakening being able to preach for revival.[167] He was educated at Harvard not at the college to become Yale, which at the time gave him more exposure to the influx of latitudinarian liberalism that was appearing in the colonies, one of the less notorious proponents of which was for a while his tutor.[168] But his early work portrays no latent liberalism, and even at the end he was convinced of Unitarianism on the basis of what he believed was taught in scripture.[169] He has even, a little unwisely no doubt, been compared not to the Emersons of this world but instead to Richard Baxter.[170] A gentler kind of Puritan, Chauncy may have been, but not without zeal and seemingly orthodox. What then was it that caused such a difference in ministry between Edwards and Chauncy?

The turning point of his life is reasonably clear. All was well, Prince writes, with the growing revival, until Davenport arrived on the scene and caused mayhem.[171] It was his arrival that also turned Chauncy into a Puritan turn-coat. Davenport, following his usual habit of pronouncing with certainty on the regeneration or otherwise of ministers, bearded Chauncy in his study uninvited and told him that he was unconverted. Ever after Chauncy was set against the awakening.[172] But this description alone, however, is not enough to account for Chauncy's Unitarianism. There were others so treated who saw Davenport as the temporally insane lunatic that he was soon pronounced to be, and ignored his ravings;[173] and, of course, others who stood against the awakening who did not end in Unitarianism.[174]

It seems insufficient, therefore, to explain Chauncy's radical divergence from the Puritan mainstream on account of his Davenport encounter. His heterodoxy derives not from a personal distaste for the friends of the revival but from a principle of spirituality. It is probable that Chauncy always believed that experience of God through the gospel was essentially a rational experience. In other words, while Chauncy sought to base his Unitarian principles upon Scripture, and in this sense was a conservative, epistemologically Chauncy had always been a liberal. The appeal of Unitarianism to such a man is plain. Believing as he did that true experience came first through the reason and only after touched the emotions, he laid himself open to a rationalisation of the gospel. While for Edwards "true religion, in great part, consists in the affections,"[175] Chauncy argues that, "The plain Truth is, an enlightened Mind, and not raised Affections, ought always to be the Guide of those who call themselves Men; and this in the affairs of Religion as other things."[176] Indeed the regulation of emotion, a reasonable and rational behaviour, for Chauncy was one important sign of true conversion.[177] He, therefore, saw the irrational behaviour of the Great Awakening as a sign of its degenerative origin, whereas for Edwards such things were to be discouraged, but were the inevitable mixed result of a powerful work of God upon sinners. To Edwards humans were emotional and would have emotional responses to God's Spirit; to Chauncy humans were emotional and God's Spirit would respond by controlling their emotions.[178]

At the centre of this difference there was an epistemological disagreement; both Chauncy and Edwards recognised this, but Chauncy never really managed to come to grips with Edwards' manner of 'philosophy.'[179] He cherished a rationalist idol within Puritanism, and as far as evangelical orthodoxy is concerned, this syncretism was his undoing. Strangely, those at the opposite end of the theological spectrum to Chauncy, the separatists, had an essentially similar epistemology of salvation. Their conclusion, however, was not that the truly converted govern their heart with their head, but that the truly converted must feel in their heart to direct their head. They were not quite governed by their emotions, but primacy of epistemological order was clearly given to them over and above reason.[180]

But it was exactly this head/heart disjunction that Edwards sought to avoid in his practising of spiritual reality. The point is discussed in other Chapters, but in this context it was such a 'whole soul' response to the gospel which was the theology that separated Edwards both from Chauncy and the Separatists. It could be argued that there is an inherent principle at stake in the war over true salvation that promoted such church disunity after the Great Awakening. The separatists and Chauncy held to the same epistemology of salvation, and pulling at opposite ends of the paradigm fell into equal if opposite errors. Some, no doubt, of a pragmatic turn of mind, watched the shenanigans of the growing religious factions and opted for a careful English-style 'balance.'[181] Edwards was not one of these; he was set apart by being able to preach not for 'balance' but for passion, 'affections,' as high and as strong as could be achieved, without becoming reactionary or fanatical, for he had an epistemology of true salvation that allowed him to hold to the feelings of his head as well as the thinking of his heart.

The practice of Edwards' theory of true salvation did not confine itself to the theological hot house of Northampton. It is true that when Edwards was forced by circumstances to take his ministry to the Indians of Stockbridge, one of the most important results was the time that it gave Edwards to write some of his most important theological works.[182] However, Edwards did not avoid the task of a missionary, radically changing his preaching style to be more effective in the context. He preached a simpler, more homely message.[183] Furthermore, the missionary Brainerd was set up by Edwards as an example of real Christian piety; not a theoretical piety, but one that resulted in great evangelistic labours.[184] Various dates could be given to the birth of the modern Protestant missionary movement, but it is not an exaggeration to say that there has been no more influential figure in promoting mission than Brainerd. Many a missionary has modelled his life upon him.[185] Brainerd was not the first Puritan to brave the wilderness with the gospel,[186] but he did embody the results of the Puritan gospel activism when presented with heathens on the door step. The situation of the Puritans in America forced them to engage in evangelism with native Americans, and the lessons there learnt were taken to Africa, India, the Middle East and South America.[187] In Brainerd there was recorded for posterity the effect of a realisation of the truth of the gospel. The Biblical clarion call to the mission field, 'how shall they believe unless they hear,' was not hidden from the church, but it took the pincer movement of a revival of spiritual reality and the presence of very real and very needy heathen to re-birth missions.

While Brainerd made no radical change to the Puritan gospel message, there was an apparent increased emphasis on the simplicity of preaching Christ crucified, and this change of emphasis may have been significant for the future development of evangelicalism. The centrality of Christ to the preaching of the gospel is the one doctrinal lesson that Brainerd records as having been taught him by his missionary labours. This he deduced from his experience on the field, finding that the kind of preaching that was effective was a preaching of Christ alone, noting that, "God was pleased to help me, 'not to know any thing among them, save Jesus Christ and him crucified.' Thus I was *enabled* to show them their *misery* without him, and to represent his complete *fitness* to redeem and save them." It was this message that God caused to bring salvation to the Native Americans, "this was the preaching God made use of for the awakening of sinners, and the propagation of the 'work of grace among the Indians.'" Such observations gave him new insight into Scripture; he recounts that before his missionary experience he could not understand how Paul so quickly introduced Christ in Romans 10, "observing him in this point very widely to differ from many of our *modern* preachers," but now, "this has not seemed to be strange, since Christ has appeared to be the substance of the gospel, and the centre in which the several lines of divine revelation meet."[188] That such a shift may be significant is underlined not only by the fact that the observation is made by a man held in as high repute as Brainerd, but also that such an understanding of the centrality of Christ to the gospel was the experience of the recipients of the gospel as well as the preachers of the gospel. To dwell on Christ crucified was also the lesson that the convert chief Tschoop sought to give, "I say, therefore, brethren, preach Christ our Saviour and his sufferings and death, if you would have your words to gain entrance among the heathen."[189]

True salvation, for Edwards, was salvation by faith alone, where that faith was supernatural. In preaching, praying and practice, the ambition was for a sense of the presence of God, for a revival of spiritual reality, so that what had been theory could be real, what had been dead could become alive, and what had been silent could be sounded to the ends of the earth. So much for the story of the past. For Edwards, to rely upon past experience was a great spiritual danger, for it would cause the soul to rot as the manna rotted when the Israelites attempted to store it for the future. A picture of Edwards' vision of revival, therefore, would not be complete without his final warning: do not let your soul "breed worms and stink" by a reliance on past experiences but instead earnestly "seek new supplies of Heavenly manna."[190]

NOTES

1. Arminianism was a genuine threat, (C.C.Goen, "Editor's Introduction," *Yale Works*, iv, 8; Ava Chamberlain, *Jonathan Edwards Against the Antinomians and the Arminians*, [Ph.D., Columbia University, 1990]).

2. Gerald R. McDermott, "The Deist Connection: Jonathan Edwards and Islam," *Jonathan Edwards's Writings*, ed., Stephen J. Stein, (Bloomington, 1996), 39–52; Kenneth P. Minkema, "The Other Unfinished 'Great Work,'" *Ibid.*, 55.

3. Edwards though, as this thesis shows, was far from entirely anti-Enlightenment.

4. Arminianism could be identified with these tendencies because it was seen as semi-Pelagian, emphasising human free will, (Williston Walker, *Creeds and Platforms of Congregationalism*, [New York, 1893], 284; C.C.Goen, "Editor's Introduction," *Yale Works*, iv, 8), and Deism because it was seen as anti-supernatural, emphasising a belief in natural religion but not divine revelation, (James Turner, *Without God, Without Creed: The Origins of Unbelief in America*, [Baltimore, 1985]; John Herman Randall Jr., "The Religion of Reason," *The Making of the Modern Mind*, [Cambridge, Mass., 1926], 282–307; Kerry S. Walters, *The America Deists: Voices of Reason and Dissent in the Early Republic*, [Kansas, 1992]; William Lane Craig, "The Historical Argument for the Resurrection During the Deist Controversy," *Text and Studies in Religion*, vol. 23, [Lewiston, 1985]).

5. There are many works that rein together these two, most famously his, "A Divine and Supernatural Light Immediately Imparted to the Soul by the Spirit of God, Shown to be Both a Scriptural and Rational Doctrine," (*Banner Works*, i, 12–17) and "Justification by Faith Alone," (*Banner Works*, i, 622–654).

6. The most exhaustive defence of Edwards traditional stance in relation to the much disputed covenant theology is John H. Gerstner's, *Steps to Salvation*, (Philadelphia, 1976).

7. Such inadequacy may seem less surprising when it is remembered that the fundamental question for religious history, 'what is religion?' is not one that historians have often been inclined to ask, (Patrick Collinson, "What is Religious History?" *What is History Today?* ed. Juliet Gardner, [London, 1988], 58–59).

8. K. Marx and F. Engels, *The Communist Manifesto*, (London, 1967), K. Marx, *Capital*, (Moscow, 1954); S. Freud, *Totem and Taboo*, (London, 1983), *The Future of an Illusion*, (London, 1962); Max Weber, *The Protestant Ethic and the Spirit of Capitalism*, (London, 1930), *Economy and Society*, (New York, 1968). It was Leopold Von Ranke (1795–1886) who gave rise to what is now the traditional view of history, that is to tell it 'how it actually happened,' (for a re-assessment of Ranke see, *The Theory and Practices of History*, selections of Ranke's writings, ed. G.G. Iggers, [New York, 1973]) but more recent developments in historiography have led to great scepticism as to the possibility of such objectivity. For a survey of the theory of history see: R. G. Collingwood, *The Idea of History*, (Oxford, 1946); and an analysis of modern trends is found in, *New Perspectives on Historical Writing*, ed. Peter Burke, (Cambridge, 1991).

9. Perry Miller, "Jonathan Edwards and the Great Awakening," *American Crisis*, ed. Daniel Aaron, (New York, 1952), reprinted, *Errand Into the Wilderness*, (Cambridge, Mass., 1956), 153.

10. V.L. Parrington, "The Colonial Mind, 1620–1800," *Main Currents in American Thought*, vol.1, (New York, 1927).

11. H. Richard Niebuhr, "Toward the Kingdom of God," *The Kingdom of God in America*, (New York, 1937).

12. Alan Heimert, *Religion and the American Mind: From the Great Awakening to the Revolution*, (Cambridge, Mass., 1966).

44   Chapter One

13. Perry Miller, "Jonathan Edwards and the Great Awakening," *American Crisis*, ed. Daniel Aaron, (New York, 1952), reprinted, *Errand Into the Wilderness*, (Cambridge, Mass., 1956), 154–166.

14. I am indebted to John Coffey for this use of the phrase 'booster rocket.'

15. Richard L. Bushman, *From Puritan to Yankee: Character and the Social Order in Connecticut, 1690–1765*, (Cambridge, Mass., 1967).

16. Edwin S. Gaustad, *The Great Awakening in New England*, (New York, 1957).

17. Harry S. Stout, *The Divine Dramatist*, (Grand Rapids, 1991)

18. Jon Butler, "Enthusiasms Described and Decried: The Great Awakening as Interpretative Fiction," *Journal of American History*, vol.69, (1982), 325.

19. W.R.Ward, *The Protestant Evangelical Awakening*, (Cambridge, 1992).

20. Flower and Murphy, *A History of Philosophy in America*, (New York, 1977).

21. The sociological 'secularization' paradigm, in which the decline of religion is seen as part of the phenomena of secular states, has no doubt tended to enforce a contrary mode of interpretation. But the rise of new religious movements, and the perseverance of conservative Protestantism, for instance, has in some quarters caused attempts to re-think the accepted hermeneutic for studying religion. So Richardson seeks "to establish a somewhat different interpretation of new religions which takes them more seriously and on their own terms," (James T. Richardson, "Studies of Conversion: Secularization or Re-enchantment?" *The Sacred in a Secular Age*, ed., Philip E. Hammond, [Los Angeles, 1985], 104).

22. See, William James, "The Varieties of Religious Experience," *Works*, vol. 13, (Cambridge, Mass., 1985), and C. G. Jung, *Modern Man in Search of a Soul*, (New York, 1933).

23. James Hoopes, cited in Henry F. May, "Jonathan Edwards and America," *Jonathan Edwards and the American Experience*, ed. Nathan O. Hatch and Harry S. Stout, (Boston, 1988), 30.

24. Harvey argues similarly in relation to the common mode of assessment of the Salem witch trials: "Historians of witchcraft often assume that their own explanatory theories are not culturally specific. Unlike other participants, they are engaged in discovering what 'really' happened. This is a condescending assumption that most anthropologists and historians of science and medicine try to avoid. It is necessary to recognise the limits of secularism in order to listen to the views of the contesting participants." (David Harvey, "Explaining Salem: Calvinist Psychology and the Diagnosis of Possession," *American Historical Review*, vol.101, no.2, [April 1996], 330).

25. Both Edwards' *Some Thoughts Concerning the Present Revival of Religion in New England* and Chauncy's reply *Seasonable Thoughts on the State of Religion in New England*, were engaged in a debate over whether it was correct to attribute a divine origin to the revival. See, Edward M. Griffin, *Old Brick: Charles Chauncy of Boston, 1705–1787*, (Minnesota, 1980); Alan Heimert and Perry Miller, *The Great Awakening: Documents Illustrating the Crisis and Its Consequences*, (New York, 1967), xxxviii.

26. Edwards calls the 1735 revival a "surprising work of God," "this work of God," "a very general awakening," "this remarkable pouring out of the spirit of God," ("A Faithful Narrative," *Yale Works*, iv, 128, 152, 153, 154); the 1740–1742 revival,

"the present revival of religion," "this work," "awakenings," ("Some Thoughts Concerning the Revival," *Yale Works*, iv, 290, 296, 312), a "work of the Spirit of God," ("The Distinguishing Marks," *Yale Works*, iv, 214).

27. A treatment of revival is absent from Calvin's *Institutes of the Christian Religion*.

28. Charles Hodge, *Systematic Theology*, 3vols., (Grand Rapids, 1952); Wayne Grudem, *Systematic Theology*, (Grand Rapids, 1994).

29. Finney's use of Edwards and the idea of revival has spawned a programmatic understanding of revival such that the term 'revival' is used by some to be synonymous with an evangelistic campaign, where revival experience is the inevitable result of correctly planned activity, (See Charles G. Finney, *Lectures on Revival*, ed. W.G. McLoughlin, [Cambridge, Mass., 1960]).

30. Mark A. Noll, "Moses Mather (Old Calvinist) and the Evolution of Edwardeanism," *Church History*, 49, (1980), 273–285.

31. See Chapter, "True Experience" for discussion of these works.

32. *Yale Works*, ix.

33. Iain H. Murray, *Jonathan Edwards*, (Edinburgh, 1987), 456.

34. "A body of divinity in an entire new method," (Sereno E. Dwight, *Life of President Edwards*, [New York, 1829], 569).

35. The *History of the Work of Redemption* was first published in Edinburgh and received some savage reviews in British journals, as 'pious nonsense' and an 'attempt to revive the old mystical divinity' (Iain H. Murray, *Jonathan Edwards*, [Edinburgh, 1987], 455). For an analysis of more modern hesitations concerning the purported novelty of the *History* see William J. Scheick, "The Grand Design: Jonathan Edwards' 'History of the Work of Redemption,'" *Critical Essays on Jonathan Edwards*, ed. William J. Scheick, (Boston, 1980) 177–178. Scheick's answer to the conundrum is that Edwards is innovative because he treats history as an allegory of the conversion experience. Miller sees modernity in Edwards' understanding that, "the heart of the human problem is history" (Perry Miller, *Jonathan Edwards*, [New York, 1949], 302). Smith comes closest to my view when he argues that Edwards' originality comes from the dynamism that he wrote into his history of progress and final consummation, (John E. Smith, *Jonathan Edwards: Puritan, Preacher, Philosopher*, [London, 1992], 135). I am not therefore attempting to argue that Edwards was 'modern' in his history, whatever that may mean, being in great sympathy with Wilson's view that for critical purposes analysing whether Edwards is here 'modern' or 'traditional' is far from the best approach, (John F. Wilson, "Jonathan Edwards as Historian", *Church History*, 46, [1977], 5–18), especially as belief in historical progress itself may have long lived under the guise of the doctrine of Providence, (David Bebbington, *Patterns in History*, [Leicester, 1979], 68). There is however some originality in his use of revival, as is discussed above.

36. William Robertson, *The Progress of Society in Europe*, (London, 1769). Obviously the comparison here is by way of contrast in terms of Robertson's and Edwards' purpose (John E. Smith, *Jonathan Edwards: Puritan, Preacher, Philosopher*, [London, 1992], 134), but it is by similarity in terms of progress. For comparison of the Christian view of history and the idea of progress, see C.L. Becker, *The Heavenly City of the Eighteenth Century Philosophers*, (New Haven, Conn., 1952).

37. *Yale Works*, ix, 121.

38. As a Calvinist, "for distinction's sake," ("The Freedom of the Will," *Yale Works*, i, 131) Edwards believed that the only ultimate cause was God himself. However there could be attendant causes, or 'means of Grace' as the Puritans called them. It is with these attendant causes that this discussion is concerned.

39. See the "Introduction" for a survey of the major interpretations of Edwards.

40. See Chapter "True Experience," footnote 21.

41. Reformed theology is a theology that has developed from the principle that all religious authority rests in the Bible. It is thus possible for reformed 'traditions' to change on the understanding that such a change is required by a better understanding of the Bible. In one sense, though, all such changes become traditional because they are vested with the original authority of the Bible.

42. Luke 19:42, June 1741, *MSS*, Beinecke.

43. Wesley was one of the first to accuse Edwards of having to eat his words about the revival in his heavily edited publication of Edwards' *Religious Affections*, (John Wesley, *Works*, [London, 1872; reprinted, Grand Rapids, 1958], xiv, 269–270; Richard B. Steele, *Gracious Affections and True Virtue According to Jonathan Edwards and John Wesley*, [London, 1994]).

44. Luke 19:42, June 1741, *MSS*, Beinecke.

45. "A Faithful Narrative," *Yale Works*, iv, 168.

46. "Some Thoughts Concerning the Revival," *Yale Works*, iv, 292.

47. "A Faithful Narrative," *Yale Works*, iv, 160.

48. Luke 19:42, June 1741, *MSS*, Beinecke.

49. See Chapter "True Experience."

50. "A Faithful Narrative," *Yale Works*, iv, 180.

51. *Ibid*.

52. The sermon was "remarkably blessed," (*Banner Works*, 1, 620); though he was criticised for meddling with the Armininian "controversy in the pulpit" there was "very remarkable blessing," (*Yale Works*, iv, 148–149).

53. Iain H. Murray, *Jonathan Edwards*, (Edinburgh, 1987), 125–131.

54. *Yale Works*, iv, 387.

55. Iain H. Murray, *Jonathan Edwards*, (Edinburgh, 1987),126; Wilson H. Kimnach, "Jonathan Edwards' Pursuit of Reality," *Jonathan Edwards and the American Experience*, ed. Nathan O. Hatch and Harry S. Stout, (Boston, 1981), 102.

56. *MSS*, Beinecke.

57. All of the six sermons are dated for both these dates, bar the second, which is dated only for 1756, and the fourth, which is dated only for 1740, (*Ibid*.).

58. So to split his Sunday preaching work into a morning and afternoon continuation of the same subject may have been a common practice of Edwards, (Iain H. Murray, *Jonathan Edwards*, [Edinburgh, 1987], 137).

59. It seems that the effects of the 1735 revival had worn off and Northampton prior to the onset of the Great Awakening was far from being the "powder keg" that Miller describes, (Iain H. Murray, *Jonathan Edwards*, [Edinburgh, 1987], 158).

60. The 'two parties' were a perennial problem in Northampton, ("A letter to a minister of Boston," Northampton December 12, 1743, *Banner Works*, i, lxi) and doubtless heightened the tension of the Communion Controversy.

61. Sermon 1, Matthew 13:3–4, November 1740, April 1756, "Those that God sends forth to preach the gospel are fitly compared to an husbandman that goes forth to sow seed," *MSS*, Beinecke.

62. Sermon 2, Matthew 13:3–4, [1740], May 1756, "I would shew how there are some kinds of hearers of the word preached whose hearts are like the wayside," *MSS*, Beinecke.

63. Sermon 3, Matthew 13:5–6, November 1740, May 1756, "There are many of the hearers of the word whose hearts are like a rock with a thin covering of the earth," *MSS*, Beinecke.

64. Sermon Four, Matthew 13:5–[6], November 1740, "Sudden conversions are often false," *MSS*, Beinecke.

65. Sermon Five, Matthew 13:5–6, November 1740, "That religion that arises only from superficial impressions is wont to whither away for want of root when it comes to be tried by the difficulties of religion," *MSS*, Beinecke.

66. Sermon Six, Matthew 13:7, 1740, 1756, "That the hearts of some of the hearers of the word are so carnal and worldly that they appear to be a ground that was never plowed and so is overgrown with thorns," *MSS*, Beinecke.

67. Ava Chamberlain, "Self-Deception as a Theological Problem in Jonathan Edwards's 'Treatise Concerning Religious Affections,'" *American Society of Church History*, vol. 63, no. 4, [December 1994], 541–556. I would only add to Chamberlain's valuable work that such deceit may be subconscious as well as deliberate.

68. Sermon Three, Matthew 13:5–6, November 1740, May 1756, "There are many of the hearers of the word whose hearts are like a rock with a thin covering of the earth," *MSS*, Beinecke.

69. Sermon Four, Matthew 13:5–[6], November 1740, "Sudden conversions are often false," *MSS*, Beinecke.

70. Sermon Five, Matthew 13:5–6, November 1740, "That religion that arises only from superficial impressions is wont to whither away for want of root when it comes to be tried by the difficulties of religion," *MSS*, Beinecke.

71. Sermon Six, Matthew 13:7, 1740, 1756, "That the hearts of some of the hearers of the word are so carnal and worldly that they appear to be a ground that was never plowed and so is overgrown with thorns," *MSS*, Beinecke.

72. Genesis 19:14, 1727, "Warnings of Future Punishment Don't Seem Real to the Wicked," *Yale Works*, xiv, 201.

73. *Ibid.*, 201.

74. *Ibid.*, 202.

75. *Ibid.*, 209.

76. Edwards is referring to Matthew 18:34, where "to be tortured" in the N.R.S.V. is translated as "to the tormentors" in the A.V.

77. Genesis 19:14, 1727, "Warnings of Future Punishment Don't Seem Real to the Wicked," *Yale Works*, xiv, 209–212.

78. See Chapter "True Experience" for discussion of the sense of the heart.

79. Edwards allows a role to the imagination in conviction, (no. 325, "The 'Miscellanies' a-500," *Yale Works*, xiii, 405).

80. Genesis 19:14, "Warnings of Future Punishment Don't Seem Real to the Wicked," *Yale Works*, xiv, 211.

81. There is "in Christ Jesus abundant foundation of peace and safety for those who are in fear and danger," *Banner Works*, ii, 929–936.

82. Iain H. Murray, *Jonathan Edwards*, (Edinburgh, 1987), 173.

83. Thomas Prince, *An Account of the Revival of Religion in Boston in the Years 1740–3*, (Boston, 1823), 18.

84. 'Revivalism' can be something of a theological swear-word. Peeling away the pejorative skin, the word in essence means a belief in the possibility of a human-initiated revival, as opposed to the idea that revival is the gift of God alone. Stout may have blurred the differences between the two revival epochs, (Harry S. Stout, *The Divine Dramatist*, [Grand Rapids, 1991]); Murray argues that they were quite different phenomena, (Iain H. Murray, *Revival and Revivalism*, [Edinburgh, 1994]).

85. Though it may be possible to trace a historical progression of theology from Edwards to Finney, (Allen C. Guelzo, "Oberlin Perfectionism and Its Edwardsian Origins," *Jonathan Edwards's Writings*, ed. Stephen J. Stein, (Bloomington, 1996], 159–174), Finney's central teaching that there is a method that guarantees revival is readibly distinguishable, (Charles G. Finney, *Lectures on Revival*, [Cambridge, Mass., 1960]).

86. Henry F. May, "Jonathan Edwards and America," *Jonathan Edwards and the American Experience*, ed. Nathan O. Hatch and Harry S. Stout, (Boston, 1988), 30; James Turner, *Without God, Without Creed: The Origins of Unbelief in America*, [Baltimore, 1985], 60.

87. R. E. Davies, *Jonathan Edwards and his Influence on the Development of the Missionary Movement from Britain*, (N.A.M.P. seminar, Cambridge University Divinity School, May 23, 1996). Edwards defends his 'call to united extraordinary prayer' for revival against the charges of novelty, arguing that this prayer is in obedience to Scripture, that similar means have been used in the "appointment of days and fasting and prayer for special mercies," and that this particular method has historical precedent in 1712 in Britain when there was "A serious call from the city to the country" for setting apart specific time for united extraordinary prayer, ("An Humble Attempt," *Yale Works*, v, 428).

88. Genesis 32:26–29, not dated, "The way to obtain the blessing of God is not to let God go except he bless us," *MSS*, Beinecke.

89. Matthew 10:37, "To the Children," August 1740, "He that loveth F[ather] or Mother more than me is not worthy of me," *MSS*, Beinecke. Edwards sermons to children are striking for their rigorous theological content, and their insight into the sins of youth. The principle thrust of one sermon, therefore, is to teach right behaviour in social gatherings, with the pressures of peers and the passions of tender years discouraging godliness, (Ephesians 4:29, 1740 July, "For a meeting of young people," *MSS*, Beinecke).

90. After Whitefield's October visit to Northampton, (Iain H. Murray, *Jonathan Edwards*, [Edinburgh, 1987], 161).

91. The condition in Northampton had decayed but there had been lasting changes: "Ever since the great work of God, that was wrought here about nine years ago, there has been a great and abiding alteration in this town, in many respects," ("A letter to a minister of Boston," Northampton December 12 1743, *Banner Works*, i, lvii).

92. Luke 11:13, Fast for the pouring out of the Spirit, November 1740, "Of the more excellent nature any blessing is that we stand in need of the more ready God is to bestow it in answer to prayer," *MSS*, Beinecke.

93. These were no doubt the prayer 'bills' handed to the minister on the Sabbath for inclusion in his opening prayer of intercession and thanksgiving, (Horton Davies, *The Worship of the North American Puritans, 1629–1730*, [New York, 1990], 143).

94. "Q"[Questions on theological subjects], not dated, *MSS*, Beinecke.

95. The Cambridge Platonists were not mystics, but the classic example of the potential for a similar inherent tendency is their growth in the bed-rock of Puritanism at Emmanuel College, Cambridge University, (G.R.Cragg, *The Cambridge Platonists*, (Cambridge, 1950); Daniel Walker Howe, "The Cambridge Platonists of Old England and the Cambridge Platonists of New England," *Church History*, vol.57, (1988), 470–486).

96. William Haller, *The Rise of Puritanism*, [New York, 1957], 209.

97. *Banner Works*, ii, 956.

98. *Ibid.*, 958.

99. *Ibid.*, i, 622–654.

100. *Ibid.*, ii, 3–7.

101. Edwards argued that faith "is the souls active uniting with Christ," ("Justification by Faith Alone," *Banner Works*, i, 626; John H. Gerstner, *Steps to Salvation*, [Philadelphia, 1976], 141; Conrad Cherry, "The Puritan Notion of Covenant in Jonathan Edwards' Doctrine of Faith," *Church History*, vol.34, (1965), 333.

102. Miller argued that here Edwards first displayed Lockean philosophy, (Perry Miller, *Jonathan Edwards*, [New York, 1949]).

103. Timothy Dwight, *Travels in New England and New York*, vol.4, (Cambridge, Mass., 1969), 324.

104. Background studies: Peter Y. de Yong, *The Covenant Idea in New England Theology*, (Grand Rapids, 1945); Williston Walker, *Creeds and Platforms of Congregationalism*, (New York, 1893); Geoffrey Nuttall, *Visible Saints: The Congregational Way*, (Oxford, 1957).

105. Perry Miller, "The Marrow of Puritan Divinity," *Errand Into the Wilderness*, (Cambridge, Mass., 1956), 98.

106. John E. Smith, *Jonathan Edwards: Puritan, Preacher, Philosopher*, (London, 1992), 5.

107. After Miller, Cherry continued to argue for a modified Miller-ite position, (Conrad Cherry, "The Puritan Notion of Covenant in Jonathan Edwards' Doctrine of Faith," *Church History*, vol.34, [1965], 328–341), but more recently the tide has turned, (John H. Gerstner, *Steps to Salvation*, [Philadelphia, 1976]; Carl W. Bogue, *Jonathan Edwards and the Covenant of Grace*, [New Jersey, 1975], 87]; Harry S. Stout, "The Puritans and Edwards," *Jonathan Edwards and the American Experience*, ed. Nathan O. Hatch and Harry S. Stout, [Boston, 1981], 143; see also, Mark Valeri, "The New Divinity and the Revolution," *William and Mary Quarterly*, 3rd ser., vol.xlvi, (Oct. 1989); Gerald McDermott, "Jonathan Edwards, The City on a Hill, and the Redeemer Nation: A Reappraisal," *Journal of Presbyterian History*, (Spring 1991), *One Holy and Happy Society: The Public Theology of Jonathan Edwards*, (Pennsylvania, 1992).

108. Revelation 17:14, not dated, "1. Those that are of Christ's and belonging to him, 'tis of God that they are so. 2. They belong to Jesus Christ, they are faithful to Christ," *MSS*, Beinecke.

109. Genesis 3:24, not dated, "When man fell, God drove him away from all his former blessedness," *MSS*, Beinecke.

110. "A letter to a minister of Boston," Northampton December 12, 1743, *Banner Works*, i, lix.

111. Christopher Grasso, "Misrepresentations Corrected: Jonathan Edwards and the Regulation of Religious Discourse," *Jonathan Edwards's Writings*, ed. Stephen J. Stein, (Bloomington, 1996), 19–38.

112. "The Profession of Faith," first draft, *MSS*, Beinecke.

113. The English Puritan John Preston was one of the foremost proponents of federal theology. The concept runs throughout his works, but see especially *The New Covenant, or the Saints Portion*, (London, 1629). The most influential form in which the covenant reached New England theology was probably through the writings of William Ames, particularly, *Medulla Theologica*, (London, 1642).

114. A standard Puritan distinction that Edwards employs as basic to deeper analysis (for example in "A Divine and Supernatural Light," *Banner Works*, ii, 17) and was important for leaders of the Great Awakening, (D.W. Bebbington, *Evangelicalism in Modern Britain: A History from the 1730s to the 1980s*, [London, 1989], 57).

115. "Justification by Faith Alone," *Banner Works*, i, 623–624.

116. In one sense saints are expected to continue to seek salvation, for the very action of such desire is an evidence of salvation. It is not, though, a desiring for what is not yet attained but rather a desiring for more of what is already attained.

117. The other matter Gerstner identifies is Edwards' emphasising justification as union with Christ, (John H. Gerstner, *Steps to Salvation*, [Philadelphia, 1976]), 141–142.

118. No. 301, "The 'Miscellanies' a-500," *Yale Works*, xiii, 387; see also "Charity and its Fruits," *Yale Works*, viii, 256.

119. Genesis 1:27, August 1751, To Stockbridge Indians and Mohawks, "That God has given men reason and understanding . . . man being made in God's image . . . made holy . . . ," *MSS*, Beinecke.

120. Genesis 3:11, February 1738[/9], four sermons, "The act of our first father in eating the forbidden fruit was a very heinous act," *MSS*, Beinecke.

121. Genesis 32: 26–29, not dated, "The way to obtain the blessing of God is not to let God go except he bless us," *MSS*, Beinecke.

122. The belief that preparation was natural arose from a desire to underline the doctrine that a person is not saved until she believes, (Stoddard, *The Safety of Appearing*, [Boston, 1687], 101; *Treatise Concerning Conversion*, [Boston, 1719], 37; "if this opinion [that preparation was unnecessary] would prevail in the land, it would give a deadly word to religion," (*The Sinner Guided to the Saviour*, [Edinburgh, 1848], 15). The Difference that Edwards' understanding made to his pastoral advice can be gleaned from his comment that, "we are invited to come to the Tree of Life Immediately without any conditions," (Genesis 3:24, *MSS*, Beinecke).

123. No. 27b, "The 'Miscellanies' a-500," *Yale Works*, xiii, 213–215.

124. No. 77, "The 'Miscellanies' a-500," *Yale Works*, xiii, 244–245.

125. No. 317, "The 'Miscellanies' a-500," *Yale Works*, xiii, 397–401. The dating is drawn from Schafer's table, "Editor's Introduction," "The 'Miscellanies' a-500," xiii, *Yale Works*, 90–110.

126 . In the "manner" of conversion "there is a vast variety, perhaps as manifold as the subjects of the operation; but yet in many things there is a great analogy in all." The analogy that Edwards goes on to describe is the gospel analogy of repentance and faith, ("A Faithful Narrative," *Yale Works*, iv, 160).

127. 'Steps to Salvation' is Gerstner's phrase for Edwards' preparation theology, (John H. Gerstner's, *Steps to Salvation*, [Philadelphia, 1976]).

128. No. 27b, "The 'Miscellanies' a-500," *Yale Works*, xiii, 214.

129. Perry Miller, *The New England Mind*, (Cambridge, Mass., 1939, 1953).

130. Jamieson sees that there was Arminianism latent in the doctrines of federal theology, Stoddardeanism and also preparation, (John F. Jamieson, "Jonathan Edwards's Change of Position on Stoddardeanism," *Harvard Theological Review*, vol.74, [1981], 85).

131. John Ashley Null, *Thomas Cranmer's Doctrine of Repentance*, (Ph.D., Cambridge University, 1994), 217.

132. It is not only of the more Arminian that this has been true. Spurgeon caused a stir by preaching against preparation: "The Warrant for a sinner to believe in Christ is not in himself in any sense or in any manner, but in the fact that he is commanded there and then to believe on Jesus Christ. Some preachers in Puritanic times, whose shoe latchets I am not worthy to unloose, erred much in this matter . . . These excellent men had a fear of preaching the gospel to any except those whom they styled 'sensible sinners' and consequently kept hundreds of their hearers sitting in darkness when they might have rejoiced in the light," (Charles H. Spurgeon, "The Warrant of Faith", *Metropolitan Tabernalce Pulpit*, Sermon 531, (1863), 400–401). Gerstner is one reformed evangelical who defends preparationism, but there are many others who would be loath so to do.

133. Both of these two elements have been important interpretative grids for biographical understandings of what it was that caused Edwards' break with his church. Dwight attributed the controversy to the personal and ideological enmity of the Williams clan, (Sereno E. Dwight, *The Life of President Edwards*, [New York, 1829]). This traditional interpretation has influenced many, including Miller who similarly looked to the Williamses as being Edwards' nemesis, (Perry Miller, *Jonathan Edwards*, [New York, 1949]). Winslow, however, blamed Edwards' troubles on his opposition to the rising tide of democracy in his parish and in the colonies as a whole (Ola Elizabeth Winslow, *Jonathan Edwards*, [New York, 1940]). More recently, Murray has found his own blend of these two interpretations, tracing the family struggle with the Williams as a continuum from the Northampton to the Stockbridge struggles, (Iain H. Murray, *Jonathan Edwards*, [Edinburgh, 1987]).

134. Edwards' predecessor Stoddard had initiated an ecclesiastical change to the traditional half-way covenant of New England Congregationalism, as enshrined in the Cambridge Platform of 1648. While he was not the first to formulate such an understanding of church membership, he became its champion in New England and the

doctrine was called after him. This 'Stoddardeanism' took two distinct, but sometimes confused, forms. First, and most importantly for the context of the Communion Controversy, Stoddard lowered the barrier to full, that is communicant, membership. Previously, it had been required to give a profession of personal faith or experience of grace to be allowed full membership, but Stoddard insisted that all that need be asked of a candidate was that he or she express historical faith or a belief in the fundamental doctrines of the Christian faith. Full members, therefore, did not necessarily claim to be regenerate. The privileges of full membership were many, including voting rights, access to communion, and perhaps most importantly for many, the right to have children baptised. Stoddard found such a change expedient to evangelism, helping to increase the church membership in a series of mini-revivals that he called 'harvests.' Communion, Stoddard thought, was not a privilege of the saints but a converting ordinance. Apart from giving an evangelistic edge to his ministry, Stoddard may have also found that it solved a long standing problem of half-way members, that is those who had been baptised as children but had not yet made profession of personal faith, being overly cautious before coming to communion. There is evidence that those who, to use the Cambridge Platform phrase, in the 'judgement of charity' were regenerate, were refusing to come to communicant membership for fear of abusing what they knew to be a privilege of the saints alone. It is against this Stoddardeanism that Edwards rebelled. Secondly, however, Stoddard also innovated a loose inter-church association, and to this Edwards too was drawn. Many have seen such an association as a mere step away from a more Presbyterian understanding of church relationships, and it was this ecclesiastical innovation which earned Stoddard the 'pope' Stoddard rebuke from Increase Mather, with whom he conducted a long standing disagreement over his two innovations. Both the theology and history of the matter at issue are somewhat convoluted but helpful works to consult are, David D. Hall, "Editor's Introduction," "Ecclesiastical Writings," *Yale Works*, xii; John F. Jamieson, "Jonathan Edwards' Change of Position on Stoddardeanism," *Harvard Theological Review*, 74, (1981), 79–99; Thomas A. Schafer, "Jonathan Edwards' Concept of the Church," *Church History*, 24, (1950), 51–66; Robert Lee Stuart, "'Mr Stoddard's Way:' Church and Sacraments in Northampton," *American Quarterly*, 24, (1972), 243–253; Paul R. Lucas, "'The Death of the Prophet Lamented:' The Legacy of Solomon Stoddard," *Jonathan Edwards's Writings*, ed. Stephen J. Stein, [Bloomington, 1996], 69–84); Peter Y. De Yong, *The Covenant Idea in New England Theology*, (Grand Rapids, 1945); Williston Walker, *Creeds and Platforms of Congregationalism*, (New York, 1893), especially page 285, where Walker argues that Edwards not only stood against Stoddardeanism but also against the Half-Way Covenant from which it grew.

135. Tracy sees that the theological argument is important to understand the tensions of the Communion Controversy, though not so much for the theology itself but rather because Edwards' newly expressed ecclesiology ran counter to that of the still-influential Stoddard, and, moreover, when misunderstood, as by and large it was at the time, Edwards' theology of the church seemed to invest in himself unwarranted powers, (P. J. Tracy, *Jonathan Edwards, Pastor*, [New York, 1980]). While such an analysis is insightful, it tends to so emphasise what is evidence of the importance of

the argument over ecclesiology that it encourages the deduction that the theological issues at stake were only important as fuel for an inevitable argument between Edwards and the congregation. One is left with the feeling that what matters is not what they argued about but that they argued.

136. Edwards was mistakenly associated with the Separatists. See footnote 138 & 150.

137. It is possible to argue that Stoddard's ecclesiastical edifice was built upon a distinction between 'conversion' and 'regeneration.' Those who gave a profession of historical faith could be regarded as converted to Christianity, and thus 'visible saints,' even though none, not least themselves, would claim that they were regenerate, (Robert Lee Stuart, "'Mr Stoddard's Way:' Church and Sacraments in Northampton," *American Quarterly*, 24, [1972], 243).

138. The difference between a 'pure church' and a church of 'visible saints' is important to Edwards' defence of his case. The language of a 'pure church' effectively demarked heterodoxy, it often being the brand given to the separatists position, which Edwards many times explicitly rejected, ("An Humble Inquiry," *Yale Works*, xii, 170–171). The language of the debate is, however, complicated by various factors, particularly that the term 'visible saints' was claimed by all sides. Such visible sainthood was the traditional criterion of church membership in New England, (Edwards takes this assumption as a starting point for debate, [*Yale Works*, xii, 182]; P.J. Tracy, *Jonathan Edwards: Pastor* [New York, 1980], 172) and it retained its importance in the Cambridge Platform, (Williston Walker, *Creeds and Platforms of Congregationalism*, [New York, 1893]). Furthermore, 'visible saints' had long been a technical term within congregationalism to defend the concept of a gathered church against the charge that such polity claimed to be able to distinguish between true and false professions of faith. In other words, it had been traditionally used against the same charge of a 'pure church.' As such, in the English context, the term had been a way for Congregationalists to explain themselves to Presbyterians, who did not easily empathise with the concept of a gathered church, being more content with a profession of historical faith as a requirement for membership rather than a profession of personal faith or the experience of grace, (Geoffrey Nuttall, *Visible Saints: The Congregational Way*, [Oxford, 1957], 112; 113, 134–136). So, all in all, the term itself is not enough accurately to signify what it was that Edwards wished to say, except for the important fact that by what was seen as an ecclesiological innovation he intended to be theologically traditional. It is to the heart of the congregational impulse that Edwards appeals when he cries 'visible saints.'

139. "Preface to the farewell sermon," two fragments, not dated, *MSS*, Beinecke. Edwards was willing to retain the old form of words if rightly interpreted, (*Yale Works*, xii, 181).

140. Sereno E. Dwight, *The Life of President Edwards*, (New York, 1829), 303–307; Joseph Tracy, *The Great Awakening*, (Edinburgh, 1989).

141. P. J. Tracy, *Jonathan Edwards, Pastor*, (New York, 1980); Kevin Sweeney, *River Gods and Related Minor Deities*, (Ph.D., Yale University, 1986); Paul R. Lucas, "'The Death of the Prophet Lamented': The Legacy of Solomon Stoddard," *Jonathan Edwards's Writings*, ed. Stephen J. Stein, [Bloomington, 1996], 80).

142. David D. Hall, "Editor's Introduction," *Yale Works*, xii, 60–61.

143. *Ibid.*, 77–84.

144. There is no doubt rhetoric in his appeal to the authority of his grandfather at the start of his defence in the Communion Controversy, yet, surely, there is at least a vein of truth in his description of Stoddard as, "one whose memory I am under distinguishing obligations, on every account, to treat with great respect and honor," (*Yale Works*, xii, 167).

145. Sereno E. Dwight, *The Life of President Edwards*, (New York, 1829), 308.

146. See footnote 134 above; Edwards to John Erskine, Northampton, 5 July 1750, Sereno E. Dwight, *The Works of President Edwards*, (New York, 1829–1830), i, 412; no. 90, "The 'Miscellanies' a-500," *Yale Works*, xiii, 254.

147. Edwards to Thomas Foxcroft, May 24 1749, *A Jonathan Edwards Reader*, ed. John E. Smith, (New Haven, Conn., 1995), 309.

148. The theological war that embroiled Edwards was a part of perhaps the single most important doctrinal shift since the reformation, for it involved the much disputed problem of Church/State relations, the separation of which was only gradually to receive formal legal recognition in modern times; Christopher Grasso, "Misrepresentations Corrected: Jonathan Edwards and the Regulation of Religious Discourse," *Jonathan Edwards's Writings: Text, Context, Interpretation*, (Bloomington, 1996), 20.

149. The citation is placed in parenthesis at the end of a somewhat circuitous discussion of the effects of baptism upon the future godliness of children. It is not an exaggeration to say that in terms of church polity Edwards was only one step away from being a baptist. His church/society separation puts him near to that camp. Even on the practice of baptism itself he was uncertain, ("The Miscellanies," 595, *MSS*, Beinecke).

150. The separatists had clearly hoped to have the weight of Edwards on their side. One of their leaders, Ebenezer Frothingham, uses Edwards arguments in the communion controversy, sadly lamenting that he did not go further in this matter. He concludes his book, "earnestly praying, That God would give Mr. Edwards to see wherein he has opposed and stood against God's Work of late in the Land . . . and that God would once more make his Face as a Flint . . . and that he might be made as a Flame of Fire, in dispensing the everlasting Gospel. *Amen.*" (Ebenezer Frothingham, *The Articles of Faith and Practice that is confessed by the Separate Churches of Christ in General in this Land*, [Newport, 1750], 432). But by the end of the same year, if they had any lingering hopes that he might join them, Edwards made his position plain. He tells the lecture at Westfield that he had had cause to converse with the leaders of the Separatists, and he has concluded that "many of their notions as to the essence of Rel[ig]ion] saving Exp[erience] . . . are to the highest degree corrupt and dangerous." He lists many of the common abuses that they were known for, but the principle behind these abuses he sees as "pretended immediate Rev[elation] of supposed Truths not to be found in the Bible" and a false notion of "X[Chris]tian Exp[erience]," (Jude 19, December 1750, "Prepared for a lecture at Westfield," "To Canaan": "There was a sort of persons in the apostle's day who separated themselves from the steady ministers and churches that pretended to be very spiritual, but who really were carnal and had not the spirit of God," *MSS*, Beinecke).

151. "Misrepresentations Corrected," *Yale Works*, xii, 355.
152. *MSS*, Beinecke.
153. See the Chapter "True Experience."
154. For the argument that concerning assurance English Puritanism differed from the Reformers, see Basil Hall, "Calvin Against the Calvinists," *John Calvin*, ed. G.E. Duffield, (Abingdon, 1966); R.T.Kendall, *Calvin and English Calvinism to 1649*, (Oxford, 1979), David Bebbington draws from this understanding of the Puritan notion of assurance in his *Evangelicalism in Modern Britain: A History from the 1730s to the 1980s*, (London, 1989). For the argument to the contrary, see Joel R. Beeke, *Assurance of Faith: Calvin, English Puritanism, and the Dutch Second Reformation*, (New York, 1991).
155. It seems Jonathan Edwards Jr. did not quite agree: he made sure that the emphasis was switched from the particular certainty to the uncertain perhaps by underlining "may" to give the impression of 'maybe.'
156. "A Faithful Narrative," *Yale Works*, iv, 176.
157. Doctrine of sermon on 1 John 5:1–4, July 1750, *MSS*, Beinecke.
158. 'Arminian' is used here as defined in the first paragraph of this Chapter.
159. 1 John 5:1–4, July 1750, *MSS*, Beinecke.
160. 1 John 5:2, June 1736, "Tis commonly so with the saints, that some graces are more sensible in them than others," *MSS*, Beinecke.
161. Jonathan Edwards M.A. "Quaestio" was written in Latin; I am grateful to George Levesque for a preview of his translation of this then unpublished work, (*Yale Works*, xiv, 60–64).
162. 2 Timothy 1:1, A.V.
163. 1 John 5:1–4, July 1750, *MSS*, Beinecke.
164. It is correct to see Chauncy as Edwards' antagonist, but there have been times when he has been caricatured as, "a nasty 'heavy' out of nineteenth century melodrama. One could almost hear the scholars and critics hiss each time they brought him into their pages," (Edward M. Griffin, *Old Brick: Charles Chauncy of Boston, 1705–1787*, [Minnesota, 1980], vii).
165. He was not a Deist but did become a Unitarian, (*Ibid.*, 4).
166. It was not until after the Great Awakening, during the period 1745–60, that he became heterodox, (*Ibid.*, 94).
167. In June 1740 he preached on the signs of true regeneration, (*Ibid.*, 55). On May 13, 1741, "For the Outpouring of the Holy Ghost," urging, "Let us pray . . . for the out-pouring of the SPIRIT upon our land," (*Ibid.*, 64, 65).
168. Wigglesworth was his tutor, (*Ibid.*, 21).
169. About his proposed new system of divinity he wrote that, "The whole is written from the scripture account of these matters, and not from any human scheme. It will not, I believe, comport with what is called orthodoxy, but I am verily persuaded it contains the real truth," (*Ibid.*, 111).
170. Norman Bantley Gribbs has argued for the similarity between Chauncy and Baxter (*Ibid.*, 109).
171. Thomas Prince, *An Account of the Revival of Religion in Boston in the Years 1740–3*, (Boston, 1823), 32.

56   Chapter One

172 . Edward M. Griffin, *Old Brick: Charles Chauncy of Boston, 1705–1787*, (Minnesota, 1980), 67; "Editor's Introduction," Charles Chauncy D.D., *Seasonable Thoughts on the State of Religion in New England*, (New York, 1975), 4w.

173. Davenport was slandered by Chauncy, (Charles Chauncy D.D., *Seasonable Thoughts on the State of Religion in New England*, [Reprint, New York 1975], 70–80), and in fact was much loved and admired before and after his brief sojourn into fanaticism. But in June 1742 Davenport was pronounced "disturbed in the rational faculties of his mind," (Iain H. Murray, *Jonathan Edwards*, [Edinburgh, 1987], 225–226).

174. C.C. Goen, *Revivalism and Separatism in New England*, (New Haven, Conn., 1962).

175. "The Religious Affections," *Yale Works*, ii, 99.

176. Charles Chauncy D.D., *Seasonable Thoughts on the State of Religion in New England*, (New York, 1975), 326.

177. For Chauncy, "the marks of faith were reverence, moral living and rational action," (Edward M. Griffin, *Old Brick: Charles Chauncy of Boston, 1705–1787*, [Minnesota, 1980], 36).

178. Chauncy could not grasp the point of the distinction that Edwards made. For him if the work was often attended with such effects then it should be concluded that the work caused such effects, and therefore the work could not be supported, (Charles Chauncy D.D., *Seasonable Thoughts on the State of Religion in New England*, [New York 1975], 307).

179. Chauncy acknowledges that Edwards "himself, under this very Head, made use of more Philosophy (and in a manner not altogether exceptionable, as we may see afterwards, if I can find room), than any one I know of, who has wrote upon the Times," (Edward M. Griffin, *Old Brick: Charles Chauncy of Boston, 1705–1787*, [Minnesota, 1980], 87); Edwards argues that Scripture is the one rule to judge of experiences, but says that people have wrongly understood the Scripture because they have come to it with a philosophical bias to judge a priori, ("Some Thoughts Concerning the Revival," *Yale Works*, iv, 293–297).

180. Frothingham fails to discern the emotional effects of the Spirit when he writes that, "The sudden Impulses upon the Mind, that come from a false Spirit, serve to lead a Person away from God . . . These sudden Influences that are from God's Spirit, never lead a Person contrary to the Scriptures," (Ebenezer Frothingham, *The Articles of Faith and Practice that is confessed by the Separate Churches of Christ in General in this Land*, [Newport, 1750], 425).

181. David Harlan, *The Clergy and the Great Awakening in New England*, (Ann Arbor, Mich., 1980), 7.

182. Those that are usually referred to in this vein are *The Freedom of the Will, Original Sin, The End for which God Created the World, The Nature of True Virtue*, and *A History of the Work of Redemption*.

183. There is a fascinating comparison of Edwards treatment of Psalm 14:1 in Northampton with the treatment of the same verse in Stockbridge. On the former occasion there are long philosophical arguments for the reason for atheists to be indeed 'fools;' in the latter Edwards preaches in an 'All Creatures Great and Small' style:

"When we look up to Heaven & see the sun shine in his Brightness who made it & Gave it it [sic] Light . . . who made so many sorts of creatures . . . all sorts made there is a He one & she one . . . The eyes to see Ears to hear . . . Hands to work Feet & legs to walk Teeth to eat . . . Thus you can see how certain it is that there is a G[od]." There is no doubt that Edwards was engaged in the task of reaching his new audience for Christ. (Psalm 14:1 (a), not dated, probably late 1730s: "A principle of Atheism possesses the hearts of all ungodly men;" Psalm 14:1 (b), December 1752, Preached to Stockbridge Indians: "There certainly is a God;" *MSS*, Beinecke).

184. "The Life of David Brainerd," *Yale Works*, vii.

185. The role call of Brainerd's influences on missionaries includes Carey, Livingstone, Henry Martyn, and more recently Jim Eliott, (Norman Pettit, "Editor's Introduction," "The Life of David Brainerd," *Yale Works*, vii).

186. John Eliot, missionary to the native Americans of Massachusetts Bay colony, was the early pioneer in this regard (Cotton Mather, *Magnali Christi Americana*, [Edinburgh, 1979], i, 526–583).

187. I am referring again to Carey, Livingstone, Martyn and Eliott.

188. David Brainerd, *The Gospel the only true Reformer*, (New York, 1856), 12.

189. The full text is fascinating: "Brethren, I have been a heathen and have grown old amongst the heathen: therefore I know how heathen think. Once a preacher came and began to explain to us there was a God. We answered: 'Dost thou think us so ignorant as not to know that? Go back to the place from whence thou camest.' Then again another preacher came and began to teach us: 'You must not lie nor steal nor get drunk,' etc. We answered: 'Thou fool, dost thou think that we dont know that? Learn first thyself, and then teach the people to whom thou belongest to leave off these things. For who steals, or lies, or is more drunken than thine own people?' And thus we dismissed him. After some time, brother Christian Henry Rauch came into my hut and sat down by me. He spoke to me nearly as follows: 'I come to you in the name of the Lord of heaven and earth: he sends to let you know that he will make you happy and deliver you from the misery in which you lie at present. To this end he became a man, gave his life a ransom for man, and shed his blood for him' etc. When he had finished his discourse, fatigued by the journey, he lay down upon a board and fell into a sound sleep. I then thought what kind of a man is this? Here he lies and sleeps. I might kill him and throw him out into the wood, and who would regard it? But this give him no concern. However, I could not forget his words; they constantly recurred to my mind. Even when I was asleep I dreamed of that blood which Christ shed for us. I found this to be something different from what I had ever heard, and I interpreted Christian Henry's words to the other Indians. Thus, through the grace of God, an awakening took place among us. I say, therefore, brethren, preach Christ our Saviour and his sufferings and death, if you would have your words to gain entrance among the heathen," (Cited by Talbot W. Chambers in his Introduction to, *Ibid.*, iv).

190. Exodus 16:20, October, 1741, "For persons to lay up past experiences to live upon them . . . ," *MSS*, Beinecke.

Chapter Two

True Experience

"Randy shared a short message and soon the laughing, crying and falling down was touching many.... As Randy prayed his way through the crowd at the front, it was not long before he was standing in front of me. As he interceded for me, I felt this overwhelming sense of the peace and power of God come over me, and then it felt like someone turned out the lights. I don't know how long I was out, but I had this incredible sense of the immanent presence of the Holy Spirit resting on me. Throughout the evening, every time I would try to get up, someone would pray, 'Touch him again, Lord. More, Lord. More, Lord!' And out I would go again, each time resting deeply in the peace and presence of the Lord. I think it was around 3.00 A.M. when I finally managed to navigate my way out. This went on for days. I felt and acted very intoxicated. I couldn't talk, except in short cryptic phrases. I don't remember a whole lot, and I don't really want to believe the reports of how I acted! But as time passed I felt more cleansed and calm deep down on the inside. I felt the manifest presence of the Holy Spirit all the time, and continued to soak in a state of blissful abandonment."[1]

Such is one personal record of an experience of the presence of God. But is it true experience?[2] How is it possible to know that such an experience is indeed an experience of God and not of a disfunctioning psychology? Edwards also recorded experiences. Compare the above account of a purportedly genuine encounter with God, with the following from Edwards, his paradigmatic description of a heightened experience of God:

The person, "more than once continuing for five or six hours together, without any interruption, in that clear and lively view or sense of the infinite beauty and amiableness of Christ's person, and the heavenly sweetness of his excellent and transcendent love; so that (to use the person's own expressions) the soul remained in a kind of heavenly Elysium, and did as it were swim in the rays of Christ's love, like a little mote swimming in the beams of the sun, or streams of his light that came in at a window . . . extraordinary views of divine things, and religious affections, being frequently attended with very great effects on the body, nature often sinking under the weight of divine discoveries, the strength of the body was taken away, so as to deprive of all ability to stand or speak; sometimes the hands clinched, and the flesh cold, but senses still remaining; animal nature often in a great emotion and agitation, and the soul very often, of late, so overcome with great admiration, and a kind of omnipotent joy, as to cause the person (wholly unavoidably) to leap with all the might, with joy and mighty exultation of soul . . ."[3]

In many ways these two accounts are quite similar. There is a like experience of joy and transcendence or power, a like increased reality to the presence of God, and even like physical effects. It is not surprising, then, that justification for experience as described in the first account is explicitly sought in the historical precedence as recorded in the second.[4]

Such comparisons of experiences are certainly important for Edwards. By publishing descriptions of true experience others are exalted to seek God in like fashion. By observation true experience can be discerned from false: these are things, "which must be distinguished by the skill of the observer,"[5] that are "found by observation and experience,"[6] and "experience proves."[7] Description rarely avoids a subliminal enforcement of the norm, and Edwards made no attempt to remove such instructive value from his descriptions, rather ladening them with pedagogical intent. So it is made plain in the above observations that there are places to which true experience should not lead. There will be no appearance of flippancy: "spiritual joys in this person never were attended . . . with the least appearance of any laughter or lightness of countenance, or manner of speaking."[8] There will be no claim to new revelation: "These transporting views and rapturous affections are not attended with any enthusiastical disposition to follow impulses, or any supposed prophetical revelations."[9] There will be no monastical denial of the world: "worldly business has been attended with great alacrity, as part of the service of God; the person declaring that, it being done thus, 'tis found to be as good as prayer."[10] There will be no thought of personal perfection: "no disposition to the opinion of being now perfectly free from sin, (according to the notion of the Wesleys and their followers, and some other high pretenders to spirituality in these days), but exceedingly the contrary."[11] Finally, there will be no pharisaic hypocrisy: "And one more thing may be added, viz. That these things have been attended with a particular dislike of placing religion much in dress, and spending much zeal about those things that in themselves are matters of indifference, or an affecting to show humility and devotion by a mean habit, or a demure and melancholy countenance, or anything singular and superstitious."[12] While many other true experiences will be "not so pure and unmixed, and so well regulated,"[13] yet still what the experiences are 'attended with' is significant to discern their truth or falsity. Accurate comparison of descriptions, attention to detail, is therefore vital to Edwards: it allows correct identification of experience.[14]

However, important though it is, description for Edwards is only a means to the end of right evaluation. It provides the information but does not supply the answers.[15] Comparing one description of an experience with another can never be enough; if manifestations of true and false experience did not initially seem similar there would be no difficulty in discerning between them.[16] Manifestations of experiences must be compared not to themselves, but to Scripture. Scripture is "in itself a sufficient rule to judge of such things by."[17] Not acknowledging this is one "foundation-error" of those who wrongly discern experiences. Some make "philosophy, instead of the Holy Scriptures, their rule of judging of this work,"[18] others make "history, or former observation" their rule.[19] So, "many are guilty of not taking the Holy Scriptures as a sufficient and whole rule, whereby to judge of this work."[20] Such statements are particularly important as Edwards was careful to combine the proof of Scripture with the proof of reason; the impression that he sometimes gives of basing his findings on argument rather than on text, is due to his aim to persuade rather than to theology: "Lest I may mention a great many things, and places of Scripture, that the world will judge but frivolous reasons for the proof of what I drive at, not to mention such as I fear it of as what I depend on for proof, but to bring 'em in so that the force of the reasons will naturally and unavoidably be brought to the mind of the reader."[21] But his commitment to Scriptural proofs is unwavering: "'Tis abundantly safer therefore, to follow the light of Scripture, than to draw up rules from our own experiences."[22] Whatever one may think of the possibility of genuinely holding to a 'biblicist' approach, it is clearly one that Edwards' owned, and is the rock of Edwards' epistemology of experience.[23]

It is from the Scriptures that Edwards claims to find two sets of principles that are to be used to distinguish true from false experience. So in an important sermon he asks, what are the "sure signs of the saving grace of God's Spirit?" and answers, "those exercises and affections which are good evidences of grace, differ . . . in two things, *viz.* their *foundation* and their *tendency*."[24] The first, the foundation, concerns the 'sense of the heart', the second, the tendency, concerns 'marks' or 'signs.' In this way his aim is to distinguish both what is the nature of true experience and what is the effect of true experience. This chapter will explicate the 'sense,' then the 'signs,' and then relate them to the contemporary epistemological debate concerning religious experience.[25]

THE SENSE OF TRUE EXPERIENCE

Edwards' sense is a 'sense of the heart.'[26] If we fail to grasp the importance of the heart for Edwards, it is not an overstatement to say that we are likely to fail to understand his theology of experience. Under God, Edwards was a preacher of the heart, a theologian of the heart, a man of the heart: "for who will deny that true religion consists, in a great measure, in vigorous and lively actings of the inclination and will of the soul, or the fervent exercises of the heart?"[27] It is not deniable because, he argues, "God, in his word, greatly insists upon it, that we be in good earnest, fervent in spirit, and our hearts vigorously engaged in religion."[28]

How, though, is Edwards' doctrine of the heart to be understood? His appeal to the heart is not an appeal to emotion as such, because Edwards' concept of the soul is not polarised between reasoning and feeling. Edwards did see the human psyche as divisible into two faculties, identifying the heart with the junction of the will and the emotions as distinct from the understanding: "God has endued the soul with two principal faculties: The one, by which it is capable of perception . . . is called the understanding. The other, that by which the soul is . . . some way inclined with respect to the thing it views or considers . . . This faculty is called by various names: it is sometimes called the *inclination*; and, as it has respect to the actions that are determined and governed by it, is called the *will*; and the *mind*, with regard to the exercises of this faculty, is often called the *heart*."[29] But this important statement needs to be read with considerable care and in context, for Edwards is not arguing an essential division between the faculties but only a notional one.[30] In other words, the understanding is distinct from the will only in the sense that a person can be a "neutral observer;" once the person understands that something is desirable or not desirable the will and emotions are engaged, causing a whole-soul response, that Edwards terms 'affections.'[31] 'Affection' devotion is whole-person devotion, not emotion alone.[32]

Implies a Unique Spiritual Understanding

The unity of these two, understanding and heart, is of the essence of the uniqueness of spiritual understanding.[33] For, Edwards argues, spiritual understanding primarily consists in a "sense of the supreme beauty . . . or moral perfection of divine things." This sense of the supreme beauty of God Edwards calls a "sense of the heart," or in other words a 'perception' (a function of the understanding) of the will/emotion that is the heart, as it is not only "speculative knowledge" but also "delight" and "taste, inclination, and will."[34] So it is that there cannot be, "a clear distinction made between the two faculties of understanding and will, as acting distinctly and separately, in this matter." Their edges are blurred for this is a "sensible knowledge," where the heart is inclined, but there is still "instruction in it," in the same way that "he that has perceived the sweet taste of honey, knows much more about it, than he who has only looked upon and felt it."[35] Once there is this "sight of the divine beauty of Christ," then "not only the understanding, but the will and the whole soul, receives and embraces the saviour."[36] There are two ways of judging of the "good" of anything, either when the mind is sensible whether something is "agreeable to the law of the country or law of God," or when the mind is sensible "of the beauty and amiableness of the thing" so that it is, "sensible of pleasure and delight in the presence of the idea of it." This kind of sensibleness, "carries in it an act of the will, or inclination, or spirit of the mind, as well as the understanding."[37] This soul that so judges of God has a "taste," a "sight," a "sense," a "feeling" of God, because its understanding of God is an experience of God.[38]

Understanding is essential; if there were none it would be a sure sign that the experience were not of God, "Now there are many affections which do not arise from any light in the understanding. And when it is thus, it is a sure evidence that these affections are not spiritual."[39] Still, this does not imply that it is intellectual stimulation that converts a person. In fact an intellectual grasp of God is exactly the kind of understanding that could be given to the unconverted person on the last day. It could be, "by explaining of them to his understanding . . . so as to make the reason and justice of things comprehensible by his reason: as probably the wicked will be convinced when they come to be judged." On the other hand, the regenerate soul is given a "sense of the glorious, holy and excellent nature of God," for, "this gives it true humility and assures it that God must be right and just in all things, and even in those things that it cannot comprehend."[40] There must be content to spiritual understanding, as "holy affections are not heat without light; but evermore arise from some information of the understanding,"[41] but intellectual comprehension does not require spiritual understanding.

A late and unpublished sermon of Edwards makes the pastoral application of his position concerning the unity of understanding and heart clear. It bears the doctrine: "A work of conversion . . . in the heart is not a meer whim or fancy but a great and certain reality" and the relevant part is worth quoting at length. Edwards is applying the doctrine to encourage his hearers to self-examination to see whether they are genuinely converted,

"you say it may be it [the experience] was certainly Something extraordinary. Something beyond your own Power & Effect. But my Question now is whether you are changed. Men may have alterations of their Ideas & a great many changes in what passes in their minds & in their feelings & in their affections & yet may not be changed. Everything that is new & extraordinary on a mans mind dont change the man any more than putting on a new Garment or going into another Room. There are many new Ideas that men have excited in 'em & new affections & very strange & extraordinary feelings that dont change the man to make him new any more than a musician playing a new Tune to him or a mans telling a new story to him that have heard before. *The Question is not whether you have met with something new but whether you are new.*"[42]

That was ever Edwards' question: he was not concerned with new feelings or with new understanding, but with being new.[43]

The 'sense of the heart,' the unity of the soul in affection devotion to God, is not all that is required to explicate the uniqueness of spiritual understanding. To be made new, does not just require a particular kind of understanding, but an entirely different kind of understanding. So Edwards says that, "there is such a thing as an understanding of divine things, which in its nature and kind is wholly different from all knowledge that natural men have."[44] It is not just the object of perception that is different, but the very way the subject perceives. The spiritual understanding of saints is entirely new in that "it must consist in their having a certain kind of ideas, or sensations of mind, which are simply diverse from all that can be in the minds of natural man," which is the same as to say, "that it consists in the sensations of a new spiritual sense."[45]

It is important to grasp that this 'spiritual sense' is not a nod and a wink towards Lockean empiricism,[46] but rather an appeal to the language of that philosophy to explain the experience of what might be termed 'spiritual appreciation.'[47] So in Miscellanies 739, entitled, "LOVE TO GOD. PREDOMINANCY OF GRACE," Edwards argues that, "He that has Gods supream [sic] excellency thus discover'd to him has a sense of heart of his being lovely above all for spiritual knowledge & conviction consists in the sense of the heart . . . "[48] The 'sense of the heart' or 'spiritual sense' is the sight that God is 'lovely above all,'[49] for everything else about God—his divinity, his power, his character—will on judgement day be plain to all, and are only "what natural men and devils can see and know, and will know fully and clearly to all eternity."[50] But appreciation of God, seeing his beauty and loveliness, is what is alone granted to saints: "Spiritual understanding primarily consists in this sense or taste of the moral beauty of divine things; so that no knowledge can be called spiritual, any further than it arises from, and has this in it."[51] He that does not have appreciation of God, a sense of his beauty, has nothing, "Unless this is seen, nothing is seen . . . Unless this is understood nothing is understood . . . " Why? Because the beauty of God is of his essence, "This is the beauty of the Godhead, the divinity of the divinity, (if I may so speak,) the good of the infinite fountain of good," so that God and ourselves and existence are worse than meaningless without it, "Without this God himself (if that were possible) would be an infinite evil, we ourselves had better never have been; and there had better have been no being." He concludes that such a spiritual sense is the foundation of knowledge, "He therefore in effect knows nothing, that knows not this: his knowledge is but the shadow of knowledge, or the form of knowledge, as the apostle calls it."[52]

It is tempting to soften the blow of the radical conclusion that the foundation of knowledge is unique to a particular group, but Edwards is consistent in holding to it. While he is careful to avoid essential exclusivity, stating that, "this new spiritual sense is not a new faculty of understanding," he is clear that it is unique, "but it is a new foundation laid in the nature of the soul, for a new kind of exercises of the same faculty of understanding."[53] He does not offer explanations of reasoned clarity, in fact he readily admits that he cannot, for "When we explain spiritual things . . . though we give the most accurate descriptions possible we do not fully explain them, no, not so much as to give any manner of notion to one that never felt them; any more than we can fully explain the rainbow to one that never saw [it], though a rainbow is a very easy thing to give a definition of."[54] But the claim that true experience involves a unique spiritual understanding underpins his epistemology from the beginning, "This way of knowing or believing is very differing from all other kinds of knowledge or belief," not just as regards the divine object of knowledge but also the experience of the subject, "It is not by discourse, neither is it by intuition as other intuition. Neither can this kind of faith, or this sort of knowledge, be exercised in any common objects; for there are no such distinguishing amiable properties, of such a force as to bear down the mind at such a rate as the divine properties."[55]

Edwards defends such an experience of God as both certain and rational. It is certain in that "this faith may be to the degree of certainty, for he may certainly intuitively see God and feel him in those ideas,"[56] and that as there is such a thing as a "conviction of the reality of the thing, that is incommunicable," as it is too complex to express or argue, so it is with the "idea of religion, which is so exceedingly complex" in those who are taught by the Spirit of God. For those who are so taught, the "idea" is so "real" and bears such "ineffable marks of truth" that it is a kind of "intuitive evidence," an evidence that "the nature of the soul will not allow it to reject." It is rational in the sense of what is meant by the testimony of the Spirit, a "sort of seeing rather than reasoning the truth of religion."[57] Indeed, Reasoning alone is very fallible, the history of the world shows us that true religion was never found by reason. "We see in fact that when man first began to speculate and reason about the things of the world, they reason'd & speculated very wrong," and when the accounts are properly analysed, "we can meet with nothing to induce us to think that the first religion of the world was introduced by the use and direction of meer natural Reason . . . without any assistance from Revelation."[58] Post-New Testament revelation is rationally defensible as an impartation of 'Light' to the individual, and this "Divine and Supernatural Light immediately imparted to the Soul by the Spirit of God, [can be] shown to be both a Scriptural and Rational Doctrine."[59] It is rational because it this light that enables reason to function, "A man that sets himself to reason without divine light is like a man that goes in the dark into a garden full of the most beautiful plants, and most artfully ordered, and compares things together by going from one thing to another, to feel of them and measure the distances; but he that sees by divine light is like a man that views the garden when the sun shines upon it."[60] No attempt is made to remove from the doctrine of 'supernatural light' the stain of the 'scandal of particularity' — In his Bible Edwards wrote next to John 1:9, "*That* was the true Light, which lighteth every man that cometh into the world:"[61] "9 i.e. there is not nor ever was nor will be any man in the world Enlightened but by Jesus & Every man that cometh into the world that ever is Enlightened is Enlightened by him."[62] Yet for Edwards, even though such a truly enlightened experiential heart understanding of God is entirely unique to the Christian, it is defensible as both certain and rational.[63]

THE SIGNS OF TRUE EXPERIENCE

Initially it might seem that to enumerate the content of Edwards' signs could be a somewhat redundant exercise. Is it not simply "all the elements that constitute sanctification" that are Edwards' signs of conversion?[64] But there is more here than meets the eye because Edwards' design is grander than a pious call to holiness. His aim is to describe sanctification in such a way as to distinguish it from unregenerate morality.[65] Or, to put it another way, Edwards attempts to answer, "the central test of Protestantism," that is, "how shall the presence of the divine spirit be discerned?"[66] By means of signs, Edwards marked out the area for true religious experience. This section shall indicate his answer by evaluating first his negative signs and then his positive signs.

In Edwards' assessment of experience it as important to understand what is not significant as what is significant. Roughly half of the content of both "The Religious Affections" and "The Distinguishing Marks" is concerned to analyse the 'negative' signs, or things that are not *signi*ficant. These are not merely a prelude to the real argument in the main body of the text, but a clearing of the decks serving to pull the reader's judgement away from what may, and to Edwards' mind often does, lead to a false assessment of experience.[67]

Edwards lists many negative signs, nine in "The Distinguishing Marks" and twelve in "The Religious Affections." While it is possible to see that these various signs are not amorphous but related,[68] it is not possible to distil specific doctrines of Edwards' from the pedagogical content of these negative signs. This is because they are not really expressions of his doctrines as such. Instead, they are a list of other people's doctrinal mistakes; their, in Edwards' eyes, mistaken interpretative grids used either for or against the experiences associated with the Great Awakening. What makes these lists of negative signs revealing for the understanding of Edwards is that they display an undergirding principle that causes him to reject these interpretations. In that sense they do not express doctrines of Edwards but a doctrine of Edwards: they are his record of the many mistakes that originate from a source error. So he argues that, "They have greatly erred in the way in which they have gone about to try this work ... in judging of it *a priori*; from the way that it began, the instruments that have been employed, the means that have been made use of ... in carrying it on. Whereas, if we duly consider the matter, it will evidently appear that such a work is not to be judged of a priori, but *a posteriori*. We are to observe the effect wrought."[69] The error is to judge by what produces the experience not by what the experience produces, *a priori* not *a posteriori*.[70]

The types of a priori signs that may be mistakenly resorted to as a basis for judgement are partly concerned with the externals of an experience. So "The Distinguishing Marks" has as negative signs various extreme or untraditional factors that might prejudice analysis. It is no sign that the work, "is carried on in a way very unusual and extraordinary," that it causes "effects on the bodies of men," that the subjects of it, "have great impression made on their imagination," that there are "some delusions of Satan intermixed with the work," that "such as were thought to be wrought upon, fall away into gross errors."[71] Similarly in "The Religious Affections" the extraordinary nature of the work is not significant, that "religious affections are very great, or raised very high," nor the physical manifestations of the work, that there are "great effects on the body."[72] But the fallacy of a priori judgement is not limited to conclusions from externals, but includes the experiential. In "The Religious Affections" there are eight negative signs that are concerned with the internal. We are told that it is no sign of the validity of experiences that "they come with texts of Scripture, remarkably brought to the mind," or that they have "an appearance of love in them," or that they are "religious affections of many kinds."[73]

According to Edwards, it is as erroneous to assume that a heart experience is the work of God because it touches the heart, as it is to assume that an experience is not the work of God because it is accompanied by means to reach the heart; as erroneous to assume that a religious experience is the work of God because it makes someone 'religious' as it is to assume that an experience is not the work of God because it is accompanied by unusual religious methods. *A priori* judgement fails: "To judge *a priori*, is a wrong way of judging of any of the works of God." Why? For two reasons. First, because of the "nature of man" these kind of effects are inevitably tied to the human condition.[74] Secondly, because there is something unknowable about the work of God in its *a priori* state, "God gives no account of his matters. . . . We know not what is the way of the Spirit, nor how the bones do grow in the womb of her that is with child; even so we know not the works of God who maketh all."[75] The only reliable way to assess an experience is *a posteriori*.

Produces a Unique Spiritual Effect

The *a posteriori* assessment that Edwards offers lies in his inter-relation of twelve positive signs, producing a positive paradigm of holiness that is inextricably linked to experience.[76] Here Edwards marks out the epistemological import of the unique spiritual effect of grace.[77] For Edwards, as true experience implies a unique spiritual understanding of God, a "sense of the heart," so that true experience produces a unique spiritual effect. While there is not an essential change (it is not a "new faculty of will" that is produced in the same way that the "sense of the heart" is not a "new faculty of understanding"), still there is a "new holy disposition of heart that attends this new sense."[78] The true disposition is unique: it is "that which the power of men or devils is not sufficient to produce the like of, or anything of the same nature,"[79] and that which the "Devil would not do if he could."[80] So the true disposition is distinguishable by its effects: Scripture teaches, "that converts are new men, new creatures, that they are renewed not only within but without."[81]

In "The Religious Affections," then, it is, indeed, not enough simply to ask "whether Edwards was 'for' or 'against' affections," because no answer of the either/or type can be given, "the point is that he was 'for' the affections, but not in any sense that you please."[82] So the first eleven positive signs of "The Religious Affections" concern true heart experience as carefully distinguished from false experience. Yet it is also not enough to see moral behaviour as necessarily spiritual fruit. In the twelfth sign Edwards identifies the kind of fruit that will only grow out of such true heart experience.

However, in "The Distinguishing Marks" Edwards does come close to suggesting a caricature of his signs, inadvertently encouraging the interpretation that if someone appears religious then that someone must be experiencing God. Here his concern is, as with "The Religious Affections," rightly to evaluate experience of God, yet his epistemological method is somewhat less subtle. In "The Distinguishing Marks" his design is to show what are "the true, certain, and distinguishing evidences" of a work of the Spirit,[83] and from these evidences confidently concludes that such and such, "is a sure sign that it is the true and right Spirit,"[84] or that because of so and so, "we may certainly conclude that it is from the Spirit of God."[85] In "The Distinguishing Marks" Edwards has near total confidence based on 'evidences' or 'marks.' In "The Religious Affections" on the other hand, while Edwards is likewise concerned to establish correct 'signs,' his specific aim is to judge of 'affections,' for "true religion, in great part, consists in the affections."[86] His epistemological focus is not so much on 'marks' but on the affections of the heart, and secondarily on the signs that will validate them. The difference is crucial to understanding the development within his thinking, and grasping his maturer position.[87] In "The Religious Affections" it is only the last positive sign that most closely covers the same ground as all the positive signs in "The Distinguishing Marks."[88]

It is true that this last sign, the fruit of practical Christian living, is the one that Edwards considers to be his most significant distinguishing mark.[89] It is "Christian practice . . . that it is the chief sign of grace."[90] This emphasis on practical fruit is characteristically Edwardean. It may be found in other places in "The Religious Affections,"[91] and in his unpublished writings.[92] In his "Miscellanies," Edwards makes it clear that signs of holiness are the epistemological indicators of true experience. The answer to the question, "what are the Best signs of Godliness?" is that a person's "Good fruits" are the "Evidences by which we are chiefly & most safely & surely" to determine godliness.[93] Late in the "Miscellanies," Edwards concludes that every other kind of indicator may mislead, "Blossoms may look fair and not only so but smell sweet Send forth pleasant odour and yet come to nothing. It is true the Fruit therefore and neither leaves nor blossoms is that by which we must Judge of the Tree. So persons talk about things of Religion may appear fair and may be exceeding savoury and the Saints may think they talk feeling they may relish their may imagine they perceive a divine savour in it as David did in Ahithophel (as he says, we took Sweet Counsel together) and yet all may prove nothing."[94] Edwards may even have run against the formidable example of his Grandfather Stoddard on this matter, so certain was he of the importance of fruit.[95]

Yet, while this is clearly an appeal to morality as the final arbiter of experience, it is not equating morality with experience. For the fruit of practical holiness to be the sign of true affections it is necessary that it be the expression of the internal acts of grace in the soul.[96] There is an inextricable connection between the internal and the external. Edwards sees that when Scripture asserts that God searches the heart the internal is most significant, "in this great evidence of sincerity that the Scripture gives us, what is inward is of greatest importance." But this prioritisation does not deny but incorporate the significance of the external, "yet what is outward is included and intended, as connected with the practical exertion of grace in the will, directing and commanding the actions of the body."[97] While it is not possible, then, to say that there is a heart for Christ without actually following him, "The main and most proper proof of a man having a heart to any thing, concerning which he is at liberty to follow his own inclinations . . . is his doing of it," there must actually be a heart for Christ.[98]

Even within the section discussing the fruit of Christian practice in "The Religious Affections," Edwards is at pains to make plain that heart experience of Christian truth is essential. In discussing fruits, "a profession of Christianity is not excluded, but supposed," defining this as holding to the "essence of Christianity" both in terms of basic doctrine, such as that "Jesus is the Messiah" and in personal application of such doctrine, "that we do with our whole hearts embrace Christ as our only saviour."[99] So he comments, "We are to know them by their fruits; that is, we are by their fruits to know whether they be what they profess to be; not that we are to know by their fruits, that they have something in them, to which they don't so much as pretend to."[100]

The same pattern is apparent in his unpublished notes "Signs of Grace." While, on the one hand the keeping of Christ's commandments that are given in Scripture as a sign are not referring to the "holy exercises of heart" for this would be to test the heart by the heart, to make it a "sign of itself."[101] Yet, on the other hand, as real morality and true experience are in collaboration not contradiction, "to have X'[Christ's] spirit and to be of a X[Chris]tian spirit are the same thing,"[102] feeling is essential. It is not a sign but it must be the signified. By feeling we can even have assurance, "by feeling that divine holy humble amiable disposition and motion in us."[103] 'Fruits' are a sign of the accuracy of that internal feeling.

In other words, morality alone can not be a sign of true religion. It is a simple misappropriation to use Edwards, as William James did, as a base for the validation of a spirituality with no base in objectivity.[104] Fruit is Edwards most important sign, but it is fruit that stems from 'root.' There must be objective truth and a foundation in genuine experience, for the sign of morality to mean anything. So, Edwards is careful to define precisely what kind of fruit he is looking for as a sign of true experience, and that such experience is essential; not just any fruit will do and the personal knowledge of Christ can not be replaced with a vacuum of 'spirituality.'

Therefore for someone who professes to be Christian to be seen as a 'good person' is not a sufficient external sign of internal grace: "Merely that a professor of Christianity is what is commonly called an honest, and a moral man

... is no great evidence of the sincerity of his profession." For such morality is not exclusive to a heart experience of Christ. What is needed is not a negative morality but, "great positive appearances of holiness in men's visible behaviour."[105]

"The Religious Affections" travels upon this unbreakable cord that runs from experience to practice.[106] The twelfth sign establishes a positive paradigm of practical holiness, which, Edwards explicitly argues, draws from the foundation of heart experience.[107] Christian practice has three particular aspects. First, total obedience: "'Tis necessary that men should be universally obedient."[108] There can be no lurking monster of sin in the depths of a persons heart, "So that it is necessary that men should part with their dearest iniquities, which are as their right hand and right eyes."[109] Secondly, complete employment: Christianity is to be "the main business of their lives." For "no man can do the service of two masters at once," and "the kingdom of heaven is not to be taken but by violence. Without earnestness there is no getting along, in that narrow way that leads to life."[110] Thirdly, final perseverance: "Every true Christian perseveres in this way of universal obedience, and diligent and earnest service of God, through all the various kinds of trials that he meets with, to the end of life."[111] Each of these is drawn from the waters of true experience.

Edwards' paradigm of practical holiness is produced from the preceding eleven signs concerning heart experience. Edwards argues that, "The *reason why* gracious affections have such a tendency and effect, appears from many things that have already been observed, in the preceding parts of this discourse."[112] Edwards gives eleven "reasons why" true experience gives rise to such practical holiness, explicitly drawn from each of the eleven positive signs concerning the heart, showing that it is this root that generates the practical fruit.[113]

In the first sign Edwards argues that true affections of the heart are "*spiritual, supernatural* and *divine*."[114] To be spiritual is not merely to be the object of the Holy Spirit's actions but to be invested with the Holy Spirit's nature.[115] So manifesting the gifts of the Spirit proves nothing because true experience manifests spiritual character not just spiritual ability.[116]

Edwards argues in signs two and three that true affections are founded on a realisation and love of the excellency of divine things "as they are in themselves,"[117] not for ulterior motives.[118] True experience aims at God himself not the experience, and therefore motivates holiness.[119]

The fourth sign argues that true heart experience is reasonable. It arises from "the mind being enlightened, rightly and spiritually to understand or apprehend divine things," for "holy affections are not heat without light" but always contain some "spiritual instruction."[120] This "shows the reason" for holiness.[121]

Fifthly, true affections are certain. They are attended with "a conviction of the reality and certainty of divine things."[122] The conviction is reasonable,[123] confident beyond the merely probable,[124] an internal gospel evidence[125] that persuades of the value of holiness.[126]

True affections are humble, "attended with evangelical humiliation," according to sign six.[127] For the true saint the sense of God's "holy beauty" is such that he inevitably feels his own moral poverty.[128] This is not 'legal' humiliation,[129] nor 'hypocritical' pretence[130] but a servant attitude that causes a willingness to obey, "Humility is that wherein a spirit of obedience does much consist."[131,132]

True affections in the seventh sign are not an external effect but an internal change that produces changed character. They are a "change of nature,"[133] a "new creature,"[134] so that "not only does the sun shine in the saints, but they also become little suns, partaking of the nature of the fountain of their light."[135]

In sign eight, the ethic that true affections produce is the character of Christ, which Edwards defines as a "spirit of love, meekness, quietness, forgiveness, and mercy . . . " According to Edwards this is specifically the "Christian spirit."[136]

True experiences in sign nine hate sin but the false love it. The subjects of false affections never grasp that grace is an escape from sin not a ticket to indulge in it: "Such persons as these, instead of embracing Christ as their *saviour from sin*, trust in him as the *saviour of their sins*."[137] The "reason why" true saints have "constant obedience" is because they have a nature to run from sin, "a dread of the appearance of evil."[138]

True affections are balanced, they have "beautiful symmetry and proportion," according to sign ten.[139] Edwards here displays his aesthetical taste for order. For him, true affections are harmonious, false affections discordant. False affections may have a love for God that is not matched by love for man, or perhaps an unbalanced zeal for some doctrine disproportionate to its importance. There is a symmetrical shape to true affections to which false affections can be compared;[140] the balance of true experience is "one great reason" why the Christian practice which flows from it is "universal, and constant, and persevering."[141]

Eleventhly, true affections desire more. They produce an increasing "spiritual appetite" whereas "false affections rest satisfied in themselves."[142] That does not mean that God does not satisfy, discovering him leads to a desire for, "no other kind of enjoyments," but an increasing desire for "more of the same."[143]

The causal link between these eleven signs and the twelfth sign of practical Christian holiness teaches that real morality is founded on real affections. Edwards' true experience is of affections that entail appreciation of the character of God, a unique sense of the heart of the beauty of God. Such affections are validated not by the intensity of the emotional experience, but by the fruit, that is the unique moral fruit that the unique affections produce. Now what remains is to evaluate Edwards' position in terms of the contemporary debate over the epistemology of religious experience.

SENSE, SIGNS AND CONTEMPORARY EPISTEMOLOGY

It is apparent that over the last twenty years or so there has been an increasing awareness of the epistemological structure of our Enlightenment heritage. By and large it is agreed that since the eighteenth century the dominant process of making epistemological judgements has been on the basis of 'foundationalism.'[144,145]

It would not be hard to argue that epistemological debate and the primacy of the foundationalist answer is the essential nature of our inheritance from the Enlightenment.[146] The genealogical tree of foundationalism has often been traced; rooted in Descartes, growing from Locke to Hume, replanted by Kant, redirected by the 'Vienna Circle,' and with contemporary defenders such as Chisholm.[147] Within this picture there are both empiricists and rationalists, and the junction of the two in Kant's 'transcendental idealism,' but all are united by their Cartesian doubt of any knowledge unless it can be shown to be based on an indubitable foundation. They are united by a certain epistemology. Kant's famous retrospective description of the Enlightenment in his answer to the question, 'Was ist Aufklärung?' was not 'dare to reason' or 'dare to think' but 'aude sapere,' 'dare to know.'[148] So the main stay of philosophical debate became how to know: "Ultimately the philosophical controversies of the Enlightenment did not focus their attention on metaphysics but turned to questions of epistemology, which remain the preoccupation of modern philosophy."[149] The foundationalism thus established by Descartes was no minor tinkering change to western thinking but a Kuhn-esque paradigm shift.[150] The ensuing history of philosophy records that Descartes' foundation principle, *Cogito ergo sum*, may be seen as an epistemological change of astronomical proportions, of Copernican dimensions.[151]

Of course, foundationalism has always had its detractors. Early on Hume exposed the resident sceptical position germinal in the foundationalist scheme, the answer to which Kant's work was dedicated.[152] Dissatisfaction with such scepticism also led to the appearance of the Scottish 'Common Sense' school and American 'Pragmatism.'[153] But currently the debate over foundationalism has reached a new stage: it rages, not just in criticism of its results, but in doubting its very cogency.[154] Epistemology has always formed itself vis-à-vis scepticism, and some defenders of foundationalism would no doubt see these attacks on their position in old fashioned sceptical dress, to which the best response is a determined re-expression of the foundationalist position, perhaps in combination with other systems.[155] Yet with body blows from the Gettier counter-examples,[156] and post-modern denial of the possibility of objective knowledge, such traditional responses are decidedly inadequate.[157]

As regards the epistemology of religious experience, these developments are highly significant. It is from this angle of the philosophy of religion that perhaps the most telling criticism of foundationalism has come, but also some real attempts at replacement systems.

It is not surprising that proponents of the reality of religious experience have been suspicious of foundationalism, at least in its 'strong' form, for it has often been used *a priori* to negate the possibility of religious experience.[158] So Plantinga is at his most incisive when he argues that foundationalism cannot possibly be satisfactory as it is self-referentially incoherent; it makes no sense on its own terms. If the principle of knowledge, he asks, is that all knowledge must be based on that which is self-evident or incorrigible, how can one possibly arrive at this principle?[159] While this obviously exposes the circularity of foundationalism, it may be felt that this is not an example of vicious circularity, or that, in other words, some circularity is inevitable when discussing the principle of knowledge. How, it may be asked, could it be possible to know any principle of knowledge without some self-referential incoherence? Be that as it may, taken in the context of the gathering momentum of criticism levelled at foundationalism, history may record such presuppositional queries as the straw that broke the foundationalist's back.

More significant, however, for our evaluation of Edwards' contribution to the contemporary debate is the answers that have been proposed to solve this, at least perceived, problem. I will briefly outline three specific responses that I take to be indicative of the two main positions, and a variation on a theme of the second. First, there is that given by Hebblethwaite in his "A Defence of Objective Theism."[160] Hebblethwaite's approach is to digress from the description of the development of modern philosophy such that it is seen as inevitably leading to religious subjectivism. Rather he cites authors to support the thesis that there is a stream of thought in defence of objectivity.[161] Then he re-expresses the traditional arguments in defence of God, emphasises the importance of the inner coherence of Christianity, so underlining his method of arguing from truth to the existence of God,[162] acknowledging that belief in God must be founded on revelation.[163] His method, in sum, is to argue from truth to God. Secondly, there is the approach of John Hick, as argued in his "Philosophy of Religion."[164] For Hick the traditional proofs of God are inadequate, which he counterpoises with revelation.[165] By this he does include the historical revelation of God in Jesus Christ, but his emphasis is on the subjective mechanism by which we come to believe. He draws from his understanding of Wittgenstein's use of puzzle pictures in the "Philosophical Investigations," that make the viewer look twice to really see, that there is seeing and then there is seeing. This second seeing he calls "Experiencing as" and this is his "epistemological pattern," for experience of God.[166] Hick's method, in sum, is to appeal to human experience to legitimise God experience. Thirdly, there is the position of William Alston, argued in his, "Perceiving God: The Epistemology of Religious Belief."[167] Alston argues for the similarity of sense perception to what he terms 'mystical perception.'[168] In the same way that sense perception can be justified circularly and only circularly, so can mystical perception. Thus mystical perception is on the same footing as the normally accepted sense perception.[169] Alston's method, in sum, is to defend mystical perception as defensible as sense perception.[170]

It is clear that there is common ground between Edwards and the current epistemological debate over religious experience. His approach bears little resemblance to the main thrust of that represented by Hebblethwaite. Edwards does not argue from truth to God or experience of God, but from God to true experience.[171] With the approach of Hick and Alston he would be closer, particularly with that of Alston, for as Alston recognises, Edwards did describe experience of God in terms of sense perception.[172] However the door to relativism that Hick has been criticised as leaving open would have abhorred him,[173] and his formation of the sense of God avoids the charge against Alston, that he has failed to establish the rationality of his mystical perception.[174]

The key point to distinguish is that Edwards is not arguing that 'mystical perception,' to use Alston's terminology, is the same kind of perception as sense perception, but that it is analogous to it. So he is not committed, as Hick may be, to arguing that all perception is 'appearing-as,' nor to agree with Alston that sense of God is a literal sense. When talking in such intangible terms the distinction between 'analogy' and being of the 'same kind' may seem to be arbitrary. To show that it is not, let us say for the sake of argument that Alston is also drawing an analogy between physical sense and sense of God. What then would be the distinction between this and Edwards' position? For Edwards the man who cannot see God is not strictly analogous to the man who can not see a tree; Edwards' sense is not analogous to the physical difference between sight and blindness, but analogous to an analogy drawn between sight and blindness. In other words, as Edwards insists, the spiritually blind can see God, in fact on the day of Judgement they will see God, but will never really see Him, because they do not recognise Him. They have no appreciation, no 'taste,' for his beauty.

A non-Edwardean metaphor may help to make the point clear. A baby with all its senses functioning normally can see as well, and quite possibly better, than an adult. Yet it is blind as to recognition: it can see its cot but does not know that it is a cot, does not appreciate it as a cot. This metaphor works as far as it goes. It is true for Edwards, as the metaphor suggests, that a lack of perception of God is not due to inability, strictly speaking, as it is for the physically blind. The cot is seen but not seen, it is not that it is not seen at all. However, the metaphor does also imply that perception can be learnt, as a child learns to see a cot, when for Edwards appreciation of God, the 'sense of his beauty,' can not be learnt because it is not a development of already resident faculties. Here we must be careful: it is not a new faculty that is given (Edwards is at pains to make this clear, and it separates him from Alston, it is not another perception), nor though is it the right development of the faculty that we already possess (again Edwards vehemently makes plain that the new sense is unique).[175]

So how, then, is it acquired? Now we reach the nub, because for Edwards it is simply not acquired, it is given. Another, more Edwardean, metaphor may help. The metaphor I have in mind is that of 'light,' a device with an Augustinian pedigree. A certain woman cannot feel God, He seems unreal, distant, imaginary. At some time her mind is enlightened; He is no longer a mental image but a spiritual sight. How did she come to see, she is asked? Did she acquire spiritual 'eyes' to perceive God? Did she learn to 'see' by religious technique? Neither of these fit the bill. In the end she stumbles that, 'God opened her eyes.' Whether the reply is thought to be naive or profound, she is witnessing to what Edwards called "A Divine and Supernatural Light," that is not acquired but given, it is "immediately imparted to the soul by the Spirit of God," and can be, "shown to be both a Scriptural and Rational Doctrine." For Edwards, the sense of God is only, to parody him, a 'new sight' as it sees by 'new light.' The sense reorientates the disposition of the mind by giving the mind light to work right.

This distinction involves three sub-distinctions that set Edwards apart from contemporary mystical perception theories: his insistence upon the mental continuity before and after experience of God, the total revolution of the orientation of the human psyche that this produces, and the utter sovereignty of God that his perception theory rest upon. God gives light, so humans now see right. God thus makes the blind see. Edwards avoids being forced to argue that all experiencing is 'experiencing as,' and so side-steps the charge of relativism. He is also able to assert the rationality of such a sense, for it is not a new mind that is acquired, but a mind made new that is given.

Edwards' true experience, then, may be philosophically defended as well as being theologically persuasive. As such, his 'sense of the heart' and 'signs of experience' provide a coherent and compelling means to and evaluation of spiritual experience.

NOTES

1. Guy Chevreau, *Catch the Fire*, (London, 1994), 150–151.
2. By engaging in the project of specifying true spiritual experience, Edwards is following a characteristic pattern of Puritan religious tradition, (William K.B. Stoever, "The Godly Will's Discerning," *Jonathan Edwards's Writings*, ed. Stephen J. Stein, [Bloomington, 1996], 85–99).
3. "Some Thoughts Concerning the Revival," *Yale Works*, iv, 332.
4. By far the longest chapter in *Catch the Fire* is, "A Well Travelled Path: Jonathan Edwards and the Experiences of the Great Awakening."
5. "Some Thoughts Concerning the Revival," *Yale Works*, iv, 297.
6. *Ibid.*, 441.
7. *Ibid.*, 473.
8. *Ibid.*, 333–334.
9. *Ibid.*, 335.
10. *Ibid.*, 340.
11. *Ibid.*, 341. Edwards here may misunderstand John Wesley's doctrine of Christian perfection. He does mention John Wesley approvingly in a 1739 unpublished sermon, (John H. Gerstner, *Steps to Salvation*, [Philadelphia, 1976], 92).
12. *Yale Works*, iv, 341. Only after such careful analysis, that Edwards made the much quoted comment, "Now if such things are enthusiasm, and the fruits of a distempered brain, let my brain be evermore possessed of that happy distemper!" ("Some Thoughts Concerning the Revival," *ibid.*, 341).
13. *Ibid.*, 341.
14. Edwards frequently appeals to his "experience" of these matters, or his knowledge of a "particular instance;" the "third cause of errors" he identified was, "being ignorant or unobservant of some particular things, by which the Devil has special advantage," (*Ibid.*, 458).
15. Expressions of piety are not sufficient sign of true experience. Commenting on the 'shibboleth' passage in Judges 12:6 Edwards argues, "we cant infer from it that we are warranted to Go as far in Judging mens state by what we think of their Rightly expressing themselves in spiritual & Experimental language," "Notes on the Scriptures," 367, *MSS*, Beinecke.
16. So the constant refrain in "The Distinguishing Marks" and "The Religious Affections" that if such and such things happen or if so and so things occur, it does not mean that it is a work of God and it does not mean that it is not: " 'Tis no argument," ("The Distinguishing Marks," *Yale Works*, iv, 234 etc.), " 'Tis no sign" ("The Religious Affections," *Yale Works*, ii, 127 etc.).
17. "Some Thoughts Concerning the Revival," *Yale Works*, iv, 296.
18. *Ibid.*, 296.

19. *Ibid.*, 306.

20. *Ibid.*, 300. Edwards' hermeneutical principle is a complex subject, and a complete analysis of it must bear in mind his expansive use of typology and his occasional hint that this implied the possibility of multi-layered interpretations, ("Notes on The Scriptures," 341; no. 851, "The Miscellanies," *MSS*, Beinecke; "Typological Writings," *Yale Works*, xi), and that despite this he believed that Scripture spoke with one gospel voice, seeing the importance of comparing Scripture with Scripture, (" 'Tis a good rule [in interpreting—crossed out] our [sic] endeavours to understand the mind of the spirit of God to compare spiritual Things with spiritual and to interpret scripture by scripture . . . " ("Notes on the Scriptures," 501, *MSS*, Beinecke). His understanding of the strategy necessary to interpret the Scriptural doctrine of spiritual experience could be summarised as 'descriptive' rather than 'prescriptive,' in search of 'analogy' rather than 'equivalence.' So he readily admits that there is no exact equivalent for some manifestations in the Scriptures, "I do not know that we have any express mention in the New Testament of any person's weeping, or groaning, or sighing through fear of hell, or sense of God's anger" and carries on in a tone of incredulity, "but is there any body so foolish as from hence to argue, that in whomsoever these things appear, their convictions are not from the Spirit of God?" He does, however, give examples of analogous occurrences in Scripture, listing as examples, for instance, the jailer who falls trembling at Paul and Silas' feet in Acts 16, and the experiences of the Psalmist in Psalm 32:3&4. He asserts that the reason why he is not here looking for direct equivalence is because of the descriptive not prescriptive nature of Scripture in this matter, "And the reason why we do not argue thus is, because these are easily accounted for, from what we know of the nature of man, and from what the Scriptures do inform us in *general*, concerning the nature of eternal things, and the nature of the convictions of God's Spirit; so that there is no need that any thing should be said in *particular* concerning these external, circumstantial effects," ("The Distinguishing Marks," *Yale Works*, iv, 233. My italics). This does not mean that Edwards limited the extent to which Scripture applied, it clearly covered every part of life, "To say that the Scriptures contain all things that are necessary in matters of faith, and not of worship [or] practice, is to talk very unintelligibly," (no. 61, "The 'Miscellanies,' a-500," *Yale Works*, xiii, 233), but that he defined the way in which it applied, "We have no grounds to assert that it was God's intent by the Scripture, in so many terms to declare every doctrine that he would have us believe; there are many things the Scripture may suppose that we know already," (no. 426, "The 'Miscellanies,' a-500," *Yale Works*, xiii, 479). For further discussion of Edwards' principle of Biblical interpretation, see Karl Dietrich Pfisterer, *The prism of Scripture: Studies on History and Historicity in the Work of Jonathan Edwards*, (Frankfurt, 1975), and Stephen Stein, "The Quest for the Spiritual Sense: The Biblical Hermeneutics of Jonathan Edwards," *Harvard Theological Review*, 70, (1977), 99–113.

21. "Scientific and Philosophical Writings," *Yale Works*, vi, 195.

22. "The 'Miscellanies', a-500," *Yale Works*, xiii, 460.

23. Variations on both of the view points that Edwards' identified as errors are often said to have been held by him. He is by some seen as 'historical,' as standing resolutely in a particular tradition. By others as 'philosophical,' as forming his theology

78   *Chapter Two*

around a particular school of thought. One of the most interesting examples of this is Perry Miller's philosophical interpretation of Edwards' sermon, "God glorified in man's dependence," (Perry Miller, *Jonathan Edwards*, [New York, 1949]). While at other times Miller does affirm that Edwards held to a biblicist use of Scripture, (though as Marsden argues, Miller may have a general tendency to undervalue the biblicism of the Puritans, George M. Marsden, "Perry Miller's Rehabilitation of the Puritans: A Critique," *Church History*, [March 1970], 91–105), one wonders, when reading this interpretation, what then Edwards meant by his introduction, "Corinth was not far from Athens, that had been for many ages the most famous seat of philosophy and learning in the world. The apostle therefore observes to them, how God by the gospel destroyed, and brought to nought their wisdom," and what he meant by the choice of a text in a chapter containing the theme, "Where is the wise? where is the scribe? where is the disputer of this world? hath God not made foolish the wisdom of this world?" (1 Corinthians 1:20, A.V.), of which Edwards quotes, that God, "chose the foolish things of the world to shame the wise," commenting that "the apostle informs them in the text why he thus did, *That no flesh should glory in his presence &c.*,"(*Banner works*, ii, 3–7). Certainly, in one sense there is much 'philosophy' here as elsewhere in Edwards, but it is hard to see this sermon as the right place to locate any philosophical programme of Edwards.

24. "True Grace Distinguished from the Experience of Devils," *Banner Works*, ii, 48.

25. A caveat should be noted at this point. It is quite clear that there is a significant development within Edwards' thinking on the matter of experience. His sometimes near-euphoric descriptions of the early Northampton revival in "A Narrative of Surprising Conversions" turned into an extended analysis of revival experience in his "The Distinguishing Marks" and "Some Thoughts Concerning the Revival," which then matured into his "The Religious Affections." No doubt the increasingly cautious tone in his writings was a response to some of the unfortunate extravagances of the Great Awakening, and the harm that was thus caused to the church. I suspect many misinterpretations of Edwards' views on experience are due to a lack of understanding of such a development, (See the "Conclusion" for an analysis of some recent popular interpretations that fall into this trap). But, it is equally essential to realise that Edwards' developing caution did not take him down the route that might be expected: he did not lean more heavily on the moral effects of an experience to discern its truth, but on its nature. Both emphases are important to Edwards throughout his writings, but the distinction between the "The Distinguishing Marks" and "The Religious Affections" is an increasing emphasis on affections not on marks, on the nature of an experience rather than its moral fruit.

26. Hoopes feels that it is important to distinguish between the 'sense of the heart,' a general term denoting emotional inclination, and the 'new spiritual sense,' Edwards' specific phrase for gracious affections. Failure to do so, to Hoopes' mind, has been a cause of significant misinterpretations, (James Hoopes, "Jonathan Edwards' Religious Psychology," *Journal of American History*, vol.69, [1982–1983], 849–865). Hoopes' view in part derives from a concern to evaluate Edwards' experiential theology as not dependant on Locke, and in part from an implied understanding of the 'affections' and the 'heart' in Edwards' writings as synonymous with 'emotions,' (*Ibid.*,

851, 857). With the first I am in sympathy (see footnote 47), but the second, besides appearing to make 'affections' anachronistic, seems to miss Edwards' constant emphasis on a whole soul response to God, a change of disposition. I, contrary to Hoopes, believe that these terms, and various others that Edwards uses, while not exactly interchangeable, are intended to convey different aspects of the same gracious experience of the true saint. The best way to understand Edwards' 'sense' descriptions of true experience is, I will argue, as 'appreciation.'

27. "The Religious Affections," *Yale Works*, ii, 99.
28. *Ibid.*, 99.
29. *Ibid.*, 96.
30. Steele is surely correct in seeing this as marking a "return to the *totus homo* doctrine of the Reformers," and may be correct in identifying the western mainstream understanding of the soul and the "regnant psychology of the day" as tripartite, a "harmonious co-operation of the 'faculties' of the soul (the intellect, the will, and the emotions)," but to say that Edwards moved from this position to affirm two faculties is too simplistic. (Richard B. Steele, *'Gracious Affection' and 'True Virtue' According to Jonathan Edwards and John Wesley* [London, 1994], 21, xi, 20). It is more correct to see in Edwards a kindling of spiritual fire as, "Will and emotions were organically bound together," (Richard L. Bushman, "Jonathan Edwards and the Puritan Consciousness," *Journal for the Scientific Study of Religion*, vol. 5, [1966], 385). There is something of a prefiguring of Edwards' position in his grandfather Solomon Stoddard, who could say on one occasion that, "understanding and the will in man being faculties of the same soul and really one and the same thing, the same act of God upon the soul that puts light into the understanding, does also suitably incline the will," (Cited by P.J. Tracy, *Jonathan Edwards, Pastor*, [New York, 1980], 32).
31. John E. Smith "Editors Introduction," *Yale Works*, ii, 13.
32. The faculties, "Join'd together & united in one constituteth saving Faith or the souls savingly embracing X[Christ]," ("Notes on the Scriptures," 304, *MSS*, Beinecke). See Chapter, "True Salvation" for comparison of this view with Chauncy's.
33. It is important to realise that when Edwards talks of beauty as recipient of a whole soul response he speaks in metaphor not equation. Human aesthetical experience is like experience of God not the same as experience of God.
34. That this is Edwards' intention by the phrase "sense of the heart" can be seen by the similarity in meaning he gives to the parallel, but linguistically different, phrase, "sense of the mind." So he argues that the first act of the Holy Spirit after conversion is "in spiritual understanding, or in the sense of the mind," and remarks that, "Indeed, the inclination of the soul is as immediately exercised in that sense of the mind which is called spiritual understanding, as the intellect." He then infers that this sense implies appreciation, by equating "sense or taste of the mind," (no. 397, "The 'Miscellanies', a-500," *Yale Works*, xiii, 463).
35. "The Religious Affections," *Yale Works*, ii, 272–3. No. 782 of Edwards' "Miscellanies," the "Sense of the Heart," that Perry Miller published as a disclosure of the thinking of Edwards, is only a fuller analysis of what was long before made public here, (See Perry Miller, "Jonathan Edwards on the Sense of the Heart," *The Harvard Theological Review*, vol.41, [1948], 123–45).

36. "True Grace Distinguished from the Experience of Devils," *Banner Works*, ii, 49.

37. No. 489, "The 'Miscellanies,' a-500," *Yale Works*, xiii, 533.

38. Edwards was not alone in the eighteenth century in so describing true Christian experience. For John Wesley, ". . . the natural man discerneth it not; partly, because *he has no spiritual senses, whereby alone we can discern the things of God*; partly, because so thick a veil is interposed as he knows not how to penetrate. But when he is born of God, born of the Spirit, how is the manner of his existence changed! His whole soul is now *sensible* of God, and he can say, by sure experience, 'Thou art about my bed, and about my path;' I feel thee in all my ways . . ." ("Privilege of Those that are born of God," *Sermons on Several occasions by the Rev. John Wesley*, sermon xix, vol. 1, [London: 1865], 251. My italics).

39. "The Religious Affections," *Yale Works*, ii, 266–7.

40. No. 470, "The 'Miscellanies,' a-500," *Yale Works*, xiii, 511–512.

41. "The Religious Affections," *Yale Works*, ii, 266.

42. 1 Corinthians 6:11, March 1747, "A work of Conversion as a great effect of God's power and grace in the heart is not a meer whim or fancy but a great and certain reality," (*MSS*, Beinecke. My italics).

43. It is also worth noting the linguistic looseness of his use of 'affections' here, when in "The Religious Affections" it is used with considerable precision. It is the concept of 'newness' that is of interest to him, and which I would argue is similar in both works, not its definition.

44. "The Religious Affections," *Yale Works*, ii, 270.

45. *Ibid.*, 271.

46. Edwards' relation to Locke has already been discussed in the "Introduction." In essence the position held is in agreement with Morris that Edwards, "used [Locke] mainly as a departure for his own thinking, rather than as a master in whose steps he would willingly follow," and hesitatingly in accord with the statement that Edwards was, "probably influenced by him more than by any other thinker," as long as this is taken to refer to 'philosophical' thinker as distinguished from the Puritan tradition in which Edwards stood, which seems the most natural way to read Morris given his earlier statement that, "There is no doubt also that the fundamental way in which he approached . . . Locke . . . was determined, before he read Locke, by his reading of the Protestant Scholastics," (William Sparks Morris, *The Young Jonathan Edwards: A Reconstruction*, [Ph.D. 1955, Brooklyn, N.Y., 1991], 576, 544). In the specific case of the 'sense' of the heart it is accepted that Edwards was influenced by Locke, but it is denied that Edwards thought to himself that, "the superstructure of theology would forever rest on shaky foundations if it could not be wholeheartedly committed to the Lockean Philosophy," (Perry Miller, "Jonathan Edwards on the Sense of the Heart," *Harvard Theological Review*, no. 41, [1948], footnote to page 124). Edwards' 'sense of the heart' is to some extent formulated in terms of Lockean empiricism, but the source of its content is Puritan and Biblical. Since work by Fiering, Anderson and Tracy on Edwards it has become common to downgrade the influence of Locke on Edwards. Hoopes goes further, arguing that Edwards use of words such as 'sense' and 'idea' are not examples of his use of empiricism to re-express traditional Puritan un-

derstanding of gracious experience; rather Edwards was embarked on an attack on the foundation of empiricism, materialism, "in order to make *it* consistent with the old view of religious experience," (James Hoopes, "Jonathan Edwards' Religious Psychology," *Journal of American History*, vol.69, [1982–83], 851). Hoopes slightly undervalues Locke's importance to Edwards, but I agree that an understanding of Edwards' 'immaterialism' is essential to grasping his doctrine of true experience. See the Chapter "True Reality."

47. Not grasping the importance of appreciation for Edwards' elucidation of the saints apprehension of the beauty of God, seems to be a serious error in William Wainwright's otherwise helpful, "Jonathan Edwards and the Sense of the Heart," *Faith and Philosophy*, vol. 7, no. 1, (Jan. 1990), 43–63. He argues that Edwards commits himself, "to the view that our knowledge of at least some necessary truths is derived from sense," which is unfortunate because, Wainwright feels, it is not possible to apprehend the moral goodness of a benevolent action without apprehending that the action is morally good. But Edwards is not so torturous: his position is that one can apprehend God (not moral goodness) without apprehending his beauty. To put it bluntly, it is possible to know the attributes of God without loving them, and this, Edwards argues, will be the situation of the devils and all unregenerate on judgement day. "Thou believest that there is one God;" Edwards would accord, "thou doest well: the devils also believe, and tremble." (James 2:19, A.V.; See Edwards' sermon on this text, "True Grace Experienced From the Experience of Devils," *Banner Works*, ii, 41–50). Actually, Edwards does not argue that "some" necessary truths are "derived" from sense, but that all truths are perceived by sense. See the Chapter "True Reality."

48. "Miscellanies," 739, *MSS*, Beinecke.

49. It is this sense of loveliness that is the cause of true spiritual feeling, a burning heart of devotion, (Luke 24:32, June 1736; Oct. 1755, " 'Tis a common [thing] with the saints that their hearts do burn within them while divine things are represented to them," *MSS*, Beinecke).

50. "The Religious Affections," *Yale Works*, ii, 272.

51. *Ibid.*, 273.

52. *Ibid.*, 274. Edwards is referring to Romans 2:20: "[thou art] an instructor of the foolish, a teacher of babes, which hast the form of knowledge and of the truth in the law," (A.V.). Some have seen Edwards' doctrine of sense to be "strikingly similar" to that of the Cambridge Platonist John Smith. We can not know for sure the extent of Smith's influence upon Jonathan Edwards, but Edwards certainly held his writings in high regard, giving him the longest footnote in "The Religious Affections" because he could not "forebear transcribing the whole of it" and remarking in his catalogue that his views had the power to take "one's eyes above the world," (John E. Smith, "Editor's Introduction," *Yale Works*, ii, 66). While some of what Smith says does bear a striking verbal similarity to Edwards phrases, such as, "That Divine things are to be understood rather by a Spiritual Sensation than a Verbal Description, or mere Speculation," one suspects that the underlying agenda is somewhat different from that of Edwards. Edwards could never have agreed that, "To seek out Divinity meerly in Books and Writings, is to *seek the living among the dead*: we doe but in vain seek God many times in these, where his Truth is not so much *enshrin'd*, as *entomb'd*: no;

intrate quare Deum, Seek to God within thine own soul," (John Smith, "A Discourse Concerning The True Way or Method of Attaining to Divine Knowledge," *Select Discourses*, [London, 1660], 1, 3).

53. "The Religious Affections," *Yale Works*, ii, 206.

54. No. 123, "The 'Miscellanies,' a-500," *Yale Works*, xiii, 286.

55. No. aa, *Ibid.*, 178. Pierce finds the appropriate description of Edwards' 'new sense' in his "Personal Narrative." Here, he argues, it is possible to see that the two conflicting strands of Edwards, philosopher and theologian, are really two contrasting ways of interpreting experience, "both of which, so to speak, are theological." Edwards unites both Puritan "order" and Enlightenment "enlargement" to see nature in a way not seen before, by encountering, a 'new sense' of glory in all nature." Such an appreciation of philosophy was made possible by the new philosophy's, "rapprochement between God and nature," shown in Edwards' 'space is God' statement and exhibited in the "Personal Narrative," (David C. Pierce, "Jonathan Edwards and the 'New Sense' of Glory," *The New England Quarterly*, vol.41, [1968], 82–91). Despite the insightful analysis of the constraining tensions of the time, and the imaginative power of this interpretation, it seems to lack insight into Edwards' new sense. Edwards' sense was unique, and therefore not essentially applicable to other kinds of appreciation though comparable with them, and divine. Edwards may well have had a greater 'sense' of the beauty of nature than his Puritan forebears, but this is not the same as his "sense of the heart."

56. No. aa, "The 'Miscellanies,' a-500," *Yale Works*, xiii, 178.

57. No. 201, *Ibid.*, 338.

58. "Miscellanies," 986, *MSS*, Beinecke.

59. *Banner Works*, ii, 12–17. The description Edwards gives of this 'light' is essentially the same as that in the "The Religious Affections" describing true affections, and as that in Miscellanies aa describing spiritual understanding, from where some of the paragraphs in "Supernatural Light" were probably imported, ("The 'Miscellanies,' a-500," *Yale Works*, xiii, 177).

60. No. 408, "The 'Miscellanies,' a-500," *Yale Works*, xiii, 470.

61. A.V.

62. This is the first of the two possible interpretations that Edwards gives for the verse. Edwards' annotation continues, "or thereby is meant that this light is not only to enlighten the Jews but that it enlightens Indifferently Every man Let him be of what nation soever it was fit that the True light when he came should be a general light Moses Enlightened only the nation of the Jews because he was not the True Light. See a very Parallel expression Col.1.23," ("Blank Bible," *MSS*, Beinecke).

63. It is this emphasis on the internal work of God in the heart that allows Edwards to sweep aside claims to experiences of, what might be called, 'external' divine action, i.e. actual visions or actual verbal suggestion. It is because these things make no impact on the heart. So in Miscellanies 394, he argues that there is real danger at times of heightened emotions that the imagination, rather than the heart, will be stimulated to mimic real spiritual awakenings, "The common people, when they are under great convictions and fears of hell, are commonly very evidently greatly under the power of imagination; they imagine they see lights, and hear voices, and see and hear many

things." So he warns that if such imaginations are encouraged, "if the main stress be laid upon such things, [Satan] may deceive persons; and God has not told us that he will not give Satan liberty." But to stress the heart, as the Bible does, is to guard against these things, as Satan can not, "imitate a Christian spirit and a Christian life; the Scripture is very careful to lay the main stress upon such things as Satan cannot imitate."(No. 394, "The 'Miscellanies,' a-500," *Yale Works*, xiii, 460). He does not deny that God can bring Scriptures to mind, but that this is not an experience of direct verbal suggestion. Rather it is by an experience of the mind, "So that the Spirit of God don't immediately suggest the places to us, as though by inspiration, but by stirring up corespondent affections of mind, whereby the mind is naturally put in mind of the text that is so agreeable to it; as much as one speech or sentence puts us in mind of another that is like it, or as one instrument of music answers of itself to another in harmony and concord," (No. 126, "The 'Miscellanies,' a-500," *Yale Works*, xiii, 290). It is more like being stimulated to feel the concave for the convex of Scripture, the female for the male, than hearing a voice.

64. John H. Gerstner, *Steps to Salvation*, (Philadelphia, 1976), 168.

65. Edwards is careful, however, to distinguish between assessing criteria of regeneration and judging individuals as regenerate or unregenerate. The latter practice he took to be an unwarranted extension of the practice of establishing 'visible saints' in the judgement of 'good charity.' Here he disagreed with the Separatists, (Psalm 55:12–14, September 1741, "Men are not sufficient positively to determine the state of the souls of others that are of God's visible people," *MSS*, Beinecke; "Every thing in the saints that belongs to the spiritual & divine Life is spoken of in SS[Scripture] as being hidden known only to God, " "Notes on the Scriptures," 365, *MSS*, Beinecke).

66. John E. Smith, "Editor's Introduction," *Yale Works*, ii, 1.

67. Edwards' concern to identify true from false experience stems from New England's experience of the religious controversies of the Great Awakening. Ward identifies a 'classic' eighteenth century agony of distinguishing between true and false religious experience, a desire to discern in response to an international plurality of religious expression, (W.R. Ward, *The Protestant Evangelical Awakening*, [Cambridge, 1992]).

68. Number four in "The Distinguishing Marks" is similar to number five in "The Religious Affections," and the first three are similar to each other.

69. "Some Thoughts Concerning the Revival," *Yale Works*, iv, 293. My italics. It is acknowledged that Edwards writes here towards the beginning of his career of assessing Religious experience, and that subsequent works, especially "The Religious Affections," evidence changes in his interpretations, but it is held that this initial statement is the appropriate summary of Edwards' doctrine of signs, from which he did not depart. The rest of the text of this section aims to establish this position.

70. This distinction is not solely to distinguish between deductive and inductive reasoning; Edwards intends 'a priori' as arguing from "the *axiomatic*," (Roderick M. Chisholm, *Theory of Knowledge* [London, 1989], 32), in what may be called the "modern" sense, that is, to indicate something that is "necessarily true or necessarily false, and can be known to be so independently of experience," (A.J. Ayer, *The Central Questions of Philosophy*, [London, 1973], 199). It is the divorce of assessment from the fruit of Christian experience that Edwards identifies as false, not deductive reasoning itself.

It is with this formula that Edwards aimed effectively to establish the nature of true religious experience in the traumatic aftermath of the Great Awakening. It may well be that Edwards' polemical target in "The Religious Affections" was the 'New Lights,' that his, "quarrel was primarily with those who accepted his presuppositions and drew from them unacceptable conclusions,"(Ava Chamberlain, "Self-Deception as a Theological Problem in Jonathan Edwards's 'Religious Affections,'" *Church History*, vol.63, no.4, [December 1994], 546), but the content of Religious Affections, as opposed to its presumed focus, was applicable to the doctrinal positions of both the Old and New Lights. Many have described the serious division that the revival brought to the Churches; Goen cites the dramatic illustration of John Marhead, a Boston Presbyterian sympathetic to the revival, writing in 1742, "Oh how Satan spews out his blood! God direct us what to do, particularly with pious zealots and cold, diabolical opposers!" The 'zealots' and the 'opposers' were the warring factions of 'new lights' and 'old lights,' as they were called, or, as the two may be characterised, of 'enthusiasts' and 'supernatural rationalists,' (ed. C.C. Goen, "Editor's Introduction," The Great Awakening, *Yale Works*, iv, 64). With such a split it was necessary for the true experiential Christianity in the revival to be defined: for Edwards not only must there be 'heat' and 'light' (reasonable Biblical content as well as high emotions), but this 'affection' must produce Biblical holiness. Edwards sought to show that experience was essential and that it essentially resulted in moral fruit.

71. "The Distinguishing Marks," *Yale Works*, iv, 228–229, 230, 234, 235, 238, 241, 243, 244, 246.

72. "The Religious Affections," *Yale Works*, ii, 127, 130, 181.

73. "The Religious Affections," *Yale Works*, ii, 142, 146, 147; also, 138, 151, 163, 165, 167.

74. "The Distinguishing Marks," *Yale Works*, iv, 231.

75. "Some Thoughts Concerning the Revival," *Yale Works*, iv, 294. This was written as a single quotation but is actually a collection of citations from Job 33:13; Psalm 36:6; Job 21:22, 36:23, 9:12; and Ecclesiastes 11:5.

76. Smith sees that, "It is a curious fact that Edwards nowhere considers the relations between the signs, whether they imply each other, whether some are more basic than others and similar questions," (John E. Smith, "Editors Introduction," *Yale Works*, ii, 24). I would agree that Edwards does not explicate which of the signs are "more basic than the others," but not that he does not consider the "relations between the signs." While I hesitate to contradict a statement of fact from such a senior Edwards scholar, it seems that Edwards does explicitly consider their inter-relationship, and the construction that he builds is important to understanding his epistemology of signs. Their relationship is discussed below in the main text.

77. Chamberlain argues that in Edwards doctrine of moral fruit he was asserting that "sanctification evidenced justification" and so was arguing against the increasing extremism of the New Lights in the same way that, "orthodox Puritans traditionally had done in order to counteract a tendency towards antinomianism." She feels that his use of this doctrine against the New Lights evinces his increasing disaffection with the radical fringe of the Awakening, in particular that they placed assurance in the "immediate experience" of conversion, thus not taking into account the potential of

human nature for "self-deception," (Ava Chamberlain, "Self-Deception as a Theological Problem in Jonathan Edwards's 'Religious Affections,'" *Church History*, vol. 63, no.4, [December 1994], 548–549). This would seem a helpful analysis, but when she argues that Edwards, "rejected immediate experience as a solution to the epistemological problem concerning the nature and means of assurance," (*Ibid.*, 555) she appears to have given insufficient consideration to the first eleven positive signs, which concern heart experience, and only evaluated the twelfth sign, concerning moral fruit.

78. "The Religious Affections," *Yale Works*, ii, 206.
79. "The Religious Affections," *Yale Works*, ii, 210.
80. "The Distinguishing Marks," *Yale Works*, iv, 258.
81. "Letter 1 to Mr. Gillespie," *Banner Works*, i, 337.
82. John E. Smith, "Editor's Introduction," *Yale Works*, ii, 17.
83. "The Distinguishing Marks," *Yale Works*, ii, 227.
84. *Ibid.*, 250.
85. *Ibid.*, 253.
86. "The Religious Affections," *Yale Works*, ii, 99.
87. While it is probable that some of the change to a more cautious tone came from Edwards' experiences of the Great Awakening, it did not cause him to retreat from professing experiential Christianity, rather motivating him better to define the nature of that experience. The development in Edwards' thinking, as Chamberlain has recently argued, is not a radical change in response to the Great Awakening, but an increasing sophistication of theological views already held before the mass revival, (Ava Chamberlain, "Brides of Christ and Signs of Grace," *Jonathan Edwards's Writings*, ed. Stephen J. Stein, [Indiana University Press, 1996], 3–18). Hence, in "The Religious Affections" Edwards not only gave increased emphasis on the positive signs of the heart but also on the negative signs of the heart, thereby endeavouring to unravel the tangled confusion that had enveloped heart experience as a result of some of the manifestations of the Great Awakening, (*Yale Works*, ii, 138, 142, 146, 147,151, 163, 165, 167).
88. The "Conclusion" discusses popular interpretations of Edwards where such a caricature is unnervingly common.
89. Edwards' insistence on 'fruit' may bear witness to some personal pain as well as theological embarrassment. After the revival, Edwards had found that more of his converts than he had expected had gone sour. As early as 1742 Edwards wrote that, "Religion in this and the Neighbouring Towns has now of late been on the decaying hand," (Edwards letter to Joseph Bellamy, Northampton Janury 21 1742, Howard C. Rice Jr., "Jonathan Edwards at Princeton: With a Survey of Edwards Materials in the Princeton University Library," *Princeton University Library Chronicle*, vol.xv, [1953–1954], 69–89). So Wesley caustically comments in his heavily edited abridgement to "The Religious Affections," that the only way for Edwards to continue to hold to the doctrine of the perseverance of the saints after many of his converts had "'turned back as a dog to the vomit,'" was by, "eating his own words, and proving, (as well as the nature of the thing would bear,) that they were no believers at all," (John Wesley, *Works*, [London, 1872; reprinted, Grand Rapids, 1958], xiv, 269–270; Richard B. Steele, *'Gracious Affection' and 'True Virtue' According to Jonathan Edwards and John Wesley*, [London 1994]).

90. "The Religious Affections," *Yale Works*, ii, 407.
91. *Ibid.*, 151.
92. Commentating on Romans 2:29, Edwards says that, "We are no where directed to judge of men of men [sic] chiefly by the account they give of their Experiences but Chiefly by their works," ("Notes on the Scriptures," 365, *MSS*, Beinecke).
93. No. 790, "Miscellanies," *MSS*, Beinecke.
94. No. 1000, "Miscellanies," *MSS*, Beinecke. For 'Ahithophel' see 2 Samuel 15:31. Edwards also comments on Ahithophel in, "The Distinguishing Marks," *Yale Works*, iv, 286.
95. Originally Stoddard had preached that, "there is no infallible sign of Grace but Grace. Grace is known only by intuition. All the external Effects of grace may flow from other causes," (John H. Gerstner, *Steps to Salvation*, (Philadelphia, 1976), 167). Edwards looked to Christian practice not intuition as the sign of grace.
96. To underestimate the importance of the source of experience in Edwards' doctrine of fruits is to fail to grasp Edwards' point altogether. He is concerned to identify true experience not to supplant its priority. When his doctrine of fruits has been divorced from his 'sense of the heart,' it has been used to countenance almost any kind of religious experience. So William James cites him favourably as supporting his phenomenological description of religious experience, not understanding that Edwards' fruits were intended to witness to the unique supernatural work of grace, (see, Wayne Proudfoot, "From Theology to a Science of Religions: Jonathan Edwards and William James on Religious Affections," *Harvard Theological Review*, vol.82, [April 1989], 163–165). This false division has also led to many popular misinterpretations of Edwards (see the "Conclusion"). Raposa does not miss this important distinction, arguing that the twelfth sign of Christian practice, Edwards' "theosemiotic," "is a sign-producing tendency, revealing grace invisible in effective practice," (Michael L. Raposa, "Jonathan Edwards' Twelfth Sign," *International Philosophical Quarterly*, vol.33, [June 1993], 153, 156). For him what distinguishes Edwards from later writers concerned with experience, such as Emerson and Pierce, is his theology, his "theosemiosis" intended to identify true grace and "election," (*Ibid.*, 160). Raposa sometimes seems to depict Edwards' theology in post-modern colours, as a background interpretation of experience rather than as the cause of the experience, but his emphasis on the theological root of Edwards' doctrine of experience is crucial, if rather more objective than post-modernity would wish.
97. "The Religious Affections," *Yale Works*, ii, 425.
98. *Ibid.*, 427. As Smith comments, it is possible to counterfeit profession, "but one cannot counterfeit the sense of the heart," (John E. Smith, "Jonathan Edwards as Philosophical Theologian," *The Review of Metaphysics*, vol.xxx, no.2, [1976], 324).
99. "The Religious Affections," *Yale Works*, ii, 412–413.
100. *Ibid.*, 415.
101. Notes titled either "Signs of Grace" (front page) or "Signs of Godliness" (page 1), *MSS*, Beinecke, page 1, section 3.
102. *Ibid.*, Page 3, Section 10.
103. *Ibid.*, Page 3, Section 10.
104. William James frequently refers to Edwards in his *Varieties of Religious Experience*. For a salient discussion see Wayne Proudfoot, "From Theology to a Science

of Religions: Jonathan Edwards and William James on Religious Affections," *Harvard Theological Review*, vol. 82, no. 2, (April 1989), 149–168.

105. "Religious Affections," *Yale Works*, ii, 418.

106. Proudfoot rightly sees that Edwards establishes a junction between behaviour and experience, though he may be in danger of so nuancing the discussion as to undervalue the importance of the experience of God and suggest a moralistic interpretation of "The Religious Affections," (Wayne Proudfoot, "Perception and Love in Religious Affections," *Jonathan Edwards's Writings*, ed. Stephen J. Stein, [Bloomington, 1996], 122–136).

107. The exhaustiveness of Edwards' description of Christian practice may have been intended to discourage the antinomianism of the New Light radicals and the prevailing self-deception of his own congregation, (William K. B. Stoever, "The Godly Will's Discerning," *Jonathan Edwards's Writings*, ed. Stephen J. Stein, [Bloomington, 1996], 96).

108. "Religious Affections," *Yale Works*, ii, 384.

109. *Ibid.*, 386.

110. *Ibid.*, 387.

111. *Ibid.*, 388; 390.

112. *Ibid.*, 392. My italics.

113. These eleven 'reasons why' can be found, *Ibid.*, 392–397.

114. *Ibid.*, 197.

115. The theological problem of the relation of grace to nature in the regenerate arises at this point. For Edwards the newness of life that is given is complete, yet there is continuity between the faculties before and after Grace. It is not a "new faculty of understanding" that is given but a "new foundation laid in the nature of the soul," ("The Religious Affections," *Yale Works*, ii, 206).

116. Grace, for Edwards, was something essentially different from miracles. Smith puts it well: "What is remarkable or unexpected has no special religious significance. The mark of the divine takes us to another dimension altogether. Grace is a matter not of wizardry but of regeneration; Edwards was no enthusiast," (John E. Smith "Editors Introduction," *Yale Works*, ii, 27). See, "The Religious Affections," *Yale Works*, ii, 201, 392.

117. "The Religious Affections," *Yale Works*, ii, 240.

118. Fear of God as a judge becomes love for him as a father: "The big difference in the converted man was that love swallowed fear," (Richard L. Bushman, "Jonathan Edwards and the Puritan Consciousness," *Journal for the Scientific Study of Religion*, vol.5, [1966], 394). "The distinguishing nature of True spiritual Light [is] that it brings divine love into the Heart with it . . . [Satan] can easier imitate what is in the head than what is in the heart. He has Great Knowl[edge] but he has no divine Love," (1 John 4:16, not dated: "The spirit of the true saints is the spirit of divine love," *MSS*, Beinecke).

119. "The Religious Affections," *Yale Works*, ii, 264, 394. Is there, then, no self-love in true affections? In "Miscellanies" number 530 Edwards argues that self-love and love to God include each other and our necessary to each other. On his view self-love is only a capacity to enjoy what the self does enjoy, or love what the self does

love, so if the self loves God then the self is only loving what it loves or enjoying what it enjoys, and therefore love to God necessarily employs self-love. So he argues that, "Self love is a mans love of his own pleasure & happiness and hatred of his own misery, or Rather 'tis only a capacity of Enjoyment or suffering for to say a man loves his own happiness or pleasure is only to say that he delights in what he delights." Therefore it is plain that, "proportionately as we Delight in Gods Good so shall we Love that Delight. a Desire of and Delight in Gods Good is Love to God, & Love to Delight is self love," (no. 530, "Miscellanies," *MSS*, Beinecke; John E. Smith "Editors Introduction," *Yale Works*, ii, 28). Edwards goes on to use this theory to deny, what some were teaching as proper to godliness, that it is possible for anyone to wish themselves damned even for the cause of the gospel, "Hence 'tis impossible for any Person to be willing to be Perfectly and finally miserable for Gods sake." Presumably, Edwards must have considered Paul's statement, "I wish that I myself were accursed from Christ for my brethren," (Romans 9:3, A.V.) as in some way theoretical, as expressive of a love to the brethren rather than of a practical willingness to be damned.

120. "The Religious Affections," *Yale Works*, ii, 266. Here Edwards exhibits his rejection of the anti-intellectualist bent of some revivalists. The sense of the heart must also include the rational, (*Ibid.*, 272).

121. *Ibid.*, 394.

122. *Ibid.*, 291.

123. *Ibid.*, 295.

124. *Ibid.*, 304, 307

125. *Ibid.*, 307. Edwards' emphasis on the internal evidence of the gospel does not exclude his employment of historical and rational arguments. See Chapter "True Light" for discussion.

126. *Ibid.*, 395.

127. *Ibid.*, 311.

128. Isaiah 6:5, 1734 July, "There is nothing like seeing what God is, to make men sensible what they are," *MSS*, Beinecke.

129. "The Religious Affections," *Yale Works*, 311.

130. Edwards is careful to identify the signs that will distinguish false from true humility. For a true saint, "all his graces and experiences appear to him comparatively small; but especially his humility,"("The Religious Affections," *Yale Works*, ii, 334; 318, 337). It is important to realise that Edwards' use of the term 'hypocrite' in this context is different from its modern connotation. His hypocrites, while unavoidably deceiving others, were doing so because they were themselves first self-deceived. In their case the "deception of others was subordinate to their own self-deception," (Ava Chamberlain, "Self-Deception as a Theological Problem in Jonathan Edwards's 'Religious Affections,'" *Church History*, vol.63, no.4, [December 1994], 543).

131. *Yale Works*, ii, 396.

132. Constant poles of Edwards' theology were the greatness of God and the helplessness of man. This was partly a response to the direct challenge to Christianity of, "the popular acceptance of a 'God more kind, and a man more worthy,'" (John Opie, *Jonathan Edwards and the Enlightenment*, [Lexington, Mass., 1966], v). For Edwards, as Bushman comments, this conviction that "complete humility" was man's

only hope for enjoying divine love was "the theme of his life." Bushman hesitatingly interprets this by means of the psychological mesh of the 'Oedipal Crisis,' seeing it as endemic to Puritan family life. Leaving aside the wide ranging opinions that there are concerning the 'Oedipal Crisis,' the problem with such interpretations of history, even when only on the "one level" that Bushman limits himself to, is that the lack of hard evidence seems to make it impossible to genuinely debate the matter. (Richard L. Bushman, "Jonathan Edwards and the Puritan Consciousness," *Journal for the Scientific Study of Religion*, vol. 5, [1966], 390). Of greater difficulty for Edwards would be the argument that his constant emphasis on human humility and divine sovereignty actually destroys human dignity. There is no doubt that some of the ways that Edwards has been interpreted, both by his supporters and detractors gives a picture of humans as ghosts of the sovereign will. So Coleridge sees that, "The doctrine of modern Calvinism as laid down by Jonathan Edwards and the late Dr. Williams, which represents a Will absolutely passive, clay in the hands of a Potter, destroys all Will, takes away its essence and definition, as effectually as in saying—This Circle is square—I should deny the figure to be a circle at all," (S.T. Coleridge "Aphorisms on Spiritual Religion B, 1," "Aids to Reflection," *Works*, vol. 9, [London, 1962], 158–159). For Coleridge this meant that, "his world was a *machine*," (*Ibid.*, footnote 6, 158). Of course Edwards would not have been frightened of the inference that the only thing real in the universe was God; in fact he positively affirmed it: " . . . there is neither real substance nor property belonging to bodies; but all that is real, it is immediately in the first being. *Corol.1* Hence we see how God is said, still more properly, to be ens entium," (Jonathan Edwards, "Things to be Considered and Written Fully About," no. 44, *Yale Works*, vi, 238; see Chapter "True Reality" for discussion). For Edwards, this devaluation of the essence of humanity did not mean lack of appreciation for its beauty (beauty in his writings primarily concerned the divine beauty, but creation was certainly beautiful by extension, as his use of creation in his typology shows), but it was always and only a dependent beauty. If Coleridge's remark that 'his world was a machine' is anything other than a romantic's expression of dislike, then it presumably refers to this emphasis of Edwards on God being the constant cause of all things. Here we come face to face with two contrary visions of humanity. The only thing that, I think, may be said in defence of Edwards in relation to Coleridge was that for him God's action did not take away human freedom but established it. He would agree with the sentiments of the hymn writer George Matheson, that, "My will is not my own/Till Thou hast made it thine; If it would reach a monarch's throne/It must its crown resign;/It only stands unbent/Amid the clashing strife/When on Thy bosom it has leant/And found in Thee its life," (*Meditations, Prayers and Poems by George Matheson*, ed. Ian Campbell Morgan, (London, 1990), 122–123).

133. "The Religious Affections," *Yale Works*, ii, 340.
134. *Ibid.*, 341.
135. *Ibid.*, 343; 395–396.
136. *Ibid.*, 345; 350, 353–356, 396.
137. *Ibid.*, 358.
138. *Ibid.*, 396.

139. *Ibid.*, 365.

140. *Ibid.*, 373–374.

141. *Ibid.*, 396.

142. *Ibid.*, 376. This distinction is crucial to the success of Edwards' whole design. Affections are not to be taken as an end in themselves, they are only the response of the soul that has found God. They are the sign of a true encounter with God not the encounter itself; it would, indeed, "be tragic if Edwards' views were taken to mean that the affections are the object of faith," (John E. Smith "Editors Introduction," *Yale Works*, ii, 39).

143. "The Religious Affections," *Yale Works*, ii, 378–379; 396–397.

144. Alvin Plantinga and Nicholas Wolterstorff, *Faith and Rationality*, (London, 1983), 4.

145. It may be helpful at this stage to clarify my working definition of 'foundationalism.' There are various different families of foundationalism that differ in accord to the field to which they relate. There are, for instance, foundationalisms in relation to value, or knowledge or belief. However, when I use the term in this discussion, I am considering what is perhaps the core foundationalism in the debate, that is what has been dubbed 'strong' foundationalism or 'classically modern' foundationalism. I hold this to be the epistemological theory that accepts knowledge if and only if it is based upon that which is either incorrigible or self-evident. There are other factors that are often part of a foundationalist scheme, but I take this definition as that which distinguishes foundationalism from other epistemological theories. Foundationalists may hold to a definition of knowledge as justified true belief, but this applies more to the output than the mechanism of production, and as such may also be held by Coherentists, for example. Foundationalism is often confused with 'evidentialism,' a less precise term, designating the belief that appropriate evidence is necessary to accordant knowledge. It is quite possible to be anti-foundationalist and yet be evidentialist. The definition of the base of foundationalism as incorrigible or self-evident is the more modern form of foundationalism, early modern proponents may have been happy with the base as self-evident or evident to the senses. The change in terminology does not indicate a real change in doctrine, but a post-Humean lack of confidence in the senses. Foundationalists are either 'internalist' or 'externalist' as regards their defence of the reliability of the base; an internalist would hold that evidence for the base is self-contained, an externalist would look for some other evidence to support the base; most are internalist. One of the best modern defenders of foundationalism is Roderick M. Chisholm; see the summary of his position in his *Theory of Knowledge*, (London, 1989).

146. *Ibid.*, 5–6. For Wolterstorff foundationalism is central to the Enlightenment heritage. It is a near truism that epistemology was forced onto centre stage by the Enlightenment; a starting point for many arguments is something like, "Since the Age of the Enlightenment, epistemology has been central to philosophy," (*Rationality and Relativity: The Quest for Objective Knowledge*, [Avebury, 1989], xi).

147. For an overview with a bias, see A.J. Ayer, *The Central Questions of Philosophy*, (London, 1973); a good general introduction is found in the article on "Epistemology" in the Encyclopaedia Brittanica; for an insightful summary and collection of

important texts, see Paul K. Moser and Arnold Vander Nat, eds., *Human Knowledge: Classical and Contemporary Approaches*, (Oxford, 1987); probably the best restatement of the classic internalist foundationalist stance is found in, Roderick M. Chisholm, *Theory of Knowledge*, (London, 1989).

148. Immanuel Kant, "Was ist Aufklärung?" *Berlinische Monatsschrift*, (reprinted, Jean Mondot, ed., *Immanuel Kant, Qu'est-ce que les Lumières?* [Paris, 1991], 71–86).

149. John Opie, ed., "Introduction," *Jonathan Edwards and the Enlightenment*, (Lexington, Mass., 1966).

150. I am referring to Thomas Kuhn's famous concept of 'paradigm shifts' in his, *The Structure of Scientific Revolutions*, (Chicago, 1962).

151. In an original study on Locke, Wolterstorff argues that Descartes is better seen as traditional, while it is Locke who marks the break to modernity. This is the correct view to take of Descartes, he feels, because the goal of his work has a distinctly medieval ring to it. Wolterstorff takes it as significant that the Latin for Descartes' use of knowledge in his "Rules for the direction of the Mind" is *Scientia*, thereby indicating that it is with the right pursuit of academic knowledge that Descartes is concerned. This, Wolterstorff feels, is a traditional medieval aim. Locke, on the other hand, is making a genuine break from the past, for he is not concerned with *Scientia* but with the appropriate regulation of belief, or opinion. This is modern because it is a response to the diversification of opinion after the post-Reformation destruction of the magisterium. It is a powerful argument, though it should be realised that there were similar assertions of the need to distinguish between knowledge and belief in the humanist search for toleration deriving out of Protestantism's experience of persecution. Such a thought structure can be found in the works of Castellio, of Acontius, and of John Hales. (William Haller, *The Rise of Puritanism*, [New York, 1957], 195–199, 244–247). However, even if his analysis is generally accepted, it does not seem to effect the above description of the Cartesian shift, for Wolterstorff seems to agree that where Descartes was new was in his insistence on certainty in the base, in his method of doubt. This, it seems to me, is precisely the point at which 'classically modern' foundationalism is established, (Drawn from discussions with Wolterstorff, Yale University 3/96, and Nicholas Wolterstorff, *John Locke and the Ethics of Belief*, [Cambridge, 1996]).

152. Locke took Descartes concept of 'idea' and introduced a gap between the external world and the idea that we have of it; I would argue that this space gave room for Hume to doubt our knowledge of the external world while still maintaining the incorrigible, that we have an idea of it, (see David Hume, *A Treatise of Human Nature*, bk. 1, [London, 1970]); Kant's response was conciliatory: he maintained that we did indeed know the external world but only as we imposed order upon it, only as the 'phenomenon,' not the world in itself, the 'noumenon,' (see Immanuel Kant, *Critique of Pure Reason*, [London, 1929]).

153. The founder of the so-called Common Sense school was Thomas Reid, see his *An Inquiry into the Human Mind*, (Chicago, 1970); William James was the most renowned founder of Pragmatism, see his, *The Will to Believe*, (London, 1897) and, *Pragmatism, a New Name for Some Old Ways of Thinking*, (London, 1907).

154. Alvin Plantinga, "Reason and Belief in God," Alvin Plantinga and Nicholas Wolterstorff, *Faith and Rationality*, (London, 1983), 65.

155. Chisholm re-asserts foundationalism in combination with 'Coherentism.' He acknowledges the importance of the recent popularity of Coherentism, but argues that foundationalism is not incompatible with it, and indeed Coherentism, if cogent, is necessarily foundationalist, (Roderick M. Chisholm, *Theory of Knowledge*, [London, 1989], 85–89). Moser feels that, "The combining of these two theories is perhaps one of the most promising efforts of contemporary epistemology," (Paul K. Moser and Arnold Vander Nat, eds., *Human Knowledge: Classical and Contemporary Approaches*, [Oxford, 1987], 15). But I see this pattern more as patch-work than real solution.

156. See the seminal article by Edmund Gettier, "Is Justified True Belief Knowledge?" *Analysis*, vol.23, no. 6, (1963), 121–123. Gettier spawned decades of as yet unresolved debate by asserting examples of justified true belief that were clearly not knowledge. This was revolutionary as it reversed the long held assumption, since Socrates' argument in Plato's "Phaedrus," that justified true belief is a sufficient criterion for knowledge. While this was unnerving to all kinds of epistemology, it was especially so to foundationalism as it seemed to effectively undermine the base epistemic certainty that it needed. After the initial shock that the article caused, for a while it was thought that Gettier's counter-examples were trivial as they seemed to be based on propositions that were falsely justified. However, since Gettier other examples have been suggested that are not obviously falsely justified but likewise produce false knowledge on the basis of justified true belief. See, Richard Feldman, "An Alleged Defect in Gettier Counter-Examples," *The Australasian Journal of Philosophy*, vol.52, no. 1, (1974), 68–69.

157. See Michel Foucault, *The Archaeology of Knowledge*, (London, 1994) and Jacques Derrida, *Dissemination*, (London, 1981).

158. A good summary of *a priori* arguments against the existence of God in general, and thus against the possibility of real religious experience, is found in Brian Davies', *An Introduction to the Philosophy of Religion*, (Oxford 1993), 1–31. Perhaps the most famous use of a version of foundationalism to argue against the possibility of real religious experience is John Wisdom's gardener story, described in his paper, "Gods," reprinted in *Logic and Language*, ed. Antony Flew, (Blackwell, 1951). In the imaginative parable Wisdom applies the later 'falsification' development of the 'Vienna Circle' to argue that because God can not be falsified He can not be real.

159. Alvin Plantinga, "Reason and Belief in God," Alvin Plantinga and Nicholas Wolterstorff, *Faith and Rationality*, (London, 1983), 65.

160. Brain Hebblethwaite, *A Defence of Objective Theism*, (Cambridge, 1988). Hebblethwaite's work is a response to Cupitt's, *Sea of Faith*, (London, 1984).

161. Brain Hebblethwaite, *A Defence of Objective Theism*, (Cambridge, 1988), 53–80.

162. *Ibid.*, 88–102.

163. *Ibid.*, 109–135.

164. John Hick, *The Philosophy of Religion*, (New Jersey, 1990)

165. *Ibid.*, 71.

166. *Ibid.*, 65–67. See also, John Hick, "Religious Faith as Experience-As," *A John Hick Reader*, ed. Paul Badham, [London, 1990], 34–48. Hick's thinking has made a significant development in his later works, moving towards a position of reli-

gious pluralism on the basis of the unity of the ultimate, or the 'real' in his terminology, to which he believes the mystical experience of different religions points. See John Hick, *An Interpretation of Religion*, (Basingstoke, 1989).

167. William Alston, *Perceiving God: The Epistemology of Religious Belief*, (London, 1991). See also, "Religious Experience and Religious Belief," *Nous*, 16, [1982, 3–12).

168. Alston's use of the term is carefully defined. He is concerned with Christian experience alone, and he intends to analyse the normal claim to experience of God's presence that a Christian might make. He does not exclude the more extravagant claims of those traditionally known as 'mystics,' and in fact draws upon them for evidence of experience, but his concern is not with defending an experience of ultimate unity, but with defending the possibility of a Christian experiencing God. So his work is not easily countered by criticisms of mystical experience in such works as Stephen Katz's, "Language, Epistemology and Mysticism," *Mysticism and Philosophical Analysis*, ed. Katz (London, 1978).

169. William P. Alston, *Perceiving God: The Epistemology of Religious Belief*, (London, 1991), 56–66.

170. Alston in no way suggests that mystical perception need be 'sensory,' that is involving seeing visions and the like. In fact he excludes such mystical experiences from his analysis, noting that many of the 'classic' mystics regarded them as inferior to other forms of mystical perception, (William P. Alston, *Perceiving God: The Epistemology of Religious Belief*, [London, 1991], 20, footnote).

171. Hebblethwaite also recognises the importance of experience, (Brian Hebblethwaite, "On Experience of God," *Preaching Through the Year*, [Oxford, 1985], 79–83).

172. William P. Alston, *Perceiving God: The Epistemology of Religious Belief*, (London, 1991), 67.

173. Davies criticises Hick as necessarily concluding that all experience is 'experience as,' and thus falling for the problems of the uniqueness of Christianity and the logical contradiction of absolute relativism, (Brian Davies, *An Introduction to the Philosophy of Religion*, [Oxford, 1993], 140). Hebblethwaite sees the question of truth as central to a response to Hick, (Brian Hebblethwaite, *Ethics and Religion in a Pluralistic Age*, [Edinburgh, 1997], 137–148).

174. Jonathan V. Kvanig, while acknowledging the importance of Alston's work at the end of his review, heavily criticises him for having loosely defined the concept of "practical rationality" that is supportive to his argument, and for failing to establish the concept as properly defendable, (Jonathan V. Kvanig, *Faith and Philosophy*, [April 1994], 311–321).

175. Davies makes short work of sense descriptions of experience of God: "The comparison between sense experience and experience of God seems a mystery rather than an explanation. The difference between God and physical objects renders it baffling, rather than illuminating," (Brian Davies, *An Introduction to the Philosophy of Religion*, [Oxford, 1993], 129). But Edwards is not strictly speaking making a comparison to sense experience itself but to an analogy drawn from sense experience. We are not to compare God with a painting, but the way we appreciate a beautiful painting with appreciation of God.

Chapter Three

True Reality

Reality for Edwards is perception dependent. In one sense this necessitates subjectivism, yet his is an 'objective-subjectivity.' Edwards' epistemology proposes a model of reality that must be inextricably intertwined with the subjective agendas of culture and history but still intends objective truth. Or rather it is a model that aspires to transcend this sterile subjective-objective dichotomy of modern thought by advancing an altogether different theory of truth.

Edwards' philosophical sparring partner was not the radical relativism of postmodernists, but the mechanistic universe found in Hobbes' writings that seemed to leave no room for God.[1] In tackling this contemporary question, Edwards, though, found a universe that avoids the crisis of modernity *and* the relativism of postmodernism. He adopted some of the starting points of the neo-platonism of the Cambridge Platonists, freeing up space and time to allow for the supernatural operation of the divine, developed Newtonian atomism to undergird his arguments, and incorporated the terminology of Lockean empiricism to explain the mode of interaction within such a system.

His was an idealist or 'immaterialist' universe, bearing striking resemblance to that of Berkeley, where the only true substance, far from being physical, was in fact the spiritual, God himself. Modern readers are unlikely to be attracted by the details of his 'immaterialism,' for the scientific basis that Edwards proposes for his position is painfully antiquated. Idealism itself is, of course, far from dead and Edwards' form of it while not ontologically persuasive achieves epistemological solidity because of the mode of interaction that operates within his system. For what is significant in Edwards' counter materialist vision of a spiritual universe is not his outdated physics, but his hermeneutics. As material objects are ideas they can be theory-laden, inseparable from the reading of the viewer, without being relative. How? The chimera is dispersed by the assertion of God. God is, as it were, the prime empiricist; His perception gives objectivity. The inescapability of individual and cultural interpretation, the hermeneutic of life, entails not relativism but 'perceptivism.' My floating perceptions remain adrift in the sea of subjectivism, but a fixed perceiver provides objective dry land. While humans are limited to a finite view of the real, the divine vision transcends such cultural and historical barriers to view reality as an entirety. God's subjective perception gives objectivity.

A grasp of the context of Edwards' perception-dependent truth is a prerequisite to understanding it, and the context argued above is readily defendable.[2] At the metaphysical level, the aspect of the Enlightenment that concerned Edwards was its inclination towards materialism.[3] It was not Hobbes' writings themselves with which Edwards dealt, he freely admitted never to have read them,[4] but the materialism that sprang from Hobbes.[5] That this materialist foil is the right contrast in which to view Edwards' doctrine of reality is supported by the position that Hobbes occupies in Edwards' metaphysical thinking.[6] While in other contexts Edwards may cite authors copiously, they are used more as a mirror for his own ideas than as matters of debate.[7] Hobbes is cited less commonly but more crucially. He acts as a kind of talisman of materialism, to which Edwards is responding with an alternative view of reality. It was "instead of Hobbes' notion that God is matter and that all substance is matter"[8] and "contrary to the opinion of Hobbes (that nothing is substance but matter)"[9] that Edwards' True Reality was formed. In his "Freedom of the Will" Edwards wanted to extricate Calvinism from being tarred with the same brush as the secular determinism of Hobbes.[10] Furthermore, Edwards' familiarity with the Cambridge Platonists, through whom he knew Hobbes,[11] gave all of his metaphysics a similarly anti-materialist tilt to that of their writings.[12] Hobbes' function as a symbol of Enlightenment materialism explains the certain scholarly disparity whereby Hobbes' significance is sawdust to the mill of the standard introductions to this area of Edwards' thought, while it is at the same recognised that Edwards never read him.[13] It also provides the contextual framework for the general scholarly consensus concerning the ammunition which Edwards uses to counter Hobbes:[14] the broad significance of the Cambridge Platonists that gave Edwards' 'immaterialism' a neo-platonic flavour,[15] Locke's 'sense' and 'idea' terminology,[16] and the new science of Newton.[17]

Much can be learnt from the mere fact of Edwards' use of these individual Enlightenment sources, not least being his appropriation of the latest contemporary science to tackle a threat from science. Without moving an inch from the primacy of Revelation as the source of human knowledge, he embraced the discoveries of science, willing to argue on the common ground of natural reason. In this matter it is well said that, "The nerve of Edwards' genius . . . [was] . . . that he took seriously both his faith and the wisdom of the world and sought to relate them."[18] He did not, though, take both equally 'seriously;' he used the one to defend the other. In modern terms, he employed the General Theory of Relativity to counter theological relativism. To focus on Edwards' method, however, could lead to overlooking the importance of Edwards' results. Opinions vary on Edwards' abilities as a scientist, "But it is probably less important to judge Edwards as a scientist, than to find in his papers the manifestation of some significant but as yet unstudied aspects of the reception of the new science in Calvinist and scholastic New England."[19] My contention is that Edwards combines these Enlightenment sources into a recipe of reality that, though inevitably eighteenth century, is in an important sense not Enlightenment but an attempted antidote to the Enlightenment. While Newton's atomic physics has become outdated, Edwards' epistemic theology retains its bite.[20]

To appreciate the force of Edwards' True Reality, it is necessary to distinguish it from the disconcertingly similar theory of Berkeley.[21] Disconcerting for Edwards because Berkeley's idealism has often been used as the straw horse of scepticism, held up to ridicule in the light of the purported certainty of physical reality, as believing "that all material objects and space and time are an illusion."[22] Such judgements, perhaps, misunderstand him.[23] But be that as it may, Edwards is not tarred with the same brush as Berkeley. Edwards' theory is neither derived from Berkeley,[24] nor are their theories coincidentally the same. For while they have obvious similarities, Edwards is rather in contradistinction to Berkeley than in parallel to him. For to speak precisely Edwards does not hold that existence is 'ideal,' if that means it is a human perception or in the human mind. Rather, he holds that all reality is God's perception or in the divine mind.[25] "*Esse is percipi*," to be is to be perceived, is Berkeley's phrase;[26] if Edwards had been given to such watch words his would have been, *esse is percipi deo*, to be is to be perceived by God. It is true that for Berkeley as for Edwards, what gives existence reality is God's perception, but for Berkeley the nature of reality is perception in general, not specifically God's perception as it is for Edwards. A cynic's quip that then Edwards is simply a Puritan Berkeley might not be far off the mark. But I would argue that the difference is crucial, because to Edwards existence is not a human idea, but a God idea, one where the only real is God. Berkeley sounds like Edwards when he says that his aim was to "inspire my readers with a pious sense of the presence of God."[27,28] The differential lies in the use of 'sense;' Edwards does not lay human sense perception as the cornerstone but inserts God perception as the essential linch pin of the universe.

The relation between Edwards and Berkeley has been read differently. Modern scholarship has tended to argue that Edwards' epistemology is significantly distinct from Berkeley, but the location of that distinction has been disputed. Rupp contends that what separates Edwards and Berkeley is their notion of qualities of substance. Edwards, he believes, continues to hold to Lockean primary and secondary qualities, though in a modified fashion, while Berkeley removes predicates of substance altogether.[29] For Anderson the conclusions of Berkeley and Edwards are similar, but the arguments by which Edwards established these conclusions are as dissimilar as the conclusions are similar.[30] It seems that the degree of emphasis that these arguments are given is untenable. I would disagree that Edwards held to primary and secondary qualities of substance in any essential fashion, and that there was the marked similarity between Edwards' and Berkeley's conclusions that Anderson suggests. Still, no doubt both the positions of Rupp and Anderson have mileage, to which might be added consideration of the differences between Edwards' by and large positive approach to the findings of the New Science with Berkeley's stance of rebel against the intellectual establishment. One finds no such side-swipe in Edwards' writings as the: "Vanity of those barren Speculations, which make the chief Employment of learned Men."[31]

But these observations all fail to appreciate the size of the gap that there is between Berkeley and Edwards. There is a *theological* chasm that divides Edwards and Berkeley, seen in the different pictures they have of the role of God in the universe. Berkeley's response to the charge of subjectivism is first only to reassert his principle *"esse is percipi;"*[32] when pushed he argues that it is not just one mind that perceives "but all Minds whatsoever."[33] His view of God's role, then, is to excite ideas in our minds,[34] for to hold a view of God's direct action without secondary causes is an "extravagant Supposition"[35] and for him to be the perceiver is a notion that "seems too extravagant to deserve a Confutation."[36] Yet it is just these 'extravagancies' that undergird Edwards' extraordinarily theocentric view of God's role, His subjective perception objectivity.[37]

The way is now clear to assess Edwards' position itself. Edwards considers existence to be inseparable from perception, arguing at the end of his life[38] that "real existence depends on knowledge or perception" and that "all existence is perception." He boldly states that "what we call body is nothing but a particular mode of perception" and he even continues that "what we call spirit is nothing but a composition and series of perceptions."[39] What is the nature of this 'perceptivism' web?

THE SUBSTANCE

Initially, the ground of his belief in a perception-dependent world seems to be that the world is mental or ideal, "we are to remember that the world exists only mentally, so that the very being of the world implies its being perceived or discovered."[40] Existence is perception because existence is ideal, a mental construct. However, if this is his basis it looks insufficient for a Christian epistemology, as is exposed by the charge that some have levelled at Edwards' idealism, that he effectively removes all reality from creation. If Edwards says that, "no matter is, in the most proper sense, matter,"[41] and that matter "is truly nothing at all, strictly and in itself considered,"[42] does this not leave the creator alone in the universe? Does Edwards' position that God is the prime empiricist actually mean that God is the only empiricist? God seems to be left eternally perceiving himself in the mirror of an ideal world.[43]

It is instructive that Edwards himself, usually so rigorous, never considered such an obvious problem. The apparent dead end suggests an alternative route. For, apart from the fact that for practical and scientific purposes Edwards was careful to insure that nothing was removed from the reality of nature,[44] the charge made against Edwards misunderstands the way that he uses a key word, 'substance.'[45] It therefore misappropriates the basis of his perceptivism. For him substance is that which "philosophers used to think subsisted by itself, and kept up solidity and all other properties."[46] As Edwards believes in God being immediately active, to believe in a substance that 'keeps up' the world is to usurp the place of God, for nothing but God is self-existent and he directly supports the world. To deny substance and to affirm an ideal world, is not to deny reality but independent reality. There must be some substance that produces solidity and "that 'something' is he by whom all things consist."[47] Independent 'Substance' signifies independence from God, and as such, "speaking most strictly, there is no proper substance but God himself."[48] To say that Edwards' perceptivism is based on his view of a mental universe, while true as far as it goes, is to talk loosely. To speak strictly, the basis is not idealism but that immediate action of God on which also the universe is founded.[49]

It can be seen, then, that for Channing to criticise Edwards as being pantheistic was an illegitimate, if understandable, conclusion to draw from Edwards' perceptivism.[50] Despite the enticing similarity between Edwards' doctrine of God as the only substance and that of Spinoza, Edwards is no pantheist. When Edwards announces that, "God is proper entity itself"[51] and that "God and real existence are the same,"[52] he shows that he is only concerned with matter in a special sense by inserting the qualifying terms, 'proper,' 'real,' or 'strictly,' indicating that it is 'substance' or independent existence that he has in his sights. The world is an "ideal one,"[53] it is a "shadow of being,"[54] because it is an utterly dependent world, where God is the only independent. This goes beyond Calvin's statement that, "our very being is nothing else than subsistence in God alone."[55] It is not just that we only exist in God but that God is the only independent existent. Edwards argues that, "God is, as it were, the only substance."[56] The *sine qua non* of Edwards' True Reality is the dependence relation of the universe upon God.

However, it has been argued that the character of this relationship is really a combination of two distinct stages of development in Edwards' thinking.[57] An early affinity to neo-platonism is seen in the More-ite statement that "Space is God,"[58] abandoned later, it is argued, in favour of idealism.[59] While there is plain development in Edwards' thinking, there is no dilemma between an earlier and later position. That Edwards himself found no puzzling paradox is apparent from the interweaving of the two doctrines in his essay "Of Being."[60] This paper was probably composed in four different sections at three separate time periods.[61] The much cited 'space is God' motif comes from the first of these sections and time periods, so it is an early sign of Edwards' familiarity with neo-platonic thought.[62] Its inclusion at this point is not, though, a sign of dissonance between it and a later idealism. The conclusions that Edwards incorporates with the 'space is God' summary are repeated, in a fuller version, in the last of the sections and time periods of "Of Being."[63] His perception doctrine is explicitly sandwiched between these two accounts, probably written during the second time period.[64] If there is development here it is a helical development; and anyway, by the time the last addition had been made to this paper, Edwards had probably already written extensively on his doctrine of perception in his "Miscellanies."[65]

If, though, both these tenets remain a constant in Edwards' thinking their presence still needs to be explained. It is here that the subjective-objective poise of the web of Edwards' perceptivism becomes apparent. The best explanation of Edwards' More-ite statement seems not to be in terms of a purported metaphysical location, though that may be the best description of its antecedents in English philosophy. More was not the first to use the 'space mystique' in discussions of God; it could be argued to be a persistent temptation in English thought to see the attributes of the divine in the infinity of space.[66] But for Edwards it is part of a commitment to an epistemological objectivity. In these "Of Being" notes, Edwards claims an objectivity for the subjective state of the universe. The universe is utterly perception-dependent; but what, he asks, of those things that we assume to exist unobserved, as of the objects in a "room close shut up"? The answer is that they only exist in "God's knowledge." Again, the world "can exist nowhere else but in the mind," but this is a mind, "either infinite or finite."[67] It is in the assertion of the infinite mind, of the unbounded 'space is God' of the cosmos, that objectivity is retained. The same pattern is seen in the Miscellanies: the implicit process of thought construction begins with 'God's knowledge' and later incorporates 'God is being,' elucidating a subjective-objectivity to reality.[68] It is, in the Hegelian phrase, pure being that is pure knowing.[69] That space is God gives existence the "objective order" that Newtonian Physics needed,[70] but that existence is perception avoids the materialism that Hobbes suggested. So, for example, if it is supposed that all consciousness ceased, then "the universe for that time would cease to be," for God also "knew nothing of it."[71] Yet God does know it and objectivity is incorporated.

Even at the theoretical level, leaving aside textual evidence for the moment, it would seem that the purpose of the 'space is God' drama in Edwards' writings was to buttress objectivity against the subjective tendencies of perception. For this interpretation is encouraged by the similar parts which 'space' and 'perception' played on the stage of the European Enlightenment. Edwards was not alone in seeing the importance of 'space' to the defence of objectivity in the eighteenth century. For many, indeed, on the concept of space, "the fate of the concept of truth in general seemed to depend."[72] The Enlightenment dogma of empiricism, at least the perceptual form of it that had developed from Locke, had planted a principle of relativism at the very heart of the Enlightenment, and the order of the universe, or the uniformity of space, became threatened. 'Space,' then, in this discourse, symbolised objective structure as opposed to subjective experience.[73] The Enlightenment in general, and the American Enlightenment in particular, felt the change from theology to theodicy to anthropology as the eighteenth century developed; it was a move from the age of objective enlightenment to the age of subjective enlightenment.[74] Edwards' attempt to construct a subjective objectivity, an experiential order, where existence is perception and space is God, is pincered in the midst of this change as a bulwark against it.

It may be thought, though, that such a conjunction is a rather tantalising blend. What does it mean to say that God's knowledge saves objectivity? The resource to knowledge as the final arbiter of objectivity effectively means that Edwards' universe is an epistemological universe, one where the knowledge of God is all there is. In such a place 'subjective' and 'objective,' ever notoriously difficult to define, take on an even more chameleon garb.

That Edwards transforms the subjective/objective definitions can partly be seen in his doctrine of 'continuous creation.' " 'Tis certain with me," Edwards writes, "that the world exists anew every moment." So that we do not miss the epistemic theological impact of this he, carries on, "Indeed, we every moment see the same proof of a God as we should have seen, if we had seen [him] create the world at first. Rev. 4:11, 'For thy pleasure they are and were created.' "[75] Some novel relation between man and his maker seems here to be proposed. For, though it is clear that Edwards considers the spiritual in some sense more 'solid' than the body,[76] continuous creation applies as much to the human soul as to the physical universe. We are guilty of original sin because, Edwards argues, our relation to Adam's sin is no more or less continuous than our relation with our own, "For we are anew created every moment."[77] It is a non-interruptive process; 'Continuous creation' is not to be thought of as punctular (every moment means 'all time' not each minute), but as the doctrine of God's immediate, constant creative activity. The Puritans, of course, commonly believed the universe to be dependent upon God for its existence. But as Edwards makes plain, though he assumes this he intends to go beyond it; he is not thinking of God just 'upholding' the world, but constantly recreating it.[78] Neither is such a universe recognisably eighteenth century, not Hobbesian nor Newtonian.[79] As such, all the associated modern problems of personhood, history, communication that group around the subjective/objective distinction find no obvious home in Edwards' universe.

THE INHERENCY OF PERCEPTION

By his idea of perception Edwards asserts God not just as the central tenet of the universe, but as the substance of the universe. In no way, as argued above, does this mean that Edwards was a pantheist. The universe is not God but is projected by God to be real; in Edwardean terms, it is a 'shadow' of the divine being. Edwards attempts to establish the coherence of this position by his understanding of perception, that perception is somehow inherent to reality.

This is best seen in his theology of the Trinity, because for Edwards the essence of God will parallel the essence of the real.[80] In his discussions of the trinitarian nature of the Godhead, he defends the doctrine by recourse to a triangle of reflective ideas. As God "views" himself he forms a "perfect idea" of himself, and as his perfect ideas must be "substantial," there is necessitated a trinitarian essence to God. The son of God is God's wisdom, as described in Proverbs and in the term the 'word of God,' and the Holy Spirit is the divine communication of love between the Father and the Son.[81] In Scripture, Christ is "called the word of God" to intend him being the "idea of God,"[82] and the Spirit is called the Holy Spirit because God's Holiness "consists in him."[83]

The obvious conclusion from his writings on the Trinity is to further confirm the significance of the influence of Locke on the formation of Edwards' thought structure. Apart from the prevalence of the term 'idea' throughout the discussion, his distinctions and concept of 'ideas' are clearly Lockean. So, he states as foundation for his argument, without attempting to prove, that, "The immediate object of the mind's intuition is the idea always; and the soul receives nothing but ideas."[84] Less noted, but no less obvious perhaps to an historian of the earlier Church, is that Edwards' doctrine of the Trinity is not as unusual as it might seem at first reading; it has in fact an Augustinian pedigree, though it diverges from Augustine in various ways.[85]

Neither of these observations, however, seem to be particularly enlightening or surprising. What does seem unusual is Edwards' strange statements that the doctrine of the Trinity can be proved by reason. Behind this assertion there is a particular understanding of the relation between Reason and Revelation that will be discussed later in the thesis, and that deals with the apparent contradiction between this and his belief in the necessity of revelation to true religion.[86] Yet, on this basis alone, to claim that the Trinity is "within the reach of naked reason"[87] or that it is "really evident from the light of reason that there are these three distinct in God,"[88] is a little idiosyncratic even for Edwards. What is it that causes such boldness?

I take it that Edwards' confidence stems from his epistemology. And in this specific instance from the way that this epistemology is rooted in metaphysics. For Edwards, it is not just ideas that are perceivable, but reality itself. Certainly Locke, it could be argued, allowed for the direct apprehension of reality through his 'ideas,' indeed his 'ideas' were in part developed so as to confirm such direct apprehension; but the thrust of his epistemological product was not concerned with the production of certainty, knowledge, but with the regulation of opinion, belief.[89] It is too often forgotten that Locke's contribution was not so much showing how much the human mind could know but how little.[90] The ensuing development of Locke's thought in sceptical directions is perhaps, then, not as surprising as is sometimes thought: the separation of the subject from the object, the phenomenon from the noumenon, until even the subject itself was dissolved by some.[91] Such a distortion of Locke's 'way of ideas' is not possible in the same way with Edwards.[92] It is not simply that he is concerned with certainty not opinion, though that is true, but that there is no inherent fault line in Edwards' thinking between the subject and the object; as ideas are the object knowledge is a universe of interlocking ideas, "the whole of human knowledge, both in the beginning and the end of it, consists in ideas."[93] Therefore the perception of the relations between these ideas is not only epistemology it is metaphysics, it is not only narrative it is metanarrative, it is "Truth."[94] For "the only foundation of error is inadequateness and imperfection of ideas; for if the idea were perfect, it would be impossible but that all its relations should be perfectly perceived."[95] Perception is not partially sighted squinting for truth, but has twenty-twenty vision.[96] It is inherent to reality.[97]

Furthermore, the map of this reality is not drawn by a human hand. To speak in terms of perception, it is God's sight that gives reality not human sight that decides what is real. At the least Edwards is putting God as the cornerstone of True Reality; He is the subject we are the object, it might be said.

But while such a statement makes an effective paradigm shift, it accords little verification of or access to that paradigm. Perception, for Edwards, is a way to give such a 'tracer' that will mark the truth of God. It is an access point to reality. So in his unpublished "Subjects of Enquiry" we find that even the true thinking of Angels, who surely have inside knowledge of God, must "begin with some kind of sensation Preceding all Reflection, Reasoning etc."[98] Perception, then, is not just something that is necessary for the bodily nature of humans, but is inherent to all true understanding, both in the physical and spiritual realms, because existence is dependent on God's perception. We perceive what is true, the "stable idea in God's mind," as it is "communicated" to our minds by God.[99]

Certainly, this inherency is no subjective perception, a perception, that is, that allows a universe with as many interpretations as there are perceivers. For although Edwards, in the same note, says in Lockean style that he is concerned with "knowledge being the Perception of the agreement or disagreement of ideas,"[100] he later distances himself from the subjective development that grew out of Locke's 'veil of ideas.'[101] Edwards displayed his disinclination towards the subjective tendencies of the empiricism of the Enlightenment, by asking himself to enquire what "intelligible meaning" it could have for someone to have a sixth sense.[102] This may be a reference to a well known eighteenth-century debate about subjectivity, or simply his own reflections on the problems of relating perception as knowledge.[103] And, while elsewhere Edwards argues that existence is perception dependent, "Individual Perception," or subjective perception, is insufficient to account for the objectivity of the space-time continuum and even the subjectivity of individuals, the "Identity of Person or Consciousness." There must be "laws" and "order" for the "very being of the corporeal world depends upon it."[104] The world can be both law-dependent and perception-dependent, because God is the legislative and the seer. God not only makes the rules he is the rules; "Truth" can be defined in the "most strict and metaphysical manner" as "'the consistency and agreement of our ideas with the ideas of God.'"[105]

Given the framework of Edwards' idealism and doctrine of continuous creation, his view of objectivity can not be pictured as a machine, he does not speak of it in 'mechanical' terms. That Edwards departs from such a common description of existence in the eighteenth century, by both theologians and scientists, is important.[106] It is another indication that he was by no means enamoured with concepts that tasted of deism and seemed to draw from Hobbesian wells. Edwards avoided a 'God of the gaps' defence against the new science by avoiding the machine. In fact Edwards formulated an alternative metaphor for objectivity, that of 'beauty.'

BEAUTY

Edwards' concept of beauty has a strong appeal to many scholars. Delattre was one of the first to argue that we need to take seriously Edwards' "frequent suggestion that beauty is the central clue to the nature of reality."[107] But that statement, and the vein of thought that it represents, is plainly overstated. Edwards to my knowledge never explicitly suggests beauty as the dominant role in his thought, and surely God alone could be the 'central clue' to reality for Edwards. What has caused such enthusiasm? The attraction may come from a desire to find a 'softer' Edwards to counterbalance the 'hell-fire' caricature.[108] So Edwards' concepts of sensibility, beauty and his typological treatment of nature all have a certain scholarly popularity. Edwards' "Personal Narrative" in particular, can seem almost Romantic in tone: "It is not without cause that the Narrative has been compared to Emerson's 'Nature' or Wordsworth's 'Tintern Abbey.'"[109] This flavour seems a new strain in Reformed theology to some.[110] At any rate it is a welcome relief to be able to conclude, that it was the "beauty of God" not the "fires of Hell" that most moved Edwards' "mind to dialectics and his tongue to eloquence."[111]

While it might be suspected that the motivation behind these arguments lies in a desire to have Edwards' sensibility without his theology, and so to drive a wedge between the two, it is surely correct that Edwards was much, if not most, moved by beauty. But it is not any feeling of beauty, but a feeling of beauty that accords with the structure of beauty as it is found in the nature of God. This is the "beauty of holiness," and this beauty is the very essence of God, and the knowledge of God and thus all knowledge whatsoever.[112]

Beauty so attracts Edwards not because it is a feeling without structure, or an individual taste without objectivity, that 'beauty is in the eye of the beholder,' as may be the reason why it attracts some today. He did not revel in subjectivity, saying, "I am certain of nothing but of the holiness of the Heart's affections and the truth of Imaginations—What the imagination seizes as Beauty must be truth . . . O for a life of Sensations rather than of Thoughts!"[113] Rather, beauty appealed to Edwards because it seemed to be a way to form a concept of objectivity that could be subjectively channelled. Edwards' central concept behind his use of 'sense,' as argued in Chapter two is that of appreciation, an appreciation of God that is given, and in this way a 'sense of his beauty.' How, though, can such a sense be defended as objective in its reference, if it remains something that even on the day of Judgement is not sensed by all, even though all their normal sensory faculties be fully functional? In Edwards' discussions of beauty he is dealing with this problem. Beauty seems to provide a way out because it is, in Edwards' understanding, something that is an expression of the structure of existence and yet may not be appreciated.

Beauty is not merely a subjective concept in Edwards' thought; it is a structural concept that accords objectivity to existence. It is the undergirding pattern to which all perfect or excellent existence accords. Excellency he understands as commonly defined in terms of "harmony" or "proportion," but unhappy with this definition, he finds that at base excellency "consists in equality." When this is "simple equality" it equates with "simple beauty," and "all other beauties may be resolved into it." So "proportion is complex beauty." To underline the definiteness of his concept of beauty he provides three geometrical figures as a reference for his equality and proportion.[114] Beauty is the jigsaw into which the various pieces of True Reality and objectivity must fall.

However, some have seen a relational or even relative side to this structure. For Edwards argues that because beauty and excellency consist in equality and complex beauty in proportion it is impossible to conceive of beauty that is not plural: "One alone, without reference to any more, cannot be excellent; for in such a case there can be no manner of relation no way, and therefore, no such a thing as consent."[115] It has been concluded from this important remark that in Edwards' theoretical framework there is an implication that not just excellence but "the universe is necessarily pluralistic," and that this sets him apart from the theological tradition in which he stood.[116] Later, indeed, Edwards does explicitly assert a relational aspect to existence itself, arguing that "being, if we examine narrowly, is nothing else but proportion."[117] However, it seems that this could only set him apart from his tradition if he were arguing for some form of religious pluralism, a proposal which is most unlikely to be true if he is to be credited with a degree of consistency. The pluralist and relativist element in Edwards is, on the contrary, precisely intended to underpin that theological tradition in which he stood and which he elsewhere so rigorously proclaimed. In Edwards' framework of excellence the emerging differentiation of the eighteenth century did not threaten objectivity, but was subsumed into a structure that was pluralist in the sense that it was harmonious. The discoveries of the Enlightenment were discoveries to enhance the "Beauty of the World" and display the "Wisdom in the Contrivance of the World."[118] Edwards does not wish to picture a universe of discordance. He sees, in fact, a "uniformity, concord, perfect Harmony" in the universe,[119] where being consents to being because "God is proper entity itself . . . so far as a thing consents to being in general, so far it consents to him."[120] Edwards is relating plurality to beautify objectivity. Discordant relativism dances in concert to divine music.

Yet there is also a subjective side to this beauty, a sense of it. There is a "pleasedness in perceiving being . . . either from a perception of consent to being in general, or of consent to that being that perceives."[121] Wainwright thinks that these two elements, the subjective and the objective, may relate in a similar way to Locke's primary and secondary qualities, so that the sense of beauty and beauty itself relate as matter and consciousness are thought to by materialists.[122] Delattre believed that the primacy must be given to the sense of beauty, that beauty is more the beautifying than the beautified, seeing that Edwards therefore rejected Hutchenson's concept of beauty.[123] Both of these seem to be helpful paradigms in considering what is a complex intermeshing of these two factors. It may be more instructive, though, rather than to establish their precise relation, to enquire what it is that makes that relation difficult to establish. What is it that necessitates the disentangling? Here it is that Edwards is enmeshing a subjective element within the structure of beauty, and thus the objective structure of being. There are three results of Edwards' employment of the notion of beauty. First, it encourages a Biblical description of God. After a description of the nature of beauty and the beauty of nature he concludes, "this is a reason that Christ is compared so often to . . . the sun of righteousness, the morning star . . . By this we may discover the beauty of many of those metaphors and similes, which to an unphilosophical person do seem so uncouth."[124] Secondly, it is intuitively appealing. So in describing holiness he is confident that it "is a most beautiful and lovely thing. We drink in strange notions of holiness from our childhood, as if it were a melancholy, morose, sour and unpleasant thing; but there is nothing in it but what is sweet and ravishingly lovely."[125] And thirdly it gives easier acceptance to Reality that is both felt and true, a taste without being a matter of taste. Minds can cope with the idea of an object being beautiful whether it is appreciated as such or not, in other words with something that is objectively so and yet needs appreciation, a sense, to be found.

To conclude, Edwards' True Reality stands against a 'God-of-the-gaps' theory of the relation of God to the New Science. To find, as some did, in the inexplicability of gravity a residue of God's activity in the world would have appeared to Edwards as grasping at straws and not only that, but as fundamentally theologically mistaken. One is as accurate to attribute the beating of my heart or the singing of a bird to the present activity of God as gravity. The ability to explain matter in mechanical or 'scientific' theorems does not pin God's arm behind his back; we are not only thinking 'God's thoughts after him' with such descriptions, we are describing God's thinking, his ideas. Solidity as much requires God's "active influence" as does gravity.[126] However, when Rupp argues that, "the conclusion of the epistemological analysis is that all reality in fact exists in the divine mind," he paints a gaudy picture when pastels would match better.[127] And even if that view of Edwards' epistemology could be held as an appropriate description it is an inappropriate conclusion, for it misses the point for which Edwards formed the epistemology. The importance of Edwards' concept of existence and his approach to the new science was in the way it made a human *feel* about God.

Another approach to the new science was far more usual. The vast majority of theologians embraced the order of Newtonian Physics, baptising it into a Christian framework. Christian apologists responded to the new science by arguing that God was the grand architect of the structure of the world, so giving the 'Teleological Argument' or 'the argument from design' a certain popularity in the eighteenth century. Famously, Paley saw God as the 'divine watch-maker.'[128] Furthermore, it was argued, God's present action in the world, that he was not just a 'prime mover,' was defended on the grounds of the inability of science to explain all phenomena. Locke found God's action in the properties of thought that could not be explained by matter and motion; for similar reasons Newton found God in gravity. There were, of course, contemporaries who disagreed with this approach to the relation of science and religion: Leibniz, in a set of exchanges with Samuel Clarke, criticised the positions of both Newton and Locke as only establishing an imperfect God.[129] However, this approach to the new science was a popular one even among the Puritans: Cotton Mather adopted Newton in his "The Christian Philosopher" adding four principles that amounted to the assertion that the world is ordered because God is a God of order.[130] And by and large this kind of allegiance between science and religion stood firm until Hume drove a wedge of scepticism between them, allowing only that "the cause or causes of order in the universe bear some remote analogy to human intelligence."[131]

Of course, in one way Edwards similarly welcomed the new science. In our post-Darwinian era it is hard to grasp that this is not what was most unusual in Edwards' approach to new learning.[132] It was a well established Puritan intuition to accept knowledge within the encyclopedia of God. Certainly, there were those within the Reformed camp who had rejected the new philosophy, arguing against Copernicus, for instance, on the basis of Biblical astronomy.[133] There were well learned methods of dealing with classical pagan learning but there was no quick route to refocusing these upon the new science. But once grasped such a substitution was readily made and not unique to Edwards, as Mather bears witness. Edwards diverges from his contemporaries in that when he welcomed the new ideas he did not transplant them wholesale into the Christian body of learning, but redefined their foundation principles on what he took to be a more Biblical and thus reasonable footing.[134] Edwards seemed to have seen further than his colleagues that the Newtonian Physics would usher in a gathering storm of materialism and of a neutered God held at a distance to his creation as the 'architect' at best, and condemned to the mists of time as the 'prime mover' at worst. In retrospect, the danger of the new science is well described by Flower and Murphy: "The heart of Puritan piety was the constant sense of the immediate presence of God . . . .while the new science had presented a description of nature which confirmed its character as God's artistry, it was an artistry curiously detached from man."[135]

Edwards' True Reality stood with a contrary vision of the foundations of the new science. As he himself affirmed, to the practical life of work and the practice of science, it made no difference.[136] The difference lay in the sight of God that it imparted. A God who alone was independent, who was constantly creating, whose perceptions formed the basis of existence, and whose activity gave a structure of objectivity that glittered with the reflective beauty of His own person, was a God who was immediately present.[137]

If this is an accurate picture of his epistemological cosmos, it can perhaps be assessed by the means that Edwards appropriates True Reality. Verification of epistemology is an inevitably slippery business, but it may be that only according to the method of knowing reality can an epistemology of reality be evaluated.[138] For Edwards these questions of how to arrive at True Reality resolve around discussions of reason and revelation, and will be discussed in the next chapter.[139]

NOTES

1. Martinich argues that Hobbes has been misinterpreted as a Deist or a near Atheist, seeing him rather as an orthodox Christian with allegiance to the Calvinist wing of the Church of England, (A.P.Martinich, *The Two Gods of Leviathan*, (Cambridge, 1992). The real issue of debate seems to be to what extent Hobbes' utterances of orthodoxy are to be taken seriously, given his well known doctrines of mechanism and the materialism of the soul. Curley believes that they are probably not to be given credence, considering the agreed reports of Hobbes' friends after his death, that he, "being but one, and a private person, pulled down all the churches, dispelled the mists of ignorance, and laid open their priestcraft," (Edwin Curley, "Calvin and Hobbes, or, Hobbes as an Orthodox Christian," *Journal of the History of Philosophy*, vol.xxxiv, no.2, [April 1996], 257–272).

2. All that is necessary to support the argument at this stage is the non-controversial point that these sources were in some way significant to Edwards' thought. Their relation to Edwards' doctrine of reality will become apparent as the discussion progresses. Of course, there is much disagreement over the exact nature of the influence of the Enlightenment on Edwards, and whether it is these 'modern' influences that have the primary formative effect on Edwards or the 'medieval' influences of the Puritans and Ramist logic. To follow this debate further the reader is asked to refer to the "Introduction."

3. In this he was not alone. Even Leibniz and Clarke could agree that the decay of religious belief, "is to be principally ascribed to the false philosophy of the materialists," (H.G. Alexander, ed., *The Leibniz-Clarke Correspondence*, [Manchester, 1965], 12)

4. "The Freedom of the Will," *Yale Works*, i, 374.

5. Enlightenment materialism reached its extreme in Baron d'Holbach's *Système de la Nature ou des Lois des Monde Physique et du Monde Moral*, [1770], trans. H.D.Robinson, *System of Nature*, [New York, 1970]).

6. More similarities than differences have been seen by some in the writings of Hobbes and Edwards. In relation to Hobbes' 'fate' and Edwards' 'freedom of the will' there are apparent similarities, as Edwards himself allowed, "if Mr. Hobbes has made a bad use of this truth, that is to be lamented: but the truth is not to be thought worthy of rejection on that account," ("Freedom of the Will," *Yale Works*, i, 374). But as concerning their doctrines of reality they could not be further apart.

7. A characteristic of Edwards' work. He often uses another author's "words as a support for the course of his own argument," (John E. Smith, "Editor's Introduction," *Yale Works*, ii, 53). Towards the end of his life his thinking seemed to become more derivative; in the last of "The Miscellanies" Edwards copies large sections of his reading into his notes.

8. *Yale Works*, vi, 235.

9. "The 'Miscellanies,' a-500," *Yale Works*, xiii, 166.

10 This is the setting in which Guelzo fixes Edwards' "Freedom of the Will." He cites Daniel Whitby as thinking that, "There is a plain agreement betwixt the doctrine of Mr Hobbes, and of these men [Calvinists], concerning this matter, as to the great concernments of religion," (Allen C. Guelzo, *Edwards on the Will: A Century of American Debate*, [Middletown, Conn., 1989], 13).

11. Though he did not read Hobbes he read his critics, "especially Henry More and the theistic followers of Isaac Newton," (Wallace E. Anderson, "Editor's Introduction," *Yale Works*, vi, 54). The extent to which this gave him an accurate understanding of Hobbes is less important than the way in which Hobbes functioned for him as a symbol of materialism.

12. The proposal requires a diffuse neo-platonic effect upon Edwards. Such an effect, in some form or other derived from the Cambridge Platonists, has long been accepted by scholars. Anderson's novelty lay in suggesting specific areas of Edwards' thought to be Cambridge Platonist, (Wallace E. Anderson, "Editor's Introduction," *Yale Works*, vi, 52–136); others have argued for a similarly close link, (Emily Stipes Watts, "The Neoplatonic Basis of Edward's 'True Virtue,'" *Early American Literature*, vol.10, [1975–76], 179–189; Daniel Walker Howe, "The Cambridge Platonists of Old England and the Cambridge Platonists of New England," *Church History*, vol.57, [1988], 470–486). There are those, such as Fiering, (Norman Fiering, *Jonathan Edwards' Moral Thought and its British Context*, [Williamsburg, Va., 1981]), who disagree with the primacy given to the Platonist source, looking rather to Malebranche for that role, but it seems hard to deny that Edwards was in some way influenced by the Cambridge Platonists, given New England's shift from Aristotelianism to Platonism, exhibited by the adopting of Henry More's "Enchiridion Ethicum" at Harvard and Edwards' use of some of his terminology, such as his famous More-ite comment that "space is God," ("Scientific and Philosophical Writings," *Yale Works*, vi, 203). Certainly, however, Edwards' work was not directed by Cambridge Platonist rationalism. His favourite text could never have been, as it was

used by the Cambridge Platonists, Proverbs 20:27, "The spirit of man is the Candle of the Lord," (A.V.).

13. Wallace E. Anderson, "Editor's Introduction," *Yale Works*, vi, 53–68; Thomas A. Schafer, "Editor's Introduction," *Yale Works*, xiii, 40.

14. *Yale Works*, vi, 52–136; *Ibid*., 39–58. I believe that this view of Edwards as manipulating the new science is the right approach to elucidate Edwards' originality yet appreciation of new ideas; DeProspo understandably tries to distance Edwards from seeming as if he were formed by the new science, but in doing so makes too little of their influence, (Robert W. Jenson, *America's Theologian: A Recommendation of Jonathan Edwards*, [New York, 1988], 22).

15. See for example the quotation from Cudworth's "Intellectual System" in "Mind," 40, *Yale Works*, vi, 359.

16. In detail, Edwards could both agree with Locke ("Mind," No. 11, *Yale Works*, vi, 342) and disagree with him ("Mind", 70 & 71, *Yale Works*, vi, 385); in general, he disagreed most strongly with Locke over the need for Revelation, that is, when Locke argued for the sufficiency of 'natural religion' it was to Edwards' mind "but a wild fancy," (no. 986, "The Miscellanies," *MSS*, Beinecke). As regards their similarities in vocabulary, Edwards' use retained some Lockean signification, though in content the Lockean remained secondary to the Puritan influences. See the "Introduction" for further discussion.

17. For explicit citation of Newton by Edwards see, for example, "Of Insects," *Yale Works*, vi, 159; and "Things to be Considered an[d] Written fully about," no.11, *Yale Works*, vi, 221. These both refer to Newton's physics, but Edwards was also appreciative of the theology of Newton. In his "Blank Bible" he cites from Doddridge's, "Rev XIII.18. The Number of the Beast] 'of all the various Interpretations given to this text I find none that pleases me so well as that of Sir Isaac Newton, that the words γαλεινοσ and The man of Latinus or of Rome whose numeral Letters taken together make 666 are here referred to and I Suppose this mentioned to signify, that the appearance of the Power whose Efforts were to continue 1260 years was to happen about 666 years after the date of the Revelations A.D.' doddr.," ("Blank Bible," *MSS*, Beinecke).

18. Claude A. Smith, "Jonathan Edwards and 'The Way of Ideas,'" *Harvard Theological Review*, lix, (1966), 153–173.

19. Wallace E. Anderson, "Editors' Introduction," *Yale Works*, vi, 52

20. Jenson opines that, one may not only ask "why was Edwards great?" but "was he right?" and not only "was he right?" but "is he?" (Robert W. Jenson, *America's Theologian: A Recommendation of Jonathan Edwards*, [New York, 1988], viii). It is in Edwards' epistemology that a rightly contextualised Edwards can be applied today.

21. Edwards may also be distinguished from other more modern idealists, at least in terms of his intention. Bradley argues for the impossibility of absolute floating ideas, so that all ideas in some way must qualify reality, and therefore holds to some kind of relativism; Edwards' metaphysics is never proposed with a subjectivist agenda, as will become increasingly apparent as the discussion above unfolds, (F.H. Bradley, *Essays on Truth and Reality*, [Oxford, 1914], 35–64).

22. Stephen Hawking, *A Brief History of Time* (London, 1988), 20.

23. To understand Berkeley is to "drop the common judgement of him as an impractical dreamer," (Colin M. Turbayne, "Editor's Introduction," *A Treatise Concerning the Principles of Human Knowledge*, [New York, 1957]); even Kant may have miscued Berkeley, (Immanuel Kant, *Critique of Pure Reason*, [London, 1929], 244). Johnson understood Berkeley better, writing in his Autobiography that, "His [Berkeley's] denying matter at first seemed shocking, but it was only for want of giving a thorough attention to his meaning. It was only the unintelligible scholastic notion of matter he disputed, and not anything either sensible, imaginable or intelligible; and it was attended with this vast advantage, that it not only gave new incontestable proofs of a deity, but moreover the most striking apprehensions of his constant presence with us and inspection over us, and of our entire dependence on him and infinite obligations to his most wise and almighty benevolence," (Flower and Murphy, *A History of Philosophy in America*, [New York, 1977], 84). See also a recent defence of the orthodoxy of Berkeley in, James S. Spiegel, "The Theological Orthodoxy of Berkeley's Immaterialism," *Faith and Philosophy*, vol. 13, no. 2, (April 1996), 216–235.

24. Despite the attempts of an earlier generation of scholars, it has proved not possible to show that Edwards read Berkeley. So now both George Rupp ("The Idealism of Jonathan Edwards," *Harvard Theological Review*, [April 1969], 211), and Wallace E. Anderson ("Immaterialism in Jonathan Edwards' Early Philosophical Notes," *Journal of the History of Ideas*, vol. 25, [1964], 181), argue for similarities and distinctives but not derivation. A recent attempt to revive interest in the possible derivation of Edwards' ideas from Berkeley makes a case for the conceptual similarity of their ethical discussions necessitating direct derivation. The essay still admits, however, that such a link can not be established with relation to the present subject, idealism, and that even with regard to ethics the evidence is by no means proof, (Richard A.S. Hall, "Did Berkeley Influence Edwards?" *Jonathan Edwards's Writings*, ed. Stephen J. Stein, [Bloomington, 1996], 101, 115). It should be noted that Edwards does refer twice to works by George Berkeley in his catalogue of books, but this list is unfortunately soft evidence for Edwards' sources. It is not clear from the catalogue alone which of the books recorded he had read, which he intended to read, which he merely had heard of and showed some interest in, ("Catalogue of Books," *MSS*, Beinecke). Edwards had no doubt heard of Berkeley, but beyond this nothing can certainly be said.

25. Neither Anderson nor Rupp dispute that Edwards is different from Berkeley. They would, however, elucidate the distinction in ways contrary to my position. See below.

26. George Berkeley, *A Treatise Concerning the Principles of Human Knowledge*, (London, 1734), 38.

27. *Ibid.*, 173.

28. Something akin to this is often seen as the design of Edwards' idealism, that is "to restore the immanency and immediacy of God in nature," (Flower and Murphy, *A History of Philosophy in America*, [New York, 1977], 167).

29. Rupp feels that this argument is defendable in the face of Edwards' claim that all is mental as he believes that Edwards uses the word in two ways, to refer to the human and also the divine, (George Rupp, "The Idealism of Jonathan Edwards," *Harvard Theological Review*, (April 1969), 209–226).

30. Wallace E. Anderson, "Immaterialism in Jonathan Edwards' Early Philosophical Notes," *Journal of the History of Ideas*, vol.25, (1964), 200.

31. George Berkeley, *A Treatise Concerning the Principles of Human Knowledge*, (London, 1734), 173.

32. Ibid., 71.

33. Ibid., 75.

34. Ibid., 82.

35. Ibid., 79.

36. Ibid., 96.

37. For an analysis of Edwards' theocentricism see Michael J. McClymond, "God the Measure: Towards an Understanding of Edwards' Theocentric Metaphysics," *Scottish Journal of Theology*, vol.47, (Winter 1994), 43–59.

38. Wallace E. Anderson estimates these as dated 1756/7 (*Yale Works*, vi, 395). Anderson's, and to a greater extent Schafer's, suggested chronology of Edwards' unpublished Miscellanies have undermined the possibility of holding that Edwards was a man who "laid aside for ever his philosophical speculations" once he became a pastor, (B.B. Warfield, "Edwards and New England Theology," *Encyclopedia of Religion and Ethics*, ed. James Hastings [Edinburgh 1912]).

39. "Notes on Knowledge and Existence," *Yale Works*, vi, 398.

40. No. 247, "The 'Miscellanies,' a-500," *Yale Works*, xiii, 360.

41. "Things to be Considered," *Yale Works*, vi, 235.

42. "Things to be Considered," *Yale Works*, vi, 238.

43. Thomas A. Schafer, "Editor's Introduction," *Yale Works*, xiii, 49.

44. See, "The Mind," [34], *Yale Works*, vi, 353–355.

45. Anderson discusses the significance of Edwards' understanding of substance in relation to his metaphysics but not his epistemology, (Wallace E. Anderson, "Editor's Introduction," *Yale Works*, vi, 65–67).

46. "Of Atoms", corol. 11, *Yale Works*, vi, 215. The idea of a substratum of supporting substance may be drawn from Locke. See John Locke, *Essay Concerning Human Understanding*, bk. II, ch. xxiii, (London, 1706), 189–210.

47. "Mind," *Yale Works*, vi, 380.

48. "Of Atoms," corol. 11, *Yale Works*, vi, 215.

49. The historiography of Edwards' scholarship shows a certain unease with the association of Edwards with idealism. Miller denied that Edwards was an idealist at all, seeing him rather as describing reality as a sequence of events with God as the one cause, (Perry Miller, *Jonathan Edwards*, [New York, 1949], 92).

50. Miller records Channing's criticism, (Perry Miller, *Jonathan Edwards*, [New York, 1949], 292). Woodbridge Riley saw pantheism as a development of Edwards' mature thinking (I. Woodbridge Riley, *American Philosophy: The Early Schools*, [New York, 1958], 127). For discussion of pantheism and panentheism in relation to Edwards' view of the universe see, Robert C. Whittemore, "Jonathan Edwards and the Theology of the Sixth Way," *Church History*, vol.35, (1966), 60–75.

51. "The Mind," *Yale Works*, vi, 337.

52. Ibid., 345.

53. Ibid., 350.

54. *Ibid.*, 335.

55. John Calvin, *Institutes of the Christian Religion*, bk.1, ch.1, (London, 1949), 37.

56. ["Notes On Knowledge and Existence,"] *Yale Works*, vi, 398. The same concept is expressed in different terminology when he says that, "God is a necessary being," (no. 27a, "The 'Miscellanies,' a-500," *Yale Works*, xiii, 213).

57. Wallace E. Anderson, "Editor's Introduction," *Yale Works*, vi, 53.

58. "Of Being," *Yale Works*, vi, 203.

59. See Wallace E. Anderson, "Editor's Introduction," *Yale Works*, vi, 74–75.

60. "Of Being," *Yale Works*, vi, 202–207.

61. The chronology used here is that drawn from Anderson, which itself is based upon the work of Schafer. See, Wallace E. Anderson, "Editor's Introduction," *Yale Works*, vi, 186–190; and Thomas A. Schafer, "Editor's Introduction," *Yale Works*, vi, 91–109.

62 . Estimated as early 1720s, perhaps Spring 1721, Wallace E. Anderson, "Editor's Introduction," *Yale Works*, vi, 186.

63. Estimated at 1732, Wallace E. Anderson, "Editor's Introduction", *Yale Works*, vi, 190.

64. Before Yale's publication most had placed this section at the end of "Of Being." Anderson realigned its location according to his estimated chronology, and it is to his chronology that I refer.

65. Anderson estimates the last addition to be approximately simultaneous with Miscellanies no. 587, Wallace E. Anderson, "Editor's Introduction," *Yale Works*, vi, 190. For examples of earlier Miscellanies on perception, see nos. gg, 1, 354, "The 'Miscellanies,' a-500," *Yale Works*, vi, 185, 197, 428.

66. David C. Pierce, "Jonathan Edwards and the 'New Sense' of Glory," *The New England Quarterly*, vol.41, (1968), 87.

67. "Of Being," *Yale Works*, vi, 204–206.

68. "The 'Miscellanies,' a-500," nos. gg, kk, ll, pp, *Yale Works*, vi, 185, 186, 186, 188. For the link between them see, Thomas A. Schafer, "Editor's Introduction," *Yale Works*, vi, 45–47.

69. "Logic," *Hegel: The Essential Writings*, ed. Frederick G. Weiss, (New York, 1974), 108.

70. George Rupp, "The 'Idealism' of Jonathan Edwards," *Harvard Theological Review*, (April 1969), 214.

71. "Of Being," *Yale Works*, vi, 204–206.

72. Ernst Cassirer, *The Philosophy of the Enlightenment*, (Princeton, 1951), 113–114.

73. Cassirer argues that as the reading of sense became to be seen as an acquired not an innate habit, and the information from senses viewed as competitive rather than correlative to truth, there emerged a relativistic and subjectivistic stream in the Enlightenment. While few became full-blown subjectivists, Enlightenment thinkers readily embraced a rough and ready relativism as a tool against religion and tradition in general. Its popularity can be seen in works such as Swift's "Gulliver's Travels," Voltaire's "Micromegas," and also Diderot's letters on the blind, deaf and dumb, (Ernst Cassirer, *The Philosophy of the Enlightenment*, [Princeton, 1951], 112–117).

74. 1. Woodbridge Riley, *American Philosophy: The Early Schools*, (New York, 1958), 17.
75. No. 125[a], "The 'Miscellanies,' a-500," *Yale Works*, xiii, 288. Modern Bible versions translate this quotation differently from the A.V.: "By your will they existed and were created" is the N.R.S.V. translation. There is a textual variation.
76. See, "The Mind", [51], *Yale Works*, vi, 368.
77. No. 18, "The 'Miscellanies,' a-500," *Yale Works*, xiii, 210.
78. "Of Being," *Yale Works*, vi, 204.
79. There are of course precedents and antecedents to Edwards' doctrine of continual creation. Certain of the scholastics saw creation in a similar way: "the *Schoolmen*, though they acknowledge the Existence of matter . . . .[it] is expounded to be a continual Creation," (George Berkeley, *A Treatise Concerning the Principles of Human Knowledge*, [London, 1734], 72). And in the Protestant tradition there is a comparable strain. From the Reformers' concern with the sovereignty of God, there emerged an emphasis on the utter dependence of creation upon God and that sole efficiency lay in mind. Together these teachings undermined the validity of secondary causes, (Charles Hodge, *Systematic Theology*, [Grand Rapids, 1952], vol.1, 592–597).
80. Edwards closely relates his understanding of excellent existence to the necessity of the trinity, arguing that as, "one alone cannot be excellent . . . Therefore, if God is excellent, there must be a plurality in God," (no. 117, "The 'Miscellanies,' a-500," *Yale Works*, xiii, 284). Lee recognises the significance of the Trinity for a right interpretation of Edwards' metaphysics by attempting to locate 'habit' there, Lee's key hermeneutic principle for understanding Edwards, (Sang Hyun Lee, *The Philosophical Theology of Jonathan Edwards*, [Princeton, 1988], 6).
81. Edwards has a long series of notes on the Trinity in his Miscellanies. The best and most thorough introduction to his thought is probably the first note, no. 94, "The 'Miscellanies,' a-500," *Yale Works*, xiii, 256–263.
82. No. 1008, "The Miscellanies," *Unpublished Miscellanies*, Beinecke Library, Yale University.
83. No. 1047, "The Miscellanies," *Unpublished Miscellanies*, Beinecke Library, Yale University.
84. No. 94, "The 'Miscellanies,' a-500," *Yale Works*, xiii, 258.
85. Augustine's I take to be distinguished from Edwards', apart from the lack of the 'idea' terminology, by Augustine's concern with what might be called a 'psychological' defence of the Trinity. He sees in the human mind a reflection of the Trinity that leads us to belief in the Trinity: "And so there is a kind of image of the Trinity in the mind itself, and the knowledge of it, which is its offspring, and love as a third, and these three are one, and one substance," (Augustine, "Treatise on the Trinity," *Works*, vol.7, [Edinburgh, 1873], bk.ix, 240).
86. See section entitled 'Reason and Revelation' in Chapter "True Light."
87. No. 94, "The 'Miscellanies,' a-500," *Yale Works*, xiii, 257
88. *Ibid.*, 262.
89. Nicholas Wolterstorff would hold this view of Locke. See his, *John Locke and the Ethics of Belief*, (Cambridge, 1996).

90. Dreyer makes this point well, see F. Dreyer, "Faith and Experience in the Thought of John Wesley," *American Historical Review*, vol.88, no.1, (1988), 24.
91. I am, as will be apparent, referring to Hume, Kant, and lastly Nietzsche.
92. The 'way of ideas' is Thomas Reid's ironical phrase. He used it to critique the scepticism that developed from Locke, arguing that the root epistemology of 'ideas' needed to be replaced with a 'common sense' theory. See, Thomas Reid, *Inquiry into the Human Mind*, (Chicago, 1970).
93. No. 94, "The 'Miscellanies,' a-500," *Yale Works*, xiii, 257.
94. "The Mind," no. 6, *Yale Works*, vi, 339.
95. *Ibid*.
96. Kant criticises empiricism as being unable to provide the requisite universality and necessity to produce a stable thought structure. It is apparent that Edwards' perception is not susceptible to this criticism, nor to that which Kant levels at Idealism, (see, Immanuel Kant, *Critique of Pure Reason*, [London, 1929], 43–44; 244–256).
97. Jinkins sees Edwards as both a 'foundationalist' and a 'coherentist,' which seems to make Edwards snug far too easily into contemporary main-line thought. If Edwards must be squeezed into the terms of contemporary technical epistemology, then it would be on the basis of the inherency of perception that he could be said to be a "coherentist," though as a full description of his position that would be a quite false label, (Michael Jinkins, "The 'Being of Beings': Jonathan Edwards' Understanding of God as Reflected in His final Treatises," *Scottish Journal of Theology*, vol.46, no.42, [June, 1993], 166).
98. "Subjects of Enquiry," *MSS*, Beinecke.
99. "The Mind," no.13, *Yale Works*, vi, 344. How can such perception be communicated to our minds? For perception to function as a tracer of God's truth it seems that there needs to be a mechanism of transference from God's perception to our perception. Scriptural revelation gives truth but does not reveal perception, which is more assumed than taught in the Bible. If it is not communicated in Scripture where else may it be communicated? Doubtless, for Edwards the nature of this communication, of the transference of perception from the divine to the human mind, was found in God's constant creative activity. Our perceptions are a part of the continuous creation of reality. Of course, it may be objected that this goes no way to solving the problems of inaccurate perceptions, of sensory errors. However, it is not Edwards primary purpose to construct such an analytical metaphysics. He, it will be argued as the discussion progresses above, was concerned to describe reality in a way that encouraged it to be pictured as a place where God was present. His, it could be said, was a phenomenological metaphysics, in the sense that his aim was the limited one of establishing a certain attitude towards reality.
100. "Subjects of Enquiry," *MSS*, Beinecke.
101. This is Rorty's phrase to suggest that the representational picture of knowledge is problematical, (Richard Rorty, *Philosophy and the Mirror of Nature*, [Oxford, 1980], 71).
102. "Subjects of Enquiry," *MSS*, Beinecke.
103. The connection of perception to the 'external' world entails the question of the relation of mind to matter, which is the question with which Berkeley worked. The

subjective tendencies of this progress of thought are identified by Molyneuex's "Optics," where the question of the compatibility of the senses was raised. What would happen if a man born blind was enabled to see? Would he immediately be able to relate that which he had previously only touched with that which he now saw? Or would it take a process of education to relate the two senses? When a person in such a situation did come to see the latter possibility was found to be so, (George Berkeley, *A New Theory of Vision*, [London, 1914], 56, 74); Ernst Cassirer, *The Philosophy of the Enlightenment*, [Princeton, 1951], 108–112). The question of the intelligibility of a 'sixth sense' is theoretically related to this discussion and may perhaps, though not necessarily, have been drawn from it.

104. "Subjects of Enquiry," *MSS*, Beinecke.
105. "The Mind," no.10, *Yale Works*, vi, 342.
106. The order of Newtonian Physics was at first embraced by theologians as well as scientists. The significance of Edwards divergence from the more common approach to the new science in his formation of True Reality is further discussed at the end of this Chapter.
107. Roland A. Delattre, "Beauty and Theology: A Reappraisal of Jonathan Edwards," *Soundings*, (Spring 1968), 60–79; reprinted, William J. Scheick ed., *Critical Essays on Jonathan Edwards*, (Boston, 1980).
108. Delattre himself suggests this, *Ibid.*, 137.
109. David C. Pierce, "Jonathan Edwards and the 'New Sense' of Glory," *The New England Quarterly*, vol.41, (1968), 86.
110. *Ibid.*
111. Roland A. Delattre, "Beauty and Theology: A Reappraisal of Jonathan Edwards," *Soundings*, (Spring 1968), 60–79; reprinted, William J. Scheick ed., *Critical Essays on Jonathan Edwards*, (Boston, 1980), 146.
112. *Yale Works*, ii, 275.
113. John Keats, "Letter to Benjamin Bailey (Saturday 22 Nov. 1817)," *The Letters of John Keats*, ed., Robert Gittings, (Oxford, 1970), 37.
114. "The Mind," no.1, *Yale Works*, vi, 332–333.
115. "The Mind," no.1, *Yale Works*, vi, 337.
116. Wallace E. Anderson, "Editor's Introduction," *Yale Works*, vi, 85.
117. "The Mind," no.1, *Yale Works*, vi, 336.
118. These are the Yale titles for two of Edwards' philosophical notes, *Yale Works*, vi, 305, 307.
119. No. 976, "The Miscellanies," *MSS*, Beinecke.
120. "The Mind," no.1, *Yale Works*, vi, 337.
121. *Ibid.*
122. William Wainwright, "Jonathan Edwards and the Sense of the Heart," *Faith and Philosophy*, vol.7, no.1, (Jan. 1990), 47.
123. Roland A. Delattre, "Beauty and Theology: A Reappraisal of Jonathan Edwards," *Soundings*, (Spring 1968), 60–79; reprinted, William J. Scheick ed., *Critical Essays on Jonathan Edwards*, (Boston, 1980), 138–140.
124. No. 108, "The 'Miscellanies,' a-500," *Yale Works*, xiii, 280.
125. No. a, "The 'Miscellanies,' a-500", *Yale Works*, xiii, 163.

126. No.61, "The Mind," *Yale Works*, vi, 376.

127. George Rupp, "The 'Idealism' of Jonathan Edwards," *Harvard Theological Review*, (April 1969), 224.

128. William Paley, "Natural Theology; or Evidences of the Existence and Attributes of the Deity, Collected from the Appearances of Nature," *The Works of William Paley*, vol.4: *Natural Theology* (Oxford, 1838), 1.

129. *The Leibniz-Clark Correspondence*, ed. H.G. Alexander, (Manchester, 1965).

130. Flower and Murphy, *A History of Philosophy in America*, (New York, 1977), 76.

131. David Hume, *Dialogues Concerning Natural Religion*, (Edinburgh, 1947), 227.

132. Edwards use of science was "quite within the spirit of the theistic scientists of the time," Wallace E. Anderson, "Editor's Introduction," *Yale Works*, vi, 48.

133. Maastricht and Leydekken re-affirmed the need to follow scripture in questions of physics, the latter denying the Copernican system of the universe on appeal to the familiar Biblical passages, (Ernst Bizer, "Reformed Orthodoxy and Cartesianism," *Journal for Theology and the Church*, vol.2, (New York, 1965), 20–32.

134. Edwards' approach, therefore, is not found under any of the four characteristic responses to the new science suggested by Turner: his is not ignorance of the new developments, nor is it rejection of the novelties, nor is it simply accepting both traditional beliefs and the new developments assuming no inconsistency, and nor is it rejecting the old beliefs in favour of the supremacy of the new science. (James Turner, *Without God, Without Creed: The Origins of Unbelief in America*, [Baltimore, 1985], 29). Edwards has a different approach, as Turner recognises, (*Ibid.*, 50).

135. Flower and Murphy, *A History of Philosophy in America*, (New York, 1977), 85. So also Pocock, while wary of generalisations concerning the Enlightenment, remarks that its common characteristic was to encourage disbelief of any claim to experience of God; there was a scepticism "of anything which could produce conviction of God's presence in the world through channels which were not those of the normal social or ecclesiastical mediations of authority," (J.G.A. Pocock, "Enlightenment and Revolution: the Case of English-Speaking North America," *Transactions of the Seventh International Congress on the Enlightenment*, [Oxford, 1989], 249–261).

136. "The Mind," no. 34, *Yale Works*, vi, 353.

137. Edwards builds on his metaphysical understanding of the presence of God to preach the presence of God to both sinners and saints. Sinners should be awakened by the, "amazing Consideration to think that they live and move in God who is angry with them every moment he is not an enemy at a distance from them nor is he only near to them he is in them and they in him . . . .," and also, "it should be of Great Comfort to saints that he that is their friend and father is alwaies present with them and In them . . . .," (Psalm 139:7–10, "That God is everywhere Present," *MSS*, Beinecke). For further discussion of Edwards' preaching of the presence of God see the Chapter "True Salvation."

138. Chisholm argues that to start an epistemological assessment it is necessary first to assume basic rationality, to be, in the jargon, "internalistic," (Roderick M. Chisholm, *Theory of Knowledge*, [London, 1989], 5). Internalism may or may not be

cogent as far as the resultant epistemology goes, but I take it as axiomatic that some kind of basic rationality must be assumed at first. The question though, of course, is what basic rationality, and while rationality is more the fuel of the epistemological system than the result, the nature of the rationality is effected by the result. So there is something of a 'chicken and egg' scenario here. If the rationality chosen to assess an epistemology is specific to another epistemology, there is the danger that home standards are imported on to a foreign epistemology, and that the results of one epistemology be used to overturn another epistemology. I will, then, throughout the discussion assume some kind of 'common-sensical' basic rationality, but also endeavour to assess Edwards' epistemology on his own terms to establish the level of inner coherence. I will, as it were, turn Edwards guns on himself.

139. I use 'revelation' to mean the "propositional" (John Hick, *The Philosophy of Religion*, [New Jersey, 1990], 56) and historical revelation as recorded in the Bible. Edwards normally uses 'revelation' to intend the revelation of the Bible, though this is inevitably a slightly blurred term because it refers both to the experience of the Old Testament prophets, for example, as well as their recorded writings. He also often discusses revelation without use of technical terms, discussing the effect of Christ etc. When Edwards intends spiritual experience *per se*, he normally uses terms such as 'sense,' 'illumination,' 'affection,' (See Chapter "True Experience").

Chapter Four

True Light

It is 'light' that illuminates Edwards' response to the Enlightenment. The concept of light bears a string of significance that is tied to a certain discourse of the age, one that begins with the acknowledgement that to be natural was to be orthodox in the Enlightenment. Whether the impulse was foiled as an appeal to reason or an appeal to the senses, whether the inclination was towards the rational or empirical sides of the divide that marked the pre-Kantian Enlightenment, nature dominated. From Locke and Newton to Rousseau and D'Alembert nature was at the core of the thought of the age.[1] Intertwined with nature was an equally common tendency to repudiate 'authorities.' Both these factors of interpretation are non-controversial,[2] but sometimes less appreciated is the correlation between these two issues, that there was an extent to which the attractiveness of nature resided in the perception that it was an alternative authority to the 'authorities.' For some, nature gave the lie to the authoritative natural philosophy of the classics,[3] for others, to the authoritative metaphysics of religion.[4] In either case, under the motif of 'reason' all things natural could be presented as a replacement for traditional authorities, for all things peripatetic or for all things supernatural.[5] Such a battle of authorities is found in the predominance of 'light' as a metaphor for the source of truth in the philosophical and theological realms,[6] of the later common designation of the period as the Enlightenment,[7] and of Edwards' concern the true light.

It is likely, then, to be no mere coincidence that a comparison of the mottoes of Harvard and Yale exhibits a debate over authority. The Latin emblazoned on the arms of these universities in modern times is a heraldry with a theology. Harvard we know was founded as an institution of *veritas*, and Yale, while the founding of the college is shrouded in myth, at least very early had adopted the essence of its developed motto, *lux et veritas*.[8] Given that many at the end of the seventeenth century saw Harvard as becoming a heterodox university, inculcating heterodox principles, and that Yale was at least in part founded as an alternative to such tendencies, the addition of *lux* is tantalisingly idiomatic.[9] To safeguard *veritas*, it seems, it had become necessary to explicitly express its foundation in *lux*, in the light of true authority. Edwards himself addressed the necessity of establishing the nature of true authority in his epistemology of light. For him, though, light and truth were not separated into parallel domains but linked by a sequential necessity. It was not *lux et veritas*, but *lux ad veritam*: light must precede the knowledge of truth. The effectiveness of Edwards' principle of true light as a counter to contemporary concepts of enlightenment, may be evaluated by a consideration of his relation of the competing claims of revelation and reason, and the persuasiveness of his apologetic of the light of nature and the light of revelation.

REASON AND REVELATION

It was not the importance of learning that was a matter of debate in New England; despite their philistine caricature, the New England Puritans were unreservedly on the side of learning, whether it be of a Christian or non-Christian origin. The more difficult question for the Puritan was of the right relation of reason to revelation. In the seventeenth century this question was mostly coupled with the problem of pagan learning, that is, how to account for it and how much to use it.[10] The vestiges of this link can be seen in Edwards' long Miscellanies arguing that all true pagan learning was had by tradition from revelation.[11] But in the eighteenth century the problem was heightened by the new challenges and confidence of Enlightenment reasoning. As the Age of Reason lumped together Aristotle and the Bible and disparaged them as 'authorities,' the cerebral question of reason and revelation became the fiery Enlightenment battle of reason against authority,[12] or, rather, between the authority of nature and the authority of revelation. The key terms in Edwards' writings that flag this war are 'light of nature,' 'natural religion,' and of course 'reason' and 'revelation,' which also indicate that in theological terms the debate had shifted from the problem of 'foreign' learning to that of 'natural' learning, or what it was that reason could teach only on the basis of the general revelation of creation.[13]

No Edwards scholar will find it surprising to argue that Edwards did not abandon natural reason in the face of the Enlightenment challenge but consistently held it in high regard. In fact so exalted is reason in Edwards' writings that it might be thought of as what some have seen as the tares in the Puritan field that later grew to deism.[14] Even in the pulpit, while wishing to affect his hearers, the effect he desired was not just emotional; in a 'plain' Puritan way they were thick with learning and logic, comparable to a "come let us reason together style."[15] Reason is even strong enough to prove the essence of the Godhead, the Trinity is "within the reach of naked reason."[16] Given such a mandate it seems that Edwards must conclude that reason is sufficient to gain knowledge of God. Perhaps the massive "A Rational Account of Christianity" that he intended was itself germinal deism?[17] For was it not the unfulfilled attempt to prove what the influx of modernity has insured can be never be proved, God? Surely, it might be argued, those who in this respect have followed in his footsteps must have found themselves with insurmountable evidential challenges, forcing them either to deism or fideism.

There are strains of a semi-fideistic dualism in Edwards' use of reason. The free market ratiocination of Edwards stems partly from a separation of reason and revelation into distinct authority realms. He sees clear water between theology and natural science: "Divinity is not learned, as other sciences, merely by the improvement of man's natural reason, but is taught by God himself."[18] His innovative approach to practical pastoring recorded in his "The Distinguishing Marks" seems to stem from a belief that revelation does not need to tell us everything but that some things are to be naturally understood.[19] His theological speculations are based on the belief that reason can advance understanding beyond explicit Biblical doctrines.[20] On the other hand, however, it can not be doubted that Edwards took a traditional Puritan approach to the Bible; it had supreme authority as the word of God. He explicitly rejects the 'deist' reasoning of Hobbes, Toland, Shaftesbury, Chubb, Hume, and Bolingbroke in favour of revelation.[21]

Can such a high view of Revelation be reconciled with reason? For Edwards, it all depended on the beginning. The dominant picture of Edwards' understanding of the relationship of reason and revelation is not the above one of separate location, but of appropriate order. Revelation comes first. Primary place in Edwards' mental authority structure was always given to Revelation.

On this matter Edwards makes his most vigorous departure from Locke. He disagrees with him that reason can teach us true religion, which he feels is but a "wild fancy," because history shows true religion began with revelation not reason; reason before revelation went "very wrong."[22] The reason which concerns Edwards is 'thinking God's thoughts after him,' reasoning after revelation.[23] Truth "now demonstrable by reason" could never be "found out before" revelation.[24] Once things have been revealed it seems "as if we could easily arrive at a certainty of them if we never had had a revelation of them." But to see a truth is reasonable "after we have been told of it" is one thing; it is "another to find it out . . . by mere reason."[25] Thus, "The light of nature teaches that Religion, that is necessary to continue in the Favour of the God that made us; But it cannot teach us that Religion, that is necessary to our being restored to the Favour of God, after we have forfeited it."[26]

So subordinating his reason to the word Edwards seemed a tragic figure to later liberal commentators.[27] However, that interpretation fails to grasp the genuine liberality that Edwards' position gave him. It can hardly be said to have caused his mind to become moribund or infertile. True intellectual freedom lay in this 'reasoning after revelation.' If he was right in the Puritan belief in reason's insufficiency to grasp the truth, not due to essential deficiency but to post-lapsarian corruption of the mind,[28] revelation had the effect of releasing captive reason. In reason's submission to revelation as a "handmaid to religion" it became a "means of a glorious advancement of the kingdom of his [God's] Son."[29] Edwards' reason is indeed not the rationalism of Chauncy, there is emotion in his reason due to his 'whole-soul' view of the human psyche,[30] but neither is it reason as a slave to outmoded dogma. In fact, as many have seen, Edwards is in some ways far more 'modern' than the proto-typical liberals of Chauncy and the like.[31]

It may be problematic for Edwards' reasoning after revelation that there are no obvious criteria by which to assess the results of such reasoning. If revelation is only the starting point for reasoning there do not seem to be obvious means to distinguish between right and wrong conclusions. However, Edwards' intention is not to provide infallibility for the conclusions of reason but a sure foundation from which to reason. There are limits to the type of conclusions that may be made, set by the boundaries of revelation, and, as is argued later in this chapter,[32] by the assessable[33] moral and spiritual dimension to understanding. But primarily the criteria for right thinking are directive rather than restrictive: it is the trajectory of reason that is determined by the spiritual character of the reasoner and the starting point of revelation.

Two matters need be grasped to appreciate Edwards' use of reason. The first is that he does accord it emphasis. For one who is so 'sense' orientated, who, it is argued, saw reality as perception-dependent, who, at least in some definition of the word, was inclined towards empiricism, such a dichotomy is not easily understood. Indeed his inclusion of reason with sense brings to mind the attempts of Kant to reconcile a somewhat similar seeming dichotomy. The second is his 'reasoning after revelation,' reason as a good servant but a bad master. Here Edwards found a solution that others, such as Kant and his followers, have missed. In bringing reason within the bounds of revelation, not the reverse, reason was allowed to be reasonable and sense to be sensible. Edwards never moved from holding to the primacy of Scripture, and in fact if the proportion of space accorded it in his Miscellanies is anything to go by, he became increasingly convinced of the importance of 'reasoning after revelation.'[34]

Philosophically speaking, the clue to understanding Edwards' solution lies in the kind of reason that he sees as not distinguishable from perception. It is this principle, not Edwards' indebtedness to a Stoic-Ramist mentality, that is the reason for Daniel's remark that Edwards has frustrated attempts to force him into the, "empiricist-rationalist continuum that characterizes much of the historiography of modern Philosophy."[35] For Edwards, it is the initial act of reason that is perception, not the process of reasoning. He explicitly defines reason as the power or faculty that intelligent beings have to judge of truth that is either "immediately" by intuition *or* is built upon such immediate intuitions.[36] That this implies perception as the base of reason is apparent in his characteristically enigmatic statement that in some sense reason can also be resided into perception-dependence. "Demonstrative reasoning," reasoning that in Edwards' definition has no "act of the will about it," is perception dependent, for all demonstrative reasoning is the knowledge of self-evident truths, and these do "not differ from perception."[37] But the construction of reason, the "act of the judgement," is "different from mere perception," though it is mere perception that is at work in the initial act of reasoning, the "mere presence of an idea in the mind."[38] Edwards envelops the more empirical and the more rational concept of reason in a division between the initial act and the ensuing process. Such a division gives him empirical/rational balance. And it allows him to 'reason after revelation,' after God gives the sense of the heart of the truth of Biblical revelation in the true experience unity of reason and emotion, reason can be used to advance the kingdom of God.[39]

Edwards uses reason to defend Biblical revelation as historical. He is known for his typology, but it is a real not a fictional typology,[40] based on a belief in the "Evidence of the Truth of the FACTS [sic] that were the ground of the X[Chris]tian Faith."[41] With classical citations and general historical observation, he argues that true knowledge of God, even pagan understanding[42] and "Mahometan" knowledge of God,[43] stems from the Bible. He gives various historical proofs for the divine origin of Scripture[44] (on occasion stated vis-à-vis the claims of false religions[45]), to show that Scripture has a real spatio-temporal location, that it sets "forth things just as they happened."[46] He defends the historicity both of the Old Testament, the Pentateuch[47] and the later historical books,[48] and the New Testament, the Gospels[49] and Acts and Epistles.[50] Edwards pens a reconciliation of the Gospel accounts of the Resurrection,[51] seeing this event as the factual cornerstone of the Christian faith.[52]

Edwards also reasons that Biblical Revelation is rational. By this Edwards does not mean to distil revelation into rationality, to make revelation equate with reason as a quasi-deist might. Rather, he intends to show that it is reasonable that there be a revelation, and that reason teaches that the Bible is that revelation.[53] Indeed revelation teaches things that are beyond human comprehension, but that it so teaches is rationally necessary and what it teaches can be shown to be reasonable.[54] Edwards does allow place for mystery; in heaven what is now dark will be made plain by divine light.[55] Still, after revelation has shown the way it seems that there is nothing of any major gospel significance that is not capable of being proved utterly reasonable. Again, 'reasoning after revelation' is Edwards' manner; after revelation the Christian religion can be shown to be "most agreeable to reason,"[56] but reason can not establish true religion.

Edwards, therefore, responds to the Enlightenment tendency to replace revelation with reason by reasoning after revelation. He offers a paradigm of revelation and reason not as competing alternatives but as sequential necessities. What, though, was Edwards' apologetic for this doctrine? It is one thing for him to have formed a cogent theology of reason and revelation, it is quite another for him to have found a way to defend it successfully. His defence is found in certain public messages delivered from the press and from the pulpit. The language he chooses is designed to appeal to the rhetoric of the age of 'light' and 'enlightenment.' The content is a two pronged defence. Edwards preaches that: "There two lights that G[od] gives to the chil[dren] of man to discover things to em concerning their true interest . . . viz. the light of nature & the light of Revelation."[57]

THE LIGHT OF NATURE

The dominant theological debate of the Enlightenment age may be characterised as focused on the sufficiency of nature to lead to a true understanding of God. A convenient chronology for the start of the centrality of this concern for revelation can be constructed from the beginning of the Boyle lectures in 1692.[58] Tindal's "Christianity as Old as Creation" may be a notorious type of the pattern, but in one form or another these deistical concerns with natural revelation set the tone at an early stage in the period.[59] The figure of the Deist appears in many of Edwards' sermons and unpublished notes.[60] Tindal himself is argued against,[61] as are other Deists, and it is not hard to see the spectre of the Deist behind the apologetic thrust of much of his sermon rhetoric.[62] Edwards' response to the claim of Deism itself, that the truths of Christianity could be discovered from nature alone, was to assert the priority of revelation, the necessity of reasoning after revelation. However, deism was not formed in a vacuum but as a considered response to the spirit of the Enlightenment, the replacement of traditional authorities with the authority of reason. Deism may be seen as an attempt to meet fire with fire, reason with reason, to undermine or to maintain Christianity.[63] Either way, underlying deism was the Enlightenment claim to a 'metanarrative' of reason,[64] and to this more essential claim there was necessitated a more radical response. Edwards grasped something of this need to redefine the epistemological roots of the age, and as such for him it was not sufficient to meet enlightened demands for a rational defence of Christianity in deistical fashion, nor though was it sufficient merely to deny that fallen rationality could fully discover Christianity, to deny the metanarrative of reason.

I believe that there is a sense in which Edwards replied with a natural theology.[65] The concept of an 'Edwardean natural theology,' if natural theology be defined as the attempt to prove or demonstrate the existence of God without recourse to special revelation,[66] is not something that appeals to contemporary scholarship. While for Edwards the concept of authority and of revelation and of their correlation with the light of nature are foundational to his theology, the secondary literature, which elsewhere abounds with fascination with Edwards, is relatively silent on this. One might candidly remark that the reverse of the usual rule of thumb for Edwards scholarship applies: instead of forte discussion where Edwards is piano there is piano where Edwards is fortissimo.[67]

A prime instance of Edwards' natural theology is his proof of the existence of God. Edwards' line of argument is usually seen as a form of the ontological argument.[68] He tries to show the necessity of being, therefore the necessity of universal being, and therefore what Edwards calls 'Being in General,' that is God.[69] This approach does have certain factors in its favour. By starting one step back from Anselm's 'greatest conceivable being' he side-steps the classic 'greatest conceivable island' rebuttal to the ontological argument.[70] It also involves within it the intuitive force (*pace* Hume) of cause and effect, more usually associated with the cosmological argument, thus appealing to a less specialised, more common 'reasonableness.'[71] Still debates over the proofs of God have gone on for centuries, and will no doubt for centuries more; it is unlikely that any agreement could be reached on Edwards' form of one of the arguments.

Edwards, however, saw that the very susceptibility of Christianity to such natural reasoning was an important argument for its truth.[72] Thus when Edwards comes to what is a fundamental matter for one who holds revelation in high regard, that of how to discern between competing revelations, it is to reason that he appeals. The grand difference between Islam and Christianity is that while Christianity was established by "Light, Instruction & Knowledge, Reason & Enquiry," "Mahometanism was propagated not by Light & Instruction but by darkness; not by Encouraging Reasoning and Search; but by discouraging Knowledge & learning."[73] The reasonableness of Christianity is what separates it from false revelations.

Edwards places great importance on evidence and reason. Christianity is rational: he is willing "to observe HOW RATIONAL & CONGRUOUS to Reason all the Parts of Christian Religion are."[74] Theology is reasonable: a set of theological questions that may well have been formed a basis for discussion with young candidates for ministry is frequently of the 'this is taught, but how may we reason it to be so' type.[75] Natural theology is evidential: in one short section of the "The Freedom of the Will" treatise, Edwards constructs in outline a framework of natural theology, arguing that while in theory the existence of God might be known without evidence, in practice humanity requires *a posteriori* arguments from causation to believe in God's existence.[76] So it might be said that according to Edwards the existence of God is self-evident but to human mental capacity it is not self-evidently self-evident.

Is Edwards' apologetic, then, purely rational and evidentialist? If the section in the "Freedom of the Will" is taken as paradigmatic for Edwards' approach, on the grounds that it is a late and published statement, it would seem that Edwards inclines towards rationalism:[77]

"We first ascend, and prove *a posteriori*, or from effects, that there must be an eternal Cause; and then secondly, prove by argumentation, not intuition, that this Being must be necessarily existent; and then thirdly, from the proved necessity of his existence, we may descend, and prove many of his perfections *a priori*."[78]

However, before it is assumed that this establishes Edwards as a somewhat wooden evidentialist, Edwards' succinct statement needs to be contextualised in two ways. First, it is in the context of an appeal to the necessity of causation to shore up the reformed understanding of free will that Edwards asserts that without causation we could not even have the knowledge of the existence of God. In other words, Edwards is relying on a contemporary horror at the idea of a society that did not even believe in God. At a time when such atheism is at least claimed widely, it must not be missed that Edwards' primary purpose is to base cause on the commonly accepted knowledge of God, not, as a modern would be tempted to read the passage, to base the knowledge of God upon cause. So if it seems that Edwards is claiming that cause arguments are a certain process by which knowledge of the existence of God can be attained, this may at least in part be an extraneous conclusion from his real concern to prove the certainty of causation in general. Edwards, like all practitioners of the noble art of rhetoric, aims his data at the target of his purpose, and this must not be forgotten in an assessment of the data itself. Secondly, it is important to realise that while Edwards appeals to 'argumentation,' and thus to some form of rationality, he does not here make clear by what process these arguments can become effective to the human mind. He is recording a method of argument not a description of belief. It is this question of faith, of appropriation of argument, that gives Edwards' natural theology its bite. The short section of the "Freedom of the Will" is not a proof text but a tip of the iceberg, suggestive of the far more expansive foundations to Edwards' natural theology in his preaching.

There are two sermons which are particularly instructive in this regard, one on Romans 1:20 and one on Psalm 14:1. In these it becomes plain that Edwards' natural theology is persuasive because of the distinction he makes between the actual knowledge of God resident in nature and the process of attaining to such knowledge. Edwards does not qualify natural theology's ability to prove God but the ability of people to see that God is proven, to believe.

From the same text cited in the "Freedom of the Will" section, Romans 1:20, Edwards proclaims the existence of God.[79] Here there is much more material to work with than in the published discussion; it was a massive sermon, both in conception and elucidation, was preached twice, once in Northampton and once in Stockbridge,[80] the second time after the first publication of "Freedom of the Will." It is, therefore, in terms of chronology and size alone, a notable piece. In subject matter it is a sermon of natural theology. It has a threefold goal, to show "that there is some understanding Being that is the cause of this world," that this "cause is but one," and that this Being is the Biblical God, "is such a Being as we are taught that God is." All this without recourse to special revelation but "by the light of na[ture]."[81]

The arguments that Edwards amasses to support the existence of God bear characteristically Edwardean touches on traditional themes. He gives a brief variation of his own version of the ontological theory to argue that either the world or some being was from eternity,[82] from the cosmological argument he draws upon causation to argue that "there must be a first and eternal cause,"[83] from the design argument he attempts to show that this cause can not be the world but "the Being of . . . understanding cause that has made these things."[84]

These lengthy discussions of evidences are insightful and at times compelling arguments for God,[85] but for our purposes it is the degree to which Edwards believes these arguments prove God that is most instructive. The arguments are not intended to produce a persuasion of mere probability but of certainty. It seems likely that Butler's response to the Enlightenment metanarrative of reason was at the back of Edwards' mind at this point, for the largest single section of the sermon is given over not to the arguments of natural theology themselves, but to prove the extent of these arguments. There are eleven subsections, each expressly concerned to show the 'clearness of the evidence' for God's existence.[86] Butler had attempted to defend revealed religion against proponents of natural religion by recourse to an 'analogy' of equal probability before reason's attack.[87] These evidences, however, do not, according to Edwards, give "meer probability" or "strong presumption" or even "much evidence" but rather "absolute certain & full infallible demonstration." It is the ease and the "clearness of the evidence" that Edwards is determined to impress on his hearers, arguing that " 'Tis impossible for us to conceive how G[od] could have [given] Greater Evid[ence] of his being than he has done," for even "if we would see millions of miracles wrought i.e. things out of any steady course of nature could see no more in such works than in the works we see."

No doubt many, even if after reading the full text of Edwards' arguments and pondering them with greatest sympathy, would fail to be convinced of his claim to the absolute clarity of the evidences mustered. This, however, is just the point. For Edwards' conclusion is not 'hence we all know that God certainly exists,' but rather "APPLICATION 1. Hence the Great folly of atheism," and furthermore, "3. Hence a Great Evid[ence] of the blindness of mans mind & how exceedingly the fall of man has depraved man when that he has so much atheism in His Heart." The evidence, Edwards believes, which God has given us in nature is that which no greater can be considered, but this does not mean that all immediately know that God exists, or even that all will agree with careful demonstrations of the evidence of God from nature. It may be a folly to countenance atheism, but it is a folly that abounds. However, atheism abounds not due to lack of evidence to the mind, but to the lack of the mind's ability to grasp the evidence. For post-lapsarian humanity is in a condition of noetic depravity; he can not see the light of nature because of "the blindness of mans mind." Romans 1:20 is a sermon with a dual postulation: the blinding light of nature is coupled with the blindness of humanity's inability to see the light.

The other most important unpublished sermon that bears on the issue of natural theology takes the dual postulation of Romans 1:20 a step further.[88] In order to show that immorality is atheistic in principle, it argues that natural blindness has not an intellectual but a moral cause. Preaching from Psalm 14:1, Edwards maintains the doctrine that, "A principle of Atheism possesses the hearts of all ungodly men."[89] As the heart in scripture is "the whole soul Including all the faculties,"[90] so the atheism that is described in the Psalm is not atheism only of the will or only of the reason but "as sin has dominion over the whole soul so atheism is what taints all the faculties." Therefore atheism is more a condition of moral decay than a state of rational cognition.

This central insight structures Edwards sermon; he is concerned to show first "1. That there is an atheistical Inclination," secondly "2. There is a principle of speculative atheism or atheism of judgement" in all the ungodly, and thirdly, "3. They [the ungodly] have a disposition Practically to deny G[od] or to live as if there were no G[od]."[91] Such atheistic immorality is set within a framework of natural blindness. Within beginning and ending asides to the effect that while nature is an authoritative source of true knowledge, it is the "light of nature,"[92] it is unable to produce true knowledge because human reason, the "light of his mind,"[93] Edwards places his discussion of atheism. This "natural blindness of the children of men" hides not only the revealed truths of special revelation, the incarnation or the atonement which are "above the light of nature," but also "the very first principles of natural Relig[ion]," even the existence of God.

In this framework Edwards defends his analysis of natural blindness in various ways. He observes the real cause of atheism. Atheists are not made by argument, "studying and reasoning is not the way to make perfect atheists." On the contrary, the best way for people to become atheists "is not to consider at all to exercise their Reason," but instead to darken the mind by indulging in sin. To be atheists people need to "make themselves every way as much like beasts as lies in their Power . . . to stupify their minds . . . with beastly Lusts as fast as they can. that is the Readiest way to arrive at atheism . . . "

He displays the rationality of Christianity and the moral cause of atheism by arguing that even the most hardened atheists can not help but see the force of reason for belief in God. There is so much evidence for God and it "so direct" and "so numerous" that "the atheistical Principal never can so far Prevail against the Principle of Reason as so far to hinder its exercise as wholly to put out the light of nature in this particular." The "natural faculty of Reason" may not be destroyed and continues to respond to the evidence of God, and "natural conscience [that] there is in every man will make him at least suspicious of a supreme Judge for that tells every man when he is committed wickedness that he deserves punishment." So Edwards notes that even notorious atheists have been known on occasions to fear God, especially on their death beds.

He explains why, despite the work of reason and the work of conscience, the evidences of God do not produce conviction in "ungodly men," why even if they are convinced by arguments for God, it still seems not "as a thing Real to them" but "Rather such as some Fable." Edwards advances three reasons, each arguing a prioritisation of the moral cause over the intellectual. First, because sin is of a "stupifying nature it renders the soul insensible" and makes it lazy to think. Secondly, because immorality has an "aversion to divine & spiritual" things. Thirdly, because the ungodly have a "habitual dependence on their senses" and have "Lost this relish for spiritual Enjoyment they feel their pleasure only in sensual Enjoyment," so saying that they do not believe in God because they never saw him, undervaluing the "nobler way of Perception than that of sense," that is of reason and will and inclination, they become "slaves to sense."

Therefore while the light of nature may be fully functional the light of the mind of human nature is inoperative for moral reasons. Scholarly attention to the first of these twin emphases has produced a tendency to see Edwards as following the path of the seventeenth century rationalists, as a Malebranche figure.[94] But though there is some similarity of terminology, the second emphasis pushes Edwards down a different avenue.[95] For Edwards, it is the human malady that the combined effect of the evidences of nature and reason is enough to condemn but cannot be enough to save, that "natural revelation is the power of God to damnation but never to salvation."[96] It is therefore not too much to describe the human situation in bleak terms, "the dreadfull wickedness & sottishness of the heart of man naturally," when it is considered how "obvious & numerous" are the evidences for the existence of God. The conclusion of a weighing of the evidence of the light of nature is to cast the discussion back upon the moral state of humanity, upon,

"the dismal mess that the fall has made in mans soul. that he should be so separated & Removed from G[od] that he should question his being that the light of his mind should be put out that he should question the very being of the only being & author of all things that he should be without the knowledge that is the main end of the faculty of reason."

Nature provides knowledge of God but may not be regarded as a sufficient source of knowledge of God for noetic and soteriological reasons. First, the human mind does not receive the knowledge, though the light of nature is adequate to give the knowledge. The inadequacy is due not to nature, nor, strictly, to reason, but to sinful rebellion. To speak metaphorically, the communication failure is due neither to the content of the message, nor to the quality of the receptive equipment, but to the belligerence of the radar operator. Edwards did not believe that humanity had lost the ability to reason, being willing to argue that because man still possesses reason it can be said that the image of God is retained after the fall, even though the image of God is lost in that man has lost holiness: "In one Respect he had the Image of God after the Fall as he had his Reason but he lost the Holy Im[age] of G[od]."[97] By this Edwards does not intend to deny the noetic consequences of the fall, seeing that "tho after the fall he had Reason & mind left yet without Holiness does man no Good." Humanity is not better for reason because reason no longer leads to the knowledge of God, which was the original purpose of understanding, "by this man is capable of knowing God."[98] It is Edwards' Stoddard-like doctrine of the effects of the fall that leads to an emphasis on the moral rather than the rational. As the will to righteousness was degraded, so the mind of righteousness was darkened, so the acts of righteousness were perverted. It is by this means that the mind has become "broken, Impaired, & weakened & Ruin'd," and God is not known.[99]

Secondly, even if the message of nature were received it would not communicate salvation. While nature reveals morality, it does not reveal soteriology. That a person must be righteous to know God may be found from nature, but not that this righteousness can only be gained through the righteousness of another: the "light of nature" suggests that God's favour and his reward "must be obtained by Righ[teousness]" but it does not suggest a "being saved by anothers Righ[teousness]" which "is a thing man naturally can have no conception of the propriety of."[100] Edwards, then, makes a distinction between the revelation and the reception, and between the revelation of morality and of salvation. The light of nature may reveal God's existence but its message falls on deaf ears. The light of nature may suggest the need for moral purity yet it does not preach Christ crucified. Resting solely on the authority of nature people will not see the righteousness of God nor come to a knowledge of God, for "they being not Enlightened cant see any other Righ[teousness]."[101]

Such an approach to the authority of nature is found neither in the school of 'probability' nor in the school of 'common sense.' Butler's apologetic of probability is not the model that Edwards adopts as a response to the Enlightenment metanarrative of reason; Edwards argues that God's being is demonstrative not probable. Nor is Reid's common sense argument against the later epistemological scepticism that he saw as rooted in Enlightenment rationality Edwards' approach; Edwards does not appeal to the common experience of humanity to set a bulwark against doubt spawned by the authority of nature.[102] Rather Edwards argues for the utter reasonableness of Christianity, that it is 'all most reasonable,'[103] but that it can not be found by reason. It is right to underline the importance of reasoning for Edwards, but the extent to which reason fails must not thereby be understated.[104] The Enlightenment metanarrative of reason is, for Edwards, naive. Post-lapsarian reason is still reasonable but it is biased, prejudiced against the truth and inclined to the lie. It might be thought then that in effect what Edwards gives with one hand, rationality, he takes away with the other, the noetic effects of the fall. To this dilemma Edwards does offer a solution: reason is darkened but there is a light by which it may be 'enlightened.'

THE LIGHT OF REVELATION

At this juncture Edwards most commonly provides his solution in the terminology of the contemporary debate over authority.[105] He offers 'true light,' 'true enlightenment' against, implicitly, false light authority. Adoption of this kind of terminology itself is by no means an approach unique to Edwards. Apart from its prevalence in the Bible, Edwards had considerable historical precedence for the use of the terms 'enlightened' and 'light' in the context of establishing revelation against competing alternatives. There were Augustinian, Lutheran, Calvinist, and Puritan apologetics of light, interacting and overlapping one with another. An Augustinian precedence of light as certainty against doubt; obeying the "divine command" of *tolle lege*, Augustine read the Scripture which was, "as if a light of relief from all anxiety flooded into my heart. All the shadows of doubt were dispelled."[106] A Lutheran precedence of light as the gospel against the Pope; a simple receiving of the message gives light, "Therefore if you would be enlightened . . . go where you can silently meditate and lay hold of this picture deep in your heart, and you will see miracle upon miracle."[107] A Reformed precedence of light as defending the Bible against reason and tradition; Calvin argues that "the testimony of the Spirit is superior to reason. For as God alone can properly bear witness to his own words, so these words will not obtain full credit in the hearts of men, until they are sealed by the inward testimony of the Spirit,"[108] and also uses illumination, the "enlightened" experience, as a defence of *sola scriptura* against tradition.[109] Finally, a Puritan precedence of light as the mark of true Christianity; in the midst of nominal Christianity the Puritans tended to emphasise this 'experimental' side to the Protestant heritage, so Ames asserts that there is an "outward" as well as an "inward" calling of the gospel, the outward being the proclamation of the gospel and "The inward offer is a spiritual enlightening, whereby these premises are propounded to the hearts of men, as it were by an inward word."[110]

From these wells Edwards draws an apologetic to douse natural authority. Other Evangelicals may have put their hand to the same pump. In "An Appeal to Men of Wisdom and Candour" preached before Cambridge University, so in a cross current of the new learning, Simeon argues that to the enlightened revealed religion is reasonable: "though revealed religion is neither founded on human reason, nor makes its appeal to it; yet it is perfectly consistent with reason and approves itself to the judgement of everyone whose mind is enlightened by the Spirit of God," who have, "enlightened reason."[111] Edwards' response is similar to Simeon's. They only differ in that Edwards employs enlightenment as immediate spiritual experience as well as an aid to reason. For Edwards the subjective is necessary to the authority of the objective, not merely as Simeon for that objective revelation to be accepted as revelation, but as immediate contact with God. Edwards' enlightenment comes under the heading of illumination in the terms of reformed systematics, but it is an illumination without which revelation would have no direct impact.

Yet Edwards insisted on maintaining that the Bible itself was ultimate authority. Without such a revelation he believes there would have been little knowledge of any worth and with a rejection of such revelation he finds little prospect for the future of humanity.[112] In one sense, therefore, Edwards does not believe experience of God to be immediate. Claims to immediate experience which undermine the authority of the Bible Edwards considers to be spiritually dangerous. The Bible is not the just residue of true accounts of God's dealings with people but how people now hear from God. We do not contact the divine by "immediate intuition but by the word of God."[113] In Heaven we will see "Immediately face to face" but here we see "by a medium," that is by "the intermediation of the outward means of our illumination & Knowledge of God viz. X[Christ's] ministers & the Gospel which they preach & his ordinances which they administer."[114] In another sense, however, he does believe experience of God to be immediate. We do not come to God at the end of a chain of arguments, as if he is the last step in a spiritual *quod erat demonstrandum*. It is not by "ratiocination" that we come to 'see God.' Experience of God is "to have an immediate sensible & certain understanding of Gods Glorious excellency & love." This is not "speculative ratiocination," for "if they argue that he is very merciful that wont Give sense of his Glorious Grace and mercy," it "must be a very direct & sensible view."

When preaching, therefore, Edwards is careful to distinguish between these two sorts of immediacy. While true enlightenments "are Immediate in a sense that is they dont Consist in speculation & ratiocination but yet in another sense they are more indirect that is as they are by means of the Gospel."[115] Thus he strongly counsels against allegiance to the separatists on the basis of their claims to 'immediacy,' claims which a careless reading of Edwards 'light' apologetic might suggest that he was making. Without a blush of conscience that he too was preaching for immediate revelation, he warns his hearers, "Take heed you dont follow . . . pretended immediate Rev[elation] of supposed Truths not to be found in the Bible before that Rev[elation] was made." His 'light' is not this 'light.' The illustration he chose to illuminate the difference would have hit many a nerve. Do not, he rebukes, be led astray by the kind of revelation that tells you it is the will of God that you should "preach the Gosp[el]" in a certain place, for, "if this be revealed immediately 'tis a new truth not contained in the SS[Scriptures] tho many Texts should be brought to the mind to confirm." He concludes that separation from the separatists is the only legitimate option, "so that 'tis your duty to withdraw from such Chhs[Churches]." The situation is so serious because there is no probability that the immediate revelations of the apostolic period will return, "with Regard to immediate Revelations in General How unreasonable it is to expect this Inspiration be renewed."[116]

For Edwards it was important to maintain that though experience of God is direct it is through the word, and though it is through logos it is not logic. In the metaphor of light Edwards found a picture of such immediacy through the word.[117] A person, "cannot have spiritual light without the word," but the word does not cause the light, which is a "sense of the heart" and is "immediately from the Spirit of God."[118] However, despite "supposed Light that is not spiritual Light" being a great danger,[119] experience of spiritual light was a crucial component of Edwards' response to the light of the Enlightenment metanarrative of reason. The Great Awakening may have taught him the danger of the light of enthusiasm, but the apologetic significance of 'light' was such that Edwards employed it in spite of such dangers.[120]

In a famous sermon, then, Edwards preached that a 'divine and supernatural light, immediately imparted to the soul, by the spirit of God,' is 'both a *scriptural* and *rational* doctrine.'[121] According to the teaching of the Bible, it is those who are "spiritually enlightened" that have a true sense of religion,[122] and, Edwards argues, "it is rational to suppose" that this light is beyond "the mere strength of natural reason."[123] These two may be partners because it is the excellency of the truth not the content of the truth that is communicated in light, experimental not notional knowledge, and the perception of excellency is not the work of reason, "Reason's work is to perceive truth not excellency." Light must come through the mind, but if 'reason' is taken strictly as "ratiocination, or a power of inferring by arguments" then the "perceiving of spiritual beauty and excellency no more belongs to reason, than it belongs to the sense of feeling to perceive colours." This perception is the work of "the sense of the heart."[124] Early in Edwards' ministry 'light' was established as a primary apologetic for true Christianity in the Enlightenment.

Edwards' series of sermons on 2 Peter are particularly apposite in this respect. Edwards is tapping into the background debate of the epistle, those heretical false teachers that are mentioned in the second chapter of the letter who have often been thought to display Gnostic or proto-gnostic elements.[125] A text defending the authority of true knowledge of God against false claims to alternative sources of authority of knowledge was the perfect platform for Edwards' riposte to the authority of nature. Edwards commented upon 2 Peter chapter 1 in his "Notes on the Scriptures," perhaps laying the exegetical groundwork for the sermons.[126] Three significant sermons were preached on this chapter, one on verse sixteen and two on verse nineteen.[127] The content of the verses indicate the direction that Edwards' apologetic moves regarding the issue of authority: the authority that he is wishing to establish is immediate and is illuminative, it is that which arises from being 'eyewitnesses of his [Christ's] majesty' and that which is a 'light that shineth in a dark place.'[128]

The argumentative thrust of the sermon on verse sixteen is focused on the immediacy of experience of Christ,[129] with the doctrine, "That seeing the glory of Christ is what tends to assure the heart of the truth of the gospel." Edwards' exegesis of the text amounts to the proposition that "eyewitnesses of his majesty" refers to seeing the transfiguration, and that this sight was not only of his "external glory" but also that, "There was doubtless an inward sight in him by sense of heart of X[Christ's] spiritual Glory." In the same way then, Edwards argues, those who now have this inward sight of the glory of Christ in Scripture are also 'eyewitnesses of his majesty,' in fact "much more" so than those who saw the transfiguration of Christ if they had only seen the outward glory of Christ. For Edwards the crucial revelation of Christ's glory was and is the "inward sight." Those who see Christ in the present are eyewitnesses to an extent that those who saw Christ when alive but did not see who he was, that is did not really see him, never were.[130]

This light is epistemologically significant though not epistemologically communicative. While the light does not impart knowledge, "as tho one saw a visible Glory," it reveals knowledge: "a natural man beholds spiritual things as a man beholds the things upon the face of the earth in the night . . . but the mind spiritually Enlightened beholds them as a person that looks upon things after the day has dawned." Thus people in the present become "Eyewitnesses," giving self-evident attestation to gospel truth, for "when it is seen evidences itself." As Edwards comments in the "Notes on the Scriptures," faith that is an evidence that makes "clearly seen of things that are not seen."[131] Or, as he remarks in his Miscellanies, it is an "objective light."[132] No need then for complex arguments to be assured of the truth of the gospel, for "the truth of the Gosp[el] is a thing of Gods revealing." The gospel depends not upon historical evidence; God has provided a "better foundation of faith," the self-evidence of seeing the glory of the gospel, of being 'enlightened,' for "the gospel & its fundamental doctrines do carry their own evidences along with them."[133] Learning is esteemed but the "best evidence" is to have this "marvellous light that you may be eyewitnesses of X[Christ's] majesty," for if "God pleases to open your eyes . . . you will need no other arguments to convince you of the truth of the gosp[el]." Why is this evidence the best kind? Because it is "the most real & immediate" and is not by "Painful Ratiocination" but is "a kind of Intuitive Evidence."[134]

The argumentative thrust of the two sermons on verse nineteen is focused on the illuminative nature of revelation. They were preached as a series, with some time lag in-between, the first in August 1737 and the second in November of the same year. The doctrine that Edwards seeks to establish in both sermons is that, "Divine revelation is like a light that shines in a dark place." In the first sermon he analyses how it is a "light that shines in the world," that is by scripture, in the second how it is a "light that shines in the heart of man," that is in internal experience of the truth of scripture.

The first sermon argues that without Scriptural revelation there is no true enlightenment. Retract the light of revelation and even natural light is defunct.

Pre-Christian religions abound with unnatural practices, human sacrifice for instance, and the more palatable parts, "what is called natural Relig[ion]," came not from reason but by the "tradition" of ancient philosophers who journeyed to Egypt and countries bordering Judea and "gathered something from them," so that "all these fragments of truth were originally from Revelation." After Christ, "the world which before was so dark has been enlightened by divine Revel[ation]." More recently there has been "a remarkable influence . . . of Enlightening Great parts of the world." The contrast is stark between Africa, Asia and some parts of America without revelation and those with it. But even more serious is the situation for those who reject revelation, for Islam, "popery," and "our own nation."[135] This unholy trinity is explained to show that rejecting revelation leads to unnatural beliefs, culminating with the ludicrous beliefs of those "at this day in our nation." Edwards concludes it is "evidential that the bible is the proper means for teaching the world concerning G[od]."

The section on Islam is astonishing for its litany of extraordinary beliefs to which he claims Moslems hold. His information source is not clear, but is not in the main Qu'ranic. The section is intended to show the "sottishness of the world of mankind when not Guided by Revela[tion] not withstanding all that mans natural Reason or the Light of Nature teaches."[136] His criticism of the "papist religion" is founded on the way it "sets aside the Bible" and "sets up the devices of the pope & the canon of their Chh[church] which they say is infallible" as superior and the foundation to the scriptures. Ridiculous beliefs of "popery," their "many magical kind of ceremonies," are listed again to show "the strong delusions & exceeding darkness men are subject that hant guided by the light of Revela[tion]."

Edwards' *coup de grâce* aims "at this day in our own nation" those who "Reject the bible and all Revealed religion & hold the bible is a meer human book" and believe "G[od] wont give any revelation of his mind any otherwise than by the light of nature." He names the disease as "deism" which "of late has made an amazing progress in our nation." They are those who have "set up their own reason as a sufficient guide" which has led them into "darkness." In what seems to be a sideswipe at Mandeville, Edwards shows the wide group to which 'deism' could refer, remarking that "it is a principle that has been published among them that private vices are publick benefits & plead . . . for the lawfullness of . . . adultery — murder — & Robbery."[137]

Therefore there is great necessity for revelation, "These things show that we can say what we will about the Light of nature that if once we come to cast off Revelation there is no foundation principle of the Light of nature but what man will call into question & Reject." Where would we be "if G[od] had left us alone & left us only to that own [sic] Reason & had not given a light from heaven to enlighten us." Once we have been enlightened reason may function, reasoning after revelation, "Kn[owledge] is easy to him that understands." In conclusion he appeals to the rhetoric of the age, "Let us pray for the times when that Light shall Enlighten the whole world."

The second sermon is briefer, building upon the last to establish that "divine Revelation is in the hearts of those that do truly entertain it as a light that shines in a dark place." The purpose of this internal light is to reveal the truth, as "The nature of light is to discover and manifest things to our eyes," so spiritual light reveals spiritual truth, "divine Revelation in the hearts of those that truly entertain it gives a manifestation of Sp[iritual] objects that are otherwise wholly undiscovered & unseen." The effect of it is to in fact reveal "G[od] to the soul." It is so essential to spirituality that as in nature "without true light nothing will be seen all things will be perfectly hid from us" so without the true light of revelation spiritual truth will not be seen. There is a necessity for internal illumination in order for the external illumination to be grasped.

Internal revelation opens the door to see the truth of external revelation and reason, shows the light of nature and the light of revelation to be truth. Regeneration is the key, for as in creation God made light to shine out of chaos, so "spiritual light is the first thing in the new Creation;" God says "let there be light" in the heart of human chaos.[138] In Edwards mind there is no doubt that however profound the theology, accurate the philosophy, persuasive the rhetoric, faithful the gospel, there can be no recognition of the truth without an enlightenment. The effects of the fall are such that light is required to restore the ability to see. In a sermon on Matthew chapter five, Edwards argues that when Adam fell he lost this 'holy thing,' hence corrupt nature in the bible is called 'flesh,' and that in regeneration "something of this holy principle is restored." It is only a "spark" in you, it is not thorough change before heaven, yet in regeneration light is given, "when this Light shines in the Heart it is as when the Light of the sun shines in the world after a night of Great darkness . . . a new world is appeared to view to the Regenerate Person." Without regeneration there can be no knowledge of the truth, "Natural men dont see the truth," but by regeneration, the gospel, even those "Things above the Reach of sense above Reason" are revealed to be true.[139] "G[od] Enlightens the soul" with the result that there is "such marks of truth such bright & Clear Evidence" that there is "certainty of it."[140]

Assessments of the success of Edwards' true light may follow two channels, an evaluation of the content of 'reasoning after revelation' and of the persuasiveness of 'light.'

First, probably the most debilitating factor for many a reader of Edwards' apologetic in terms of content is that in Edwards' natural light there is a surprising omission from the normal canon of natural theology: there seems to be no apologetic of evil.[141] While there is evidence of Edwards' concern for suffering itself,[142] he did not construct a defence of the 'problem of evil.'[143] There is no consideration of the question that played upon many a mind, for instance, after the Lisbon earthquake. Part of the answer may be that having an Augustinian understanding of the origin of evil,[144] Edwards may have also taken an Augustinian approach to the phenomenon of evil,[145] tending therefore to be prompted by the question of suffering not primarily to apologetics but to preach the judgement of God against evil.[146] Some form of neoplatonic influence may also have informed Edwards' ontological argument so to see evil as what is not, as formally non-existent, which may have mitigated against extensive intellectualisation of the problem of evil, even though it did not, of course, entail a denial of the actuality of evil.[147] That Edwards did not have an apologetic of 'the problem of evil' was probably because for him the problem was not evil as such but people, not on sin but sinners, and therefore his focus was upon the human responsibility for sin, the coming judgement, and the rescue from sin offered in the gospel.

Despite this omission, I believe Edwards' reasoning after revelation is persuasive. To some it may seem that to argue for reason and revelation, albeit reasoning after revelation, is epistemically untenable. One might continue to proclaim the gospel as truth as a form of subjective fideism, but not as objective rationality or, indeed, historicity. Edwards, here, it could be argued, displays his pre-modern naivety; in an age that follows the wide acceptance of the Enlightenment's metanarrative of reason, numerous debunkings of the supernatural,[148] higher criticism and the 'Jesus of history' search,[149] and a recognition of the plurality of religious sensibility,[150] such an antiquated position may seem quaint but never relevant.[151] Would not Edwards have been wiser to have ceased the ascent of reason and rested on the more accessible peak of 'revelation'? After all, it may be said, such a reliance on revelation is not a sign of the victory of modernity, a privatisation of religion, but a witness to a traditional belief in the supernaturality of Christianity, in the sense that faith is not found by natural reason but defies reason.[152]

Certainly, modern theological debates have had the effect of devaluing natural theology,[153] making Edwards' apologetics under-studied. Yet the silence may bear witness to partial hearing, an ear that is inclined more to hear the dissonance between Edwards' natural theology and a certain stream of contemporary theology's response to the Enlightenment, than to hear the resonance that there is between it and the Enlightenment itself. For in the context of the Enlightenment the apologetic implications of his natural light find their mark. His reasoning after revelation avoids the metanarrative of reason, yet is not a privatised spirituality, a subjective piety. The assertion of rationality, the validity of the light of nature is genuine; one could not fault Edwards in the thoroughness of his natural theology apologetic. Coupled with a concept of the fall and the light of revelation it is a strong position: where his hearers are not persuaded he has the light of revelation, illumination and Scripture, upon which to fall back. His apologetic framework will be given further consideration in the "Conclusion;" suffice it to say here that it is not lightly dismissed.

Secondly, Edwards' 'light' has a powerful rhetorical appeal to an age of enlightenment. The terminology holds in tension a belief in the importance of reason and yet manages to avoid worshipping at its shrine. Much of this is traditionally Puritan; there had long been an empirical spirit in Puritanism's denial of traditional authority, which Edwards maintained and employed as a trojan horse against the Enlightenment authority of nature. Preachers before him had, "made experiment a familiar word on the plane of religion and morals long before it became supreme on that of natural science," heartily supporting the new learning against the sterility of the traditional curriculum.[154] Edwards' genius was to train the Puritan guns upon the Enlightenment. Theirs was the real immediacy, the real experimentation, the true reason, the true light.

Edwards' metanarrative was the metanarrative of the gospel. When such phrases as "the illusion of the Enlightenment metanarrative"[155] are being woven into argument without comment, the question of the possibility of establishing a metanarrative with cogency is by no means irrelevant. Certainly, many would see any type of metaphysical authority, even if possible, as undesirable;[156] yet it may be also that the fragmentation of our mental structures has ravaged such disillusionment that the question of a viable metanarrative is more palatable than might be thought. If not *this* Enlightenment, then *what* enlightenment? For Edwards, true light led to truth, *Lux ad Veritam*.

NOTES

1. Based in the seventeenth century works of, among others, Boyle, Newton, Hobbes, and Locke, the Enlightenment's concept of nature was central to the ideology of the age. To Enlightenment writers, "the source of man's unhappiness is his ignorance of nature," (Baron d'Holbach, *System of Nature*, [New York, 1970], viii).

2. Jean Ehrard, *L'Idée de Nature en France*, 2 vols., (Paris 1963), Simon Schafer, "Natural Philosophy," *The Ferment of Knowledge*, ed. G.S. Rousseau and Roy Porter, (Cambridge, 1980), 55–91; G.R.Cragg, *Reason and Authority in the Eighteenth Century*, (Cambridge, 1964); Dorinda Outram, *The Enlightenment*, (Cambridge, 1995), 48.

3. Francis Bacon produced the seminal programme of natural philosophy reform as rejection of the blind worship of authorities such as Aristotle, (Francis Bacon, *Two Books of the Proficiencie and Advancement of Learning*, [London, 1808]).

4. David Hume, *Dialogues Concerning Natural Religion*, (Edinburgh, 1947). The recent trend to employ the interpretative key of literary style to the 'Dialogue,' (John

Bricke, "On the Interpretation of Hume's Dialogues," *Religious Studies*, vol.11, [1975], 1–18; Gary Shapiro, "The man of Letters and the Author of Nature: Hume on Philosophical Discourse," *Eighteenth Century*, vol.26, [1985], 115–37; Jeffrey Wieand, "Pamphilus in Hume's Dialogues," *Journal of Religion*, vol.65, [1986], 33–45), underlines its extended irony on natural religion, (Michael B. Prince, "Hume and the End of Religious Dialogue," *Eighteenth Century Studies*, vol. 25, no.3, [Spring 1992], 283–308).

5. In France alone the Enlightenment explicitly attacked Christianity, but wherever the Enlightenment was found it, "again and again opposed the attempt to solve the problem of knowledge by means of a transcendent world," (Ernst Cassirer, *The Philosophy of the Enlightenment*, [Princeton, 1951], 98). Whiggism is to be avoided, (Gerard S.J. Reedy, *The Bible and Reason: Anglicans and Scripture in Late Seventeenth Century England*, [Philadelphia 1985], 3, 141), but it can not be denied that the eighteenth century rapidly developed an understanding of Christianity as rational, a natural religion not revealed religion, hence Tindal's highly influential work, *Christianity as Old as Creation, or the Gospel a Republication of the Religion of Nature*, (London, 1732).

6. Light is a common metaphor for realisation of truth but in the eighteenth century its use is especially prevalent, (Geoffrey Cantor, "Light and Enlightenment: An Exploration of Mid-Eighteenth Century Modes of Discourse," *The Discourse of Light from the Middle Ages to the Enlightenment*, [Los Angeles, 1970]), as Pope famously remarked, "God said 'let Newton be,' and all was light," (Flower & Murphy, *A History of Philosophy in America*, [New York, 1977], 64). Edwards acknowledges the word's significance when he ironically refers to "this age of light and inquiry," ("Freedom of the Will," *Yale Works*, i, 437).

7. John W. Yolton, ed., *The Blackwell Companion to the Enlightenment*, (Blackwell, 1995), 1.

8. The history of the seals of both Harvard and Yale is complex. Harvard's original *veritas* seal dates from 1643. The modern emblem is exactly the same except that the third book is now open, (Samuel Eliot Morison, "The Founding of Harvard College," *The Tercentennial History of Harvard College and University*, vol.1, [Boston Mass., 1935], 328). Two other seals seemed to have been used a little later, the mottoes of which tell us that for the founders *veritas* was revealed truth, (ibid., 330). For Yale, while the seal is used to recall its origins, ("Yale's Christian tradition," Anson Phelps Stokes, June 17th 1951, *The 250th Anniversary of Yale University*, [New Haven, Conn., 1952], 20), and the *lux et veritas* is the official translation of the Hebrew 'urim and thummim' on the seal adopted in 1745, (Samuel Eliot Morison, "The Founding of Harvard College," *The Tercentennial History of Harvard College and University*, vol.1, [Cambridge, Mass., 1935], 332, footnote), Yale's foundation is in fact not well documented, (Edwin Oviatt, *The Beginnings of Yale 1701–1726*, [New Haven, Conn., 1916], ix, 143). But we do know that from 1745 a seal and *lux et veritas* were part of the college's self-awareness, (Richard Hofstadter and Wilson Smith, eds., *American Higher Education: A Documentary History*, vol. 1, [Chicago, 1961], 51 & 54, my italics). See also, George W. Pierson, *The Founding of Yale: The Legend of the Forty Folios*, (New Haven, Conn., 1988).

9. There were no doubt practical and political reasons for the founding of Yale but the theological longing for a college which was free of the perceived dangerous tendencies of Harvard cannot be dismissed. A letter of one of the founders of the Collegiate School tells us that it was established "because the college at Cambridge was under the tutorage of latitudinarians," another letter that it was planned as a "reserve of pure and sound principles . . . in case of change in our mother Harvard," (Edwin Oviatt, *The Beginnings of Yale 1701–1726*, [New Haven, Conn., 1916], 137).

10. Perry Miller, *The New England Mind: The Seventeenth Century*, (Cambridge, Mass., 1954), 65–88. The Puritan John Preston (Master of Emmanuel College, Cambridge), for instance, was renowned for his knowledge of the scholastics and his labour to reconcile reason and faith.

11. Miscellanies entitled "Revealed Religion" and various under the heading of "Christian Religion."

12. Robert W. Jensen, *America's Theologian: A Recommendation of Jonathan Edwards*, (New York, 1988), 21.

13. See the "Revealed Religion" and "Christian Religion" series of Edwards "Miscellanies." No. 1304, for example, argues for the necessity of "revelation" though there are certain things that the "light of nature" can teach.

14. Norman Fiering, *Moral Philosophy at Seventeenth Century Harvard*, (Williamsburg, Va., 1981), 52–62.

15. John E. Smith, *Jonathan Edwards, Puritan, Preacher, Philosopher*, (London, 1992), 140.

16. No. 94, "The 'Miscellanies,' a-500," *Yale Works*, xiii, 257. Likewise that people were created to be happy in the love of God is also "evident from mere reason," (no. 197, "The 'Miscellanies,' a-500," *Yale Works*, xiii, 336).

17. *Yale Works*, vi, 396–397.

18. *Banner Works*, ii, 158.

19. Edwards argues that there is no need for there to be explicit record of a particular physical outworking of the Spirit, "because these are easily accounted for, from what we know of the nature of man," and the general principles taught in the Scriptures, ("The Distinguishing Marks," *Yale Works*, iv, 233).

20. As "there may be deductions of reason from what has been said [in the Scripture]," so he is "not afraid to say twenty things about the Trinity which the Scripture never said," (no. 94, "The 'Miscellanies,' a-500," *Yale Works*, xiii, 257).

21. "The Miscellanies," 1297, *MSS*, Beinecke.

22. "The Miscellanies," 986, *MSS*, Beinecke.

23. I use the term 'reasoning after revelation' not because Edwards believes it desirable to discover new doctrines not found in Scripture, but because he hesitates to say that revelation is above reason if that means either that revelation is not reasonable or that revelation can be received without reason. At the back of Edwards' mind may well have been the subtitle to John Toland's *Christianity not Mysterious*: "or, a *Treatise* showing, that there is nothing in the *Gospel* contrary to *Reason*, nor above it," (London, 1702).

24. No. 140, "The 'Miscellanies,' a-500," *Yale Works*, xiii, 297.

25. No. 350, "The 'Miscellanies,' a-500," *Yale Works*, 421.

26. "The Miscellanies," 1304, *MSS*, Beinecke.

27. Paul Helm, "Editor's Introduction," *Treatise on Grace and Other Posthumously Published Writings by Jonathan Edwards*, (Cambridge, 1971), 21.

28. No. 249, "The 'Miscellanies,' a-500," *Yale Works*, xiii, 361.

29. "A History of the Work of Redemption," *Yale Works*, ix, 441.

30. Discussed in "True Experience."

31. Miller's view of Edwards as modern is far from dead: "Edwards was actually more radically 'modern' than Miller himself might have realised," (Sang Hyun Lee, *The philosophical theology of Jonathan Edwards*, [Princeton, 1988], 3).

32. Under 'The Light of Nature.'

33. The Chapter "True Experience" discusses Edwards' method of assessment.

34. Many of his later Miscellanies are variations on this theme.

35. Stephen H. Daniel, *The Philosophy of Jonathan Edwards*: A Study in Divine Semiotics, (Bloomington, 1994), 1. Daniel argues for Edwards' debt to the "Stoic-Ramist" heritage.

36. "The Miscellanies," 1340, *MSS*, Beinecke; reprinted (without Edwards' indication that this is his definition) *Banner Works*, ii, 479.

37. Even reasoning that does have an act of the will about it may also be meant by Edwards to be thought of as not different from perception, as it is "not of a different nature to demonstrative reasoning," ("The Mind," no. 58, *Yale Works*, vi, 373).

38. "Subjects to be Handled in the Treatise on the Mind," no. 28, *Yale Works*, vi, 390.

39. See Chapter "True Experience" for elucidation of the sense of the heart.

40. See for a good example of Edwards typology, "The Miscellanies," 1069, *MSS*, Beinecke.

41. "The Miscellanies," 1324, *MSS*, Beinecke.

42. "HEATHENS had they what they had of truth in divine things by TRADITION from the first Fathers of nations or from the Jews . . . Plato . . . tells us plainly that they the Grecians received letters from the Gods by certain Barbarians more rational than themselves," ("The Miscellanies," 959, *MSS*, Beinecke). Not all "natural religion" before Christ must stem from revelation but "most," (no. 350, "The 'Miscellanies,' a-500," *Yale Works*, xiii, 423).

43. By the revelation of Christ "the Mahometan parts of the world came to acknowledge the true God," (no. 443, "The 'Miscellanies,' a-500," *Yale Works*, xiii, 491).

44. Nos. 131, 202, 276, 382, 465, "The 'Miscellanies,' a-500," *Yale Works*, xiii, 293, 338, 376, 451, 507; nos. 981, 984, 1002, *MSS*, Beinecke; "Notes on the Scriptures," 220, 222, 445, *MSS*, Beinecke.

45. The rite of circumcision selects the "Jewish Religion" as of "divine authority" as it contradicts human pride and lust: "False religions always spare those two lusts of lasciviousness and pride," (no. 311, "The 'Miscellanies,' a-500," *Yale Works*, xiii, 393–4).

46. No. 6, "The 'Miscellanies,' a-500," *Yale Works*, xiii, 203; nos. 465, 266, 203, 444, *Yale Works*, xiii, 507, 372, 339, 492.

47. Edwards aims to show what "Evidences There are that the Facts of the MOSAIC HISTORY never could be forged," ("Subjects of Inquiry," *MSS*, Beinecke, page 14).

48. Edwards expects historical accuracy: the "Great difficulty" that Ahaziah seems to be two years older than his father in 2 Chronicles 22:1–4 is resolved by arguing that the number refers not to Ahaziah's age but to the age of his household, thereby including the years of his father to match the total recorded, ("Notes on the Scriptures," *MSS*, Beinecke, page 222).

49. For Edwards the accounts of the gospel are "the Facts of the X[Chris]tian Religion," ("Rough Notes on the Truth of the Christian Religion," *MSS*, Beinecke).

50. Edwards reminds himself "In reading the ACTS & the EPISTLES to observe the Evidences of the Fact of X'[Christ's] Resurrection & other Chief Facts Relating to X[Christ]," ("Subjects of Inquiry," *MSS*, Beinecke, page 17).

51. Despite the reference to the four evangelists in the note's title, it is only in fact the synoptic gospels that Edwards cites: "The accounts of the four Evangelists Concerning the Resurrection of Christ Reconciled," ("Notes on the Scriptures," *MSS*, Beinecke, page 220).

52. He argues that Christ really died as he did not feign death or "swoon," (no. 152, "The 'Miscellanies,' a-500," *Yale Works*, xiii, 302); that the Resurrection was a full proof of Christ's authority as "witches juggling is at an end when they are dead," (no. 313, *ibid.*, 395), and the Old Testament argues it as a proof of a prophet, (no. 321a, *ibid.*, 402); and that Christ's resurrection is the fact that separates Christianity from Islam, ("The Miscellanies," 1334, *MSS*, Beinecke).

53. "The Miscellanies," 1340, *MSS*, Beinecke.

54. "Miscellanies," 1156, *MSS*, Beinecke.

55. "But the more perfect views that the saints have of Gods Glory & love in another world is what is Especially Called seeing of G[od] then they shall see him as he is their light which now is but a Glimmering will be brought to Clear sunshine that which is here but the dawning will become Perfect day," (Matthew 5:8 [1], *MSS*, Beinecke); "even under the gospel dispensation we see by a reflex light we see through a looking glass in comparison of what we shall see in the future state," ("The Miscellanies," 710, *MSS*, Beinecke); "MYSTERIES in Religion . . . doubtless many truths will hereafter appear Plain, when we come to look on them by the bright light of Heaven, that now are involved in mystery and darkness," (*Ibid.*, 765).

56. "The Miscellanies," 1156, *MSS*, Beinecke.

57. 2 Peter 1.19: "Divine Revelation is like a light that shines in a dark place," (August 1737, February 1758), *MSS*, Beinecke.

58. McDonald argues that the Boyle lectures produced an extensive body of literature dealing with evidences for Christianity, thus exhibiting a rising concern for the defence of special revelation against the claims of nature, (H.D. McDonald, *Ideas of Revelation: An Historical Study, 1700–1860*, [London, 1959], 3). While Boyle has often been seen as a founder of modern science, it is also important to realise, and less often noticed, that he worked within and out of personal religious convictions, (Robert Marley, "Robert Boyle In and Out of His Time," *The Eighteenth Century*, vol.35, no.3, [Autumn 1994], 280–286).

59. Matthew Tindal's, *Christianity as Old as Creation*, (London, 1732), is and was probably the most cited of the deistical works, though there was much else in a similar vein. Earlier than Tindal, and perhaps even more controversial, was John Toland's,

Christianity Not Mysterious, (London, 1702); G.R.Cragg, *Reason and Authority in the Eighteenth Century*, (Cambridge, 1964); R.E. Sullivan, *John Toland and the Deist Controversy: A Study in Adaptions*, (Cambridge, Mass., 1982).

60. Explicit and implicit references to the deist are numerous. The collection of posthumous sermon notes, published as one sermon under the title of "Man's Natural Blindness in the Things of Religion," *Banner Works*, ii, 247–256: Since the Reformation many have fallen away, "to atheism, deism, and gross infidelity; and others to Arminianism," (*Ibid.*, 249); deistical concerns occur in his distinctions between true and false faith: "But if it be not seated in the will, it is no more a holy faith, than the Faith of deists," (1 John 5:1–4, July 1750, *MSS*, Beinecke); The miscellanies have notes explicitly directed against the deists, ("The Miscellanies," 1297, *MSS*, Beinecke; no. 127, "The 'Miscellanies,' a-500," *Yale Works*, xiii, 291), and generally much of the Miscellanies series 'Christian Religion' is written to show the necessity of special revelation; Edwards' Catalogue of reading records, "alciphon or the minute Philosopher in 2 vols on octavo against the deists by George Berkeley," and various deist authors are also listed, ("Catalogue of Books," *MSS*, Beinecke).

61. "The Miscellanies," 1340, *MSS*, Beinecke. A somewhat rearranged version is published in *Banner Works*, ii, 479–485.

62. Edwards shows his wide knowledge of deist writings in "The Miscellanies," 1297, *MSS*, Beinecke; Johnson concluded from his analysis of Edwards' reading that not only was Edwards "thoroughly familiar" with Hobbes, Chubb and Tindal, but that "considering that Edwards' later writings were directed against deism," he must have known about other deists, including Charles Leslie, John Toland, Anthony Collins, and William Woolston, (Thomas H. Johnson, "Jonathan Edwards' Background of Reading," *The Publication of the Colonial Society of Massachusetts*, vol.xxviii, [1931], 212, footnote); disentangling the oratorical punch of past sermons, much of which is by insinuation, is no easy business, but the rhetoric of a sermon with the doctrine, "They who are in a natural condition are in a dreadful condition" seems, while obviously traditionally Calvinist in its appeal to the Biblical correlation of 'flesh' as sinful nature, to be touching the nerve of a common social respect for the condition of nature, (*Banner Works*, i, 817–829).

63. Contemporaries had differing opinions as to the validity of the deistic type of response, seeing it as a capitulation or veneration of the truth, (Ezio Vailati, "Leibniz and Clarke on Miracles," *Journal of the History of Philosophy*, vol. xxxiii, no.4, [October 1995], 543–562). The categorisation of 'deists' is slippery; Hobbes has been seen as a deist, an atheist and as an orthodox Christian, (Edwin Curley, "Calvin and Hobbes, or, Hobbes as an Orthodox Christian," *Journal of History of Philosophy*, vol. xxxiv, no.2, [April 1996], 257–272). Kant believed that the God of Deism was the only kind that could be reached by the arguments of 'speculative reason' alone, (Immanuel Kant, *Critique of Pure Reason*, [London, 1929], 553)

64. Francois Lyotard uses the phrase 'metanarrative' or 'grand récit' to describe the way in which narratives (popular stories, myths, legends) bestow legitimacy on social institutions, and legitimate a certain type of knowledge. For Lyotard the hero of the Enlightenment metanarrative is one who uses reason to 'work toward a good ethico-

politico end—universal peace,' (*The Postmodern Condition: A Report on Knowledge*, [Manchester, 1984], xxiv). His definition of metanarrative is the one employed in this Chapter.

65. Edwards reflected on the method of natural theology, asking "How far the unity of the Godhead may be argued from the manner of Creation" and "Whether the unity of the Godhead can be demonstrated a priori," ("Q"[Questions on theological subjects], *MSS*, Beinecke).

66. A broader definition, without reference to the exclusion of 'special revelation,' seems unhelpfully to bias a discussion in favour of the necessity of some form of natural theology, (John Beversluis, "Reforming the 'Reformed' Objection to Natural Theology," *Faith and Philosophy*, vol.12, no. 2, [April 1995], 189).

67. No major work deals with Edwards' concept of authority and revelation, and while there is discussion in various places of Edwards' arguments for God, they tend to be dealt with piece-meal and somewhat cursorily rather than as an integral part of the overall structure of his theology. A scholarly work such as John E. Smith's *Jonathan Edwards: Puritan, Preacher, Philosopher*, (London, 1992) lacks a thorough discussion of authority. Schafer incorporates a section on 'spiritual light' in his introduction but analyses the concept solely in terms of Edwards' understanding of the experience of grace not of the source of grace, (Thomas A. Schafer, "Editor's Introduction," *Yale Works*, xiii, 49–52). The tome which comes closest to centering on these debates is John H. Gerstner's, *The Rational Biblical Theology of Jonathan Edwards*, 3 vols., (Powheton, Va., 1991–1993).

68. Edwards' argument differs from Anselm's in that he does not argue for God on the basis of the greatest conceivable being but on the basis of being itself.

69. The "Being" series in Edwards' Miscellanies, especially, nos. pp. 27a, 91, 167, 186, 267, 268, 269, 274, 312, 365, "The Miscellanies a-500", *Yale Works*, xiii, 188, 213, 254, 322, 330, 373, 373, 375, 394, 436; also, "Of Being," *Yale Works*, vi, 204–206; "The Mind," no. 12, *Yale Works*, vi, 343, (Wallace E. Anderson, "Editor's Introduction", *Yale Works*, vi, 68–75).

70. Gaunilo's response to Anselm was that if Anselm's argument is cogent it can be argued that the most wonderful island that can be imagined must also exist, but, as Plantinga has pointed out, this is not an effective reply because one can always imagine a greater island, (Brian Davies, *An Introduction to the Philosophy of Religion*, [Oxford, 1993], 60–61); in other words Gaunilo's argument is not based on the category of being itself but a subset of being. By starting with the concept of being Edwards underlines the strength in the argument at this initial stage.

71. Gerstner believes that Edwards argues for general being in the "Of Being" notes without employing causation, (John H. Gerstner, "The Apologetics of Jonathan Edwards," *Bibliotheca Sacra*, vol. 133, [January-March 1976], 7). Whether or not this is an accurate exegesis of that text, it is apparent that Edwards employs causation as integral to his general being argument and at least in one place elsewhere makes that relation explicit. Edwards does not only argue that there must be being now because we can not conceive nothing, but that being must have existed always and everywhere, which is an inherent reliance on some cause and effect string in the universe. Edwards makes this conjunction explicit, (no. 91, "The 'Miscellanies,' a-500," *Yale*

Works, xiii, 254–256). He sparingly makes use of the design argument, (second half of "The Miscellanies," 1156, *MSS*, Beinecke).

72. Edwards disagrees with the unnamed author of "Christianity not founded on argument" because he tried to show that arguing for the truths of natural religion had "done more harm than good." To Edwards he made Christianity seem unreasonable by denying the reliability of reason, ("The Miscellanies," 1297, *MSS*, Beinecke).

73. "The Miscellanies," 1334, *MSS*, Beinecke; Gerald R. McDermott, "The Deist Connection: Jonathan Edwards and Islam," *Jonathan Edwards's Writings*, ed. Stephen J. Stein, (Bloomington, 1996), 39–51.

74. "Subjects of Enquiry," *MSS*, Beinecke, page 8.

75. "How far the voice of Reason concurs with the voice of Revelation in the doctrine of a publick General Judgement at the end of the world," ("Q" [Questions on theological subjects], *MSS*, Beinecke).

76. The apologetic grid that Edwards here forms admits that there may be in nature a foundation "without any evidence" or a "foundation of intuitive evidence" for the existence God. Appropriation of knowledge of God by this method, however, would only be possible if humanity's mental power was considerably greater than it is, "if we had strength and comprehension of mind sufficient, to have a clear idea of universal being." For Edwards, therefore, the existence of God is not a practical self-evident existence to the weak capacity of the human mind, even though actually his existence is self-evident. If we could grasp it, "I suppose we should most intuitively see the absurdity of supposing such being not to be," but we can not, (*Yale Works*, i, 182).

77. Gestner's interpretation of Edwards' apologetics is rooted in a prioritisation of Edwards' writings, whereby this late and published section is accorded precedence over other Edwards material that impinges on the matter, (John H. Gerstner, "The Apologetics of Jonathan Edwards," *Bibliotheca Sacra*, vol.133 [January–December, 1976], 3–10; 99–107; 195–201; 291–298).

78. *Yale Works*, i, 182.

79. Romans 1:20, "The Being and Attributes of God are Clearly to be Seen by the Works of Creation," (June 1743, August 1756), *MSS*, Beinecke.

80. Given its intellectual content, the sermon was probably preached to the more educated English congregation in Stockbridge not the Native Americans.

81. Romans 1:20, "The Being and Attributes of God are Clearly to be Seen by the Works of Creation," (June 1743, August 1756), *MSS*, Beinecke.

82. "I. Prop[osition] something is from et[ernity] Something now is Theref[ore] something alwaies alwaies [sic] was or else there was a Time when there was nothing & then in process of Time something made it self or something started into Body of itself. Theref[ore] it follows that some being alwaies was from et[ernity] & if it be so then it follows that either the world was of itself from Et[ernity] or that there is some being that has produced it," *Ibid*.

83. "II proposition may be that the world was not of it self from Et[ernity] . . . That the world is of a fading nature . . . Thus the world is corruptable in its nature & cant be from Et[ernity] 2. That the world is is [sic] not from Et[ernity] appears not only by the Gradual diminishing of it but by the gradual increase of some things in it . . .

Theref[ore] the world must have a beginning & Hence it must be produced 3. It appears thus the world cannot be from eternity from the Impossibility of an Et[ernal] succession actually passed . . . There must be a first man or class of man the contrary is full of absurdities & contradictions & Hence there must be a first and an eternal cause . . . Thus I have shown the world cannot be from Et[ernity].
2. If that should be supposed that the world was from Et[ernity] yet it would follow nonetheless that it cant be of itself from Et[ernity] . . . The things of the world cant be of thems[elves] from Et[ernity] because we see that in their own nature they are dependent The nature of things shows that they are made things dependent things determined by a cause." (*Ibid.*).

84. "SECONDLY. that the world is produced by [sic—'eternal understanding being' understood] appears by by [sic] . . .
1. The works of nature are formed and disposed in such a manner that there is a manifest design in them . . . [long list of examples from plants and animals, day and night] . . . . differences between works of nature & art . . . Let it be consid[ered] how great this proof is of some understanding will being that had made the world . . . if we should Go somewhere into a desolute Island & find a curious structure—

curiously understanding contrived machine or found Letters in a Book so as form a curious poem. This argument concludes inevitably for an understanding cause of the world against all possible evasions.
But here I would Insist on two Effects more particularly that do most Entirely show the being of a G[od].
1. The Generation & propriation of plants & animals.
what I mean is its being so contrived now Let us Go upon what supposition we will the being of a Great &
wise cause & contriver appears in a most Glorious Light . . .
2. The other Instant is the being & faculties of the soul of man
we know that there are such things . . .
Hence is the most clear Evidence of the being of G[od] Let us Go upon what supposition we will some have [?] supposed the soul to be material
our souls are wonderf[ul] Let us consid[er] what has been done & what is daily done by Human souls," (*Ibid.*).

85. See, John H. Gerstner, "The Apologetics of Jonathan Edwards", *Bibliotheca Sacra*, vol.133, (January-December, 1976), 3–10; 99–107; 195–201; 291–298.

86. They are all insightful but too long to cite in full. Two of the eleven will give a taste of Edwards' arguments:
"I come now in the SECOND Place to note some things concerning the clearness of the Evidence that there is of the being of a G[od] from the work of crea[tion] clearly seen
1 . . . the nature of the Evid[ence] not probable but demonstrative
There are various kinds manifestations or arguments for the Truth of any thing. meer probability. strong presumption. much evidence. absolute certain & full infallible demonstration . . .
8. 'Tis impossible for us to conceive how G[od] could have Greater Evid[ence] of his being than he has done
cant devise ways

148 Chapter Four

...if we should see millions of miracles wrought
...being out of any steady course would be less evidential of a divine head
more Room to argue that they were not the effects of Intelligence & wisd[om]
if we should hear thousands of voices from Heaven
or G[od] should speak to us by voices miraculously made
attended with evid[ence] this would be Less clear."
(Romans 1:20, "The Being and Attributes of God are Clearly to be Seen by the Works of Creation," [June 1743, August 1756], *MSS*, Beinecke).

87. Butler's attempt to defend revealed religion against proponents of natural religion may be best described in his own terms as an "analogy," though the term itself does not often occur in the book of the same name. He argued that natural religion was in fact no more certain and immune from the attacks of reason than was revealed religion, it was 'analogous' to it. To later commentators this method of defence seemed deeply ironic. Butler wished to undermine natural religion to return people to revealed religion; he may have succeeded more in casting doubt on both schemes. Central to his thesis was the assertion of the basic assumption of 'probability' as the guide to all human life and thought: "Probable evidence, in its very nature, affords an imperfect kind of information . . . [God has no need of probability] . . . But to Us probability is the very guide of life," (Joseph Butler, *The Analogy of Religion, Natural and Revealed, to the Constitution and Course of Nature*, [New York, 1900], 2; Terence Penelhum, *The Arguments of the Philosophers: Butler*, [London, 1985]).

88. Its significance for Edwards is evidenced by his use of the material not only at Northampton but also in a fascinating reworking of the material to suit the lesser educative abilities of the Native Americans at Stockbridge, (Psalm 14:1, December 1752: "There certainly is a God", *MSS*, Beinecke).

89. Psalm 14:1, not dated: "A principle of Atheism possesses the hearts of all ungodly men," *MSS*, Beinecke.

90. Chapter "True Experience" discusses Edwards' application of this insight to assessments of spiritual experience.

91. Psalm 14:1, not dated: "A principle of Atheism possesses the hearts of all ungodly men," *MSS*, Beinecke.

92. *Ibid.*

93. *Ibid.*

94. Fiering argues for the strong possibility not just of the association of ideas but communication of concepts between Edwards and Malebranche, (Norman Fiering, *Jonathan Edwards' Moral Thought and its British Context*, [Williamsburg, Va., 1981]), 40–44.

95. Malebranche argues for "being in general," that "we see all things in God," and that "the mind cannot entirely rid itself of this general idea of being, because it cannot subsist outside of God." Despite the similarity of terminology, it seems dubious to suggest a great deal of analogy of content behind the expressions; Malebranche argues that "the inclination for the good in general" is in fact a cause of error, which seems antithetical to Edwards' use of the concept of being in general in his "True Virtue," (*The Search After Truth*, [Columbus, 1980], 230, 241)

96. John H. Gerstner, "The Apologetics of Jonathan Edwards," *Bibliotheca Sacra*, vol. 133, (October-December 1976), 291.

97. Genesis 1:27, August 1751, preached to Stockbridge Indians and Mohawks: "That God has given men reason and understanding . . . man being made in God's image . . . made holy . . . ," *MSS*, Beinecke.

98. *Ibid*.

99. Genesis 3: 24, not dated: "When man fell, God drove him away from all his former blessedness," *MSS*, Beinecke.

100. *Ibid*.

101. *Ibid*.

102. Thomas Reid, *An Inquiry into the Human Mind*, (Bristol, 1990), 20.

103. Isaiah 1:18–20, "All God's Methods Are Most Reasonable," *Yale Works*, xiv, 167.

104. John H. Gerstner, "The Apologetics of Jonathan Edwards," *Bibliotheca Sacra*, vol.133, (January-December, 1976), 3–10; 99–107; 195–201; 291–298; Michael Jinkins, "The 'Being of Beings:' Jonathan Edwards' Understanding of God as Reflected in his Final Treatises," *Scottish Journal of Theology*, vol.46, no.42, (1993), 161–191.

105. It is in preaching on the effects of the fall that Edwards tells his hearers to go to Christ to be "enlightened" (Genesis 3:17–19, *MSS*, Beinecke), that being saved by another's righteousness is a thing that humanity can naturally have no conception of, if they are "not Enlightened" (Genesis 3:24, not dated, "When man fell God drove him away from all his former blessedness," *MSS*, Beinecke), and to Edwards that people do not believe the so evident truth of God's existence is a strong argument for the truth of supernatural religion: "Hence how rational is the doctrine of divine ILLUMINATION of the TEACHINGS of God re Spirit opening the blind Eyes, turning from darkness to light,"("The Miscellanies," 1156, *MSS*, Beinecke).

106. Augustine, *Confessions*, VIII, xi, 29, (Oxford, 1992), 153.

107. Martin Luther, "Sermon on Christmas Day, Luke 2:1–14," *Sermons of Martin Luther*, (Grand Rapids, 1983), vol. 1, 137. Luther is notoriously diverse in his assertions, but while he may often be thought of as possessing a theology centred on trusting the objective promises of God, he can be found to preach the experimental result of such faith.

108. John Calvin, *Institutes of the Christian Religion*, book i, chapter vii, section 5, [London, 1949], 72.

109. "Enlightened by him [the Spirit], we no longer believe, either on our own judgement or that of others, that the Scriptures are from God; but . . . [believe] . . . that it came to us, by the instrumentality of men, from the very mouth of God, (*Institutes of the Christian Religion*, book i, chapter vii, section 5, [London, 1949], 72). The later Reformed theologian Charles Hodge writes, "The Bible makes a broad distinction between the mere hearers of the word, and those inwardly taught by God . . . An inward teaching by the Spirit is absolutely necessary to give the truth effect," (Charles Hodge, *Systematic Theology*, vol.2 [Grand Rapids, 1952], 660.

110. William Ames, "Medulla Theologica," bk.1, (London, 1642), 32; "The word of God is said to work effectually . . . when it works powerful illumination and thorough

reformation," (Thomas Watson, "The Word Read and Preached, How Effectual," *A Body of Divinity*, [London, 1890], 375); "Heavenly truths must have a heavenly light to discern them . . . God in every converted man putteth a light into the eye of his soul, proportionable to the light of truths revealed unto him," (Richard Sibbes, "The Bruised Reed and the Smoking Flax," *Works*, vol.1, [Edinburgh, 1983], 59); the true Christian is an "enlightened soul," (John Owen, "On the Spirit," *Works*, vol.3, [Edinburgh, 1994], 404).

111. Charles Simeon, (H.D. McDonald, *Ideas of Revelation: An Historical Study, 1700–1860*, [London, 1959], 223).

112. Discussed in the section 'Reason and Revelation.'

113. "Notes on the Scriptures," *MSS*, Beinecke, Folder 1236, Page 267.

114. "Notes on the Scriptures," *MSS*, Beinecke, Folder 1237, Page 335.

115. Matthew 5:8, "But to see God is this, it is to have an Immediate sensible & certain understanding of Gods Glorious excellency & love," *MSS*, Beinecke.

116. Jude 19, 1750 December, "Prepared for a lecture at Westfield," "to Canaan:" "There was a sort of persons in the apostles' day who separated themselves from the steady ministers and churches that pretended to be very spiritual, but who really were carnal and had not the spirit of God," *MSS*, Beinecke.

117. Edwards comments on the possible contradiction of this juxtaposition, "Grace is from God as immediately and distinctly as light is from the sun & that notwithstanding the means that are improved such as word audiences," "The Miscellanies," 539, *MSS*, Beinecke.

118. "A Divine and Supernatural Light," *Banner Works*, i, 15.

119. "The Miscellanies," 539, *MSS*, Beinecke.

120. The 2 Peter sermons that are discussed below originally came from the pre-Great Awakening period, but at least one and probably two of them were re-preached in 1758. Other sermonic material post-dates the emergence of the struggles with the separatists' doctrine of light, (Matthew 5:15–16, 1746 December: "That holy thing that is in the saints is a shining light," *MSS*, Beinecke). After the Great Awakening Edwards did not abandon his use of light but defined it against other uses, as his Jude 19 sermon makes clear, (Jude 19, 1750 December, "Prepared for a lecture at Westfield," "to Canaan:" "There was a sort of persons in the apostles' day who separated themselves from the steady ministers and churches that pretended to be very spiritual, but who really were carnal and had not the spirit of God," *MSS*, Beinecke).

121. *Banner Works*, i, 12–17, my italics.

122. *Ibid.*, 14.

123. *Ibid.*, 16.

124. *Ibid.*, 17. The Chapter "True Experience" discusses the 'Sense of the heart.'

125. While scepticism as to 'gnostic' labels legitimately arises from the fact that most of the heretical teachers described in the New Testament may at some time or other have been labelled as gnostics, the point of the background to 2 Peter in this discussion is not a precise identification of the teachers, even if that were possible, but merely to note that there is a certain resonance of debate between it and Edwards' context. The evidence for certain labelling of the teachers may be slim from the description given of their teaching, yet the angle that the letter gives to its own teaching in response to the false teaching is probably indicative of a kind of teaching that was

claiming gnostic-like heresies, even if a strict historical connection between it and later gnosticism can not be established, (Eldon Jay Epp, ed., *The New Testament and its Modern Interpreters*, [Philadelphia, 1989], 383; Donald Guthrie, *New Testament Introduction*, [Leicester, 1990], 828).

126. "Notes on the Scriptures," no. 265, *MSS*, Beinecke.

127. 2 Peter 1:16, not dated: "That seeing the glory of Christ is what tends to assure the heart of the truth of the gospel;" 2 Peter 1:19, August 1737, February 1758: "Divine revelation is like a light that shines in a dark place;" 2 Peter 1:19, November 1737, same doctrine as previous, (*MSS*, Beinecke).

128. A.V.

129. Elsewhere Edwards uses the term 'immediacy' less experientially and more doctrinally to suggest the difference between the covenant of works and the covenant of grace: "There is proclaimed to us in the Gosp[el] not only such an opportunity as Adam had of Eating of the Tree if we first obey. But we are invited to come to the Tree of Life Immediately without any conditions . . . ," (Gen. 3: 24, not dated: "When man fell, God drove him away from all his former blessedness," *MSS*, Beinecke).

130. Edwards comments on this chapter in his unpublished notes make the same point about the evidential value of the light of revelation: "There was doubtless an inward sight or lively sense of heart of X'[Christ's] spiritual glory that accompanied Peters sight of the visible glory of X[Christ] . . . so that X'[Christ's] glory there was manifested to the disciples three way By the rays of light it was exhibited to their eyes by the voice it was declared to their ears and by the spirit to their souls . . . The last was the most convincing & certain evidence to them of X'[Christ's] divinity," ("Notes on the Scriptures," no. 265, *MSS*, Beinecke).

131. "Notes on the Scriptures," no. 107, *MSS*, Beinecke.

132. Edwards is arguing that the sin against the Holy Spirit is so serious because it is a sin not just against the light of nature but against the light of revelation, which is an "objective light," ("The Miscellanies," 706, *MSS*, Beinecke).

133. In another sermon Edwards preaches that the gospel does not need external evidences because "it carries its own light and evidence with it," (Ephesians 3:10, March 1733, "The wisdom appearing in the way of salvation by Jesus Christ is far above the wisdom of the angels," *MSS*, Beinecke).

134. Edwards gives four other reasons for this evidence being the best evidence: it is "more pure than any other," it is "the most abiding," it is the only evidence "that will bring the heart to rest in X[Christ] for salvation," and it is only faith upon this evidence that will "incline the heart to a holy life."

135. "in our own nation" was added after deleting 'England.' This may either be a sign of nascent national feeling striving with loyalty to the old country, or perhaps an acknowledgement of the source of much of the Enlightenment effects that he is about to cite.

136. This section is one of the most difficult parts of Edwards script that I have attempted to decipher. Question marks indicate where the script could not be read.
"1. The Mohamedans . . . forsook the SS[Scriptures] & deny it to be the true SS[Scriptures] at least the [?last] Revel[ation] that G[od] gave to mankind & the conseq[uence] is that they are become exceeding with childish & ridiculous in their notions & customs

they expect an heaven of sensual pleasures & delights that consist in gratifying their lusts . . . They hold ridiculous things about the manner in which they suppose mohammed their Great prophet was called and went through seven heavens . . . as how the angel Gabriel came to him with twenty pair of wings and went with him to the first heaven all of silver where the stars hang in [chains?] of Gold & saw angels some with in the shape of birds & others of beasts & saw among the Rest a cock as white as snow that has [?] [preached?] to the second heavens the dist[ance] of 500 days journey his wings extending from East to west that every morning go singing an hymn . . . & in the second heaven saw an angel so big that it was 70000 thousand days journey between his eyes—and immeasurable other such ridiculous fables too childish to be insisted on in an assembly met for the W[ord] of G[od] are the principles of their Relig[ion] to hear or read them is enough to fill one with astonishment . . . of the world of mankind when not Guided by Revela[tion] not withstanding all that mans natural Reason or the Light of Nature teaches."

137. Mandeville argued that society is a hive in which humanity flourishes through the economically beneficial effects of self-interest, (Bernard Mandeville, *The Fable of the Bees, or Private Vices, Publick Benefits*, [London, 1723]).

138. "The Miscellanies," no. 702, *MSS*, Beinecke.

139. Matthew 5:8, "1. Prop. that it is a thing truly happifying to the soul of man to see God. 2. Prop. That the having a pure heart is the certain and only way to come to the blessedness of seeing God," *MSS*, Beinecke.

140. Luke 24:32, June 1736, October 1755: " 'Tis a common [thing] with the saints that their hearts do burn within them while divine things are represented to them," *MSS*, Beinecke.

141. Especially surprising when one considers that the omission was far from common at the time, (James Turner, *Without God, Without Creed: The Origins of Unbelief in America*, [Baltimore, 1985], 71).

142. Samuel Hopkins, *The Life of Jonathan Edwards*, (Boston, 1765); repinted, *Jonathan Edwards*, ed. David Levin, (New York, 1969), 45; he was careful to hold up the needs of the ill for prayer before the congregation ("Q" [Questions on theological subjects], *MSS*, Beinecke, was written on the back of prayer requests from the infirm).

143. For a modern treatment of the problem of evil see, Brian Hebblethwaite, *Evil, Suffering and Religion*, (London, 1976).

144. "the evil of sin is not a positive but a negative thing," (Isaiah 1:18–20, "All God's Methods Are Most Reasonable," *Yale Works*, xiv, 167).

145. That is, arguing for suffering as a sign of God's judgement, and that if there were no suffering at all or if all the suffering was perfectly equal to the sin then we would suspect there was no final judgement.

146. The Boston earthquake of October 30th 1727 (George J. Lankevich, ed., *Boston: A Chronological and Documentary History, 1602–1970*, [New York, 1974], 17) caused a renewed interest in spiritual matters, rather than extensive questions on the problem of suffering. A Puritan understanding of calamities as evidences of God's anger and thus occasions for repentance from sin may be seen in Prince's remark that he had seen nothing like the serious effect that Whitefield has upon his hearers except in the time of the Boston earthquake. However, he was not so naive as to equate fear

of physical harm with conviction of sin, noting that this previous awakening had only been characterised by fear and not by a desire to be saved, (Thomas Prince, *An Account of the Revival of Religion in Boston in the Years 1740-3*, [Boston 1823], 9). In fact, it was his experience that such fear never resulted in genuine convictions, finding that the kind of fear produced by thunder and lightning was quite distinct from the work of God: "in all the course of thirty years have I scarce known any, by these kind of terrors brought under genuine convictions . . . No! Conviction is quite another sort of a thing . . . These discoveries are made by means of some revealed truths . . . ." (*Ibid.*, 16).

147. Haller recognises this concept of evil as commonly Puritan, (William Haller, *The Rise of Puritanism*, [New York, 1957], 334).

148. Hume's *Dialogues Concerning Natural Religion* is the seminal example of the denial of a rational or historical belief in the miraculous, but the issue was first voiced much earlier, as the famous Leibniz-Clarke debate witnesses, (Ezio Vailati, "Leibniz and Clarke on Miracles," *Journal of the History of Philosophy*, vol.xxxiii, no.4, [October 1995], 543–562).

149. Harnack employed the historical critical method to attempt to endorse a certain 'Jesus of history,' without prejudicing the Church's acceptance of the 'Christ of faith,' (H.D. McDonald, *Theories of Revelation: An Historical Study, 1860-1960*, [London 1963], 9). It was against this culture of profound objective and subjective split that Barth reacted, (Martin Rumscheidt, ed., *Revelation and Theology: An Analysis of the Barth-Harnack Correspondence of 1923*, [Cambridge, 1972]).

150. It is to religious sensibility that Kant appeals when he remarks that, "There is only one true religion, but there can be many varieties of religious creeds . . . It is, therefore, more appropriate to say: this man is of the Jewish, Mohammedan, Christian creed, than he is of this or that religion," (cited in, H.D. McDonald, *Ideas of Revelation: An Historical Study, 1700-1860*, [London, 1959], 13); in another guise William James makes essentially similar distinctions, shifting emphasis from doctrine to sensibility, in "The Varieties of Religious Experience, " *Works*, vol. 13, (Cambridge, Mass., 1985).

151. Hebblethwaite gives an insightful analysis of the problems of revelation, (Brian Hebblethwaite, *The Problems of Theology*, [Cambridge, 1980], 85–101).

152. These two sentences are not a direct appeal to any one theologian, but the line of thinking is one that may be traced to interpretations from Kierkegaard to Barth.

153. Partly in response to the perceived success of the various modern evidentialist attacks on the rational cogency of Christianity, 'neo-orthodox' theologians have caused a growing dissatisfaction with the defences of natural theology, finding support for an alternative defence in the traditional unease with natural theology that may be seen as characterising the reformed tradition, (K. Barth and E. Brunner, *Natural Theology*, [London, 1946]; K. Barth, *The Word of God and the Word of Man*, [London, 1928]; G.C. Berkouwer, *A Half Century of Theology*, [Grand Rapids, 1977]). In similar vein, more recently it has been powerfully argued that the true reformed epistemology is one that holds that it is rational to believe in God without argument or evidence, (The literature surrounding this debate is voluminous and growing, but essential reading is, Plantinga, "Is Belief in God Properly Basic?" *Nous*, xv, [1981],

41–51; Plantinga and Wolterstorff, *Faith and Rationality*, [London, 1983]; Plantinga, *Warrant: The Current Debate*, [Oxford, 1993]; *Warrant and Proper Function*, [Oxford, 1993]; by no means all are agreed that reformed epistemology is truly reformed, John Beversluis, "Reforming the 'Reformed' Objection to Natural Theology," *Faith and Philosophy*, vol.12, no.2, [April 1995], 189–206), so that some see that Natural Theology as evidentialist apologetics is inappropriate, (Nicholas Wolterstorff, "The Migration of Theistic Arguments: From Natural Theology to Evidentialist Apologetics," *Rationality, Religious Belief, and Moral Commitment*, ed. Audi and Wainwright, [Ithaca, 1986], 38–81). One result of these trends is that arguments for Christianity have increasingly tended to draw not primarily from rationality or historicity or evidence but from experience, not from objective criteria but from subjective, not from the universal domain of natural theology but from the particular appeal to special revelation.

154. William Haller, *The Rise of Puritanism*, [New York, 1957], 299. In seventeenth century Cambridge, Puritans readily allied themselves to the work of Bacon; Milton was the most prominent example of a Puritan joining the attack on the sterility of the traditional curriculum and heartily supporting the new learning, (*Ibid.*, 299–300).

155. Kim Ian Parker, "John Locke and the Enlightenment Metanarrative: A Biblical Corrective to a Reasoned World," *Scottish Journal of Theology*, vol. 49, no.1, (1996), 57.

156. It is possible to argue this antipathy to authority lies behind the present stream of disassociation with the Enlightenment dream; a metanarrative of reason too easily seems to be an instrument of power to oppress. Foucault's work on the relation of power to knowledge is highly influential in this respect, (Michel Foucault, *Power/Knowledge: Selected Interviews and Other Writings, 1972–1977*, ed. by Colin Gordon, [Brighton, 1980]).

Conclusion

Soaring above the reach of mere mortals, Edwards' theology and philosophy scales Elysian heights. Or at least in some such vein he has often been viewed.[1] The greatest American theologian or philosopher, despite his tiresome allegiance to outmoded Calvinism or because of his faithful bond with puritan biblicism, the gloss depending on the ideological location of the scholar. While these trains of thought are open to caricature, I believe that there is a certain spark to Edwards' work that requires explanation. Such the vigour, such the originality, such the insight of Edwards' mind that it has caused many to bow in awe. It is the purpose of these final words to draw the threads of the thesis together in a way that offers solution to the enigma of the enduring fascination of Edwards and suggests how this solution is relevant today.

EDWARDS PAST

I have argued that Edwards was intimately concerned with that period of thought that may for shorthand be characterised as the 'Enlightenment.'[2] The evidence for this involvement with the contemporary debate is persuasive. He knew the substance of the arguments, was familiar with the characteristic presuppositions of his age, and made recourse to respond to them. The first two propositions of that sentence have long been analysed, but the last has not before been noted. He has been seen either as a proto-modern, someone who imbibed the Enlightenment but could not shrug off his Puritanism,[3] or as a traditionalist, someone who imbibed his Puritanism and shrugged off the Enlightenment.[4] Neither is correct.

It is this response which makes Edwards an important figure. He advanced what is best described as a re-formation of the Enlightenment. There were two aspects to this reformation. First, he remained within the Reformed, Puritan tradition, that was New England's heritage, and in this sense his response to the Enlightenment was a Reformed response. Secondly, his response to the Enlightenment was reformed in that it was a deliberate re-working of the Enlightenment. He reformed the Enlightenment by re-defining the language and presuppositions of the age and interpreting them on Reformed grounds.

Many examples of the reformation can be found. The language of Lockean empiricism was incorporated in Edwards' description of spiritual experience. Newtonian physics was interwoven into a defence of theism. Theologically, the Deist agitations were opposed with a coherent structure of the relations between nature and supernature. Philosophically, the sceptical fault line of modernism first exploited by Hume, was given alternative solution in Edwards' idealistic 'perceptivism.' Permeating all, Edwards appealed to the rhetoric of the age by preaching a gospel 'enlightenment.'

What gave Edwards this dynamic and flexible interaction with the Enlightenment? What allowed his theology not to bend to foreign winds and his philosophical sails to be hoisted to catch the developments of the Enlightenment? The ability to appropriate new concepts came from a combination of Edwards' initiative and his tradition. In the right hands Puritanism could encourage such an approach. There was precedence in the Puritan attempt to use pagan and non-Christian learning. The literature of scholasticism lay before the Puritan "like an Aztec city before the plunderer,"[5] for while it had to be used with utmost care, its assimilation was of immense value. There was a theological framework in the Puritan confidence that all truth was God's truth, underlined by Ramism. This was the 'philosophy' that the Puritans were interested in, the whole 'encyclopedia' of the revelation of God.[6] Edwards' philosophical thinking was along the same lines as his forebears, bar one factor, the 'New Science.' He had a whole new problem of assimilation. No longer was the debate primarily with Aristotle and Plato, Aquinas and Scotus; now the impetus came from Descartes and Newton, Hobbes and Locke. Like the old learning, the new offered wonderful opportunities and dreadful dangers. Edwards was not the only New Englander who seized the opportunities —Cotton Mather was a respected scientist, even a member of the Royal Society.[7] Edwards, though, was the one who escaped the dangers of Scylla and Charybdis, of traditionalism on the hand and capitulation to the Enlightenment on the other.

The scholarly intrigue with Edwards is thus explained. The exacting intricacies of the analysis of Edwards' sources, the tendency to fit Edwards into moulds with which Edwards himself would plainly have been unhappy, the reactionary concern with Edwards in context, have, of course, different motivations and different degrees of validation, but all alike are symptoms of an inability to explain Edwards' 'spark.' My belief that Edwards is reforming the Enlightenment gives evident reason for his fascination. He stands at the crossroads of modernity; he understands his time; he writes with some empathy and some criticism to form a contrary enlightenment. For us irretrievably 'modern' people, who even when attempting not to be modern are forced to define ourselves in its light as 'postmodern,' Edwards is a magnet. Like moths we are drawn to his enlightenment.

Other organising principles for Edwards scholarship have come and gone with a rapidity that cause some to argue that Edwards was too diverse for such characterisation.[8] It has been suggested that the one characterisation of Edwards' work as a whole that is able to stand the test of critical acumen is the designation of Edwards as a 'theo-centrist.'[9] But while it is hard to deny that theocentricity is fundamental to Edwards' concerns, that seems no more profound than to say that he was an orthodox Christian or a Calvinist. If after hundreds of years of research and countless works on Edwards that is all that can be said, we might as well all go home.

Yet despite redundant arguments interest remains. For this reason: Edwards work is a reforming of the Enlightenment. His quest is our quest: *Was ist Aufklärung*?

EDWARDS PRESENT

I do not wish to enter into the debate of how to characterise this present time, whether it is appropriate to speak of 'postmodernism' or of another variant of modernism, but I take it as apparent that in many fields of endeavour there is a burgeoning reassessment of the heritage of the Enlightenment. If, then, Edwards was reforming the Enlightenment his work is highly relevant to our age. Here Edwards has much to offer: his project centred on epistemology, on knowledge and how it may be attained. It is the problem of epistemology that has dogged the foot steps of Enlightenment style thought, and it is the cogency of traditional epistemology that is rejected in many reassessments of the Enlightenment. Edwards advances an epistemology that is reliable because it is a 'spiritual' epistemology, a knowing the presence of God.

a) Reliable knowledge starts with revelation. The Enlightenment fascination with reason and nature is reformed by the priority Edwards gives to revelation. Reason is only reasonable if preceded by revelation, true reasoning is reasoning after revelation. Nature is an authority, it is a 'light,' but its authority is only correctly appropriated after revelation and is cognitively insufficient without revelation. This revelation is scriptural, the doctrines taught in the Bible, and is illuminative, the process by which the Spirit brings to light the doctrines taught in the Bible. Edwards' critique of more exalted philosophies of reason and nature rests on an acknowledgement of the inadequacy of reason and nature to come to reliable knowledge. For Edwards, starting with revelation does not inhibit human progress and learning, but is flexible and productive of worthwhile intellectual endeavour.

b) Reliable knowledge is monist. The Enlightenment propensity to dualist modes of thought is reformed by Edwards with a more monist approach. Edwards defies the common division of the intellect into separate realms of reason and spirit, of secular and religious, of philosophy and theology. That is not to say that knowledge is undifferentiated but that it is coherent. Reality is invested with a single truth because of the single character of God. In such knowledge there is plurality, it is even described as beautiful, but it is a plurality that is harmonious. Throughout Edwards' work there is an expectation, a recognition that knowledge is a whole.

c) Reliable knowledge is heart knowledge. Enlightenment rationalism, and the contrary tendency to more emotive 'enthusiasm,' is reformed by Edwards with heart knowledge. The heart is not feelings or emotion alone, nor thinking or ratiocination alone, nor willing or volition alone. It is rather a sum of all these to form the central disposition of a person. The heart is the feeling, thinking, willing centre of a human being. Reliable knowledge characteristically involves this whole affection, not à la Kierkegaard, at least as Kierkegaard is commonly understood, nor à la Descartes, but a combination of such factors in the heart.[10]

d) Reliable knowledge is God-dependent. The Enlightenment tendency to downgrade the spiritual is reformed by Edwards with a knowledge that is God-dependent. When Edwards speaks of the 'ideal' and the 'mental' nature of existence it is the dependent existence that he has in his sights, to show that the only substance, strictly speaking, is God. He attempts to integrate the elements of the Enlightenment into a contrary scheme of knowledge where all is reliant on God.

Effects

What would be the effect of this kind of epistemology? It would challenge some of the assumptions of secular society; it would administer an antidote to a spiritually confused church; it would counter relativism.

First, secular society is challenged by the effect that this kind of knowledge scheme would have upon the privatisation of religion.

'Secularism' is a more familiar term, but that can be a confusing term with various and changing meanings.[11] 'Privatisation' is coined here to indicate a precise definition. That is, not to emphasise the exclusion of religious bodies from political power in modern secular states, but the common reduction of religious truth claims to the realm of private opinion in modern secular states. The two may or may not be related, but it is a matter of observation to some that religion, even by its adherents, has in secular society often increasingly become seen as a matter of private opinion.[12] Though there are exceptions, and these exceptions may be growing, for many religion is a phantom of the psyche rather than a fact of metaphysics.[13] Whatever the historical genealogy of these changes,[14] it is hard to deny that the way that religious truth claims are normally heard in secular society is in terms of personal commitment rather than existential description. The claim 'God exists' is not often heard to equate to the factual claim that 'God is an objective reality,' but to the personal claim that 'for me God exists.'[15]

Edwards' reformation of the Enlightenment is apposite in various ways. Despite having, as is argued in "True Salvation," a possible inclination towards separation of church and society, Edwards has a very public vision of God. All knowledge is subject to His oversight if it monistically reflects His character. Even 'secular,' for the sake of definition, pursuits and thoughts are redundant without a spiritual mindedness, a recognition of God-dependency, a willingness to think God's thoughts after him by reasoning after revelation.

Secondly, the church is challenged by the spiritual antidote that Edwards' epistemology would administer. It may be argued that our age has a characteristic spiritual confusion; pluralistic options in spiritualities has not tended to emphasise the differences between experiences but to blur the distinctions. All religious experiences, often, are counted as essentially the same. It may also be argued that our age has a characteristic spiritual need. The growth of new religious groups and the rise of 'fundamentalism' may both bear witness to this phenomenon.[16]

Edwards' antidote gives a means to experience the spiritual and a means to evaluate that experience. It is heart experience, rational and emotional, that is needed, and which characterises neither of the extremes of Charismatic or non-Charismatic evangelicalism that claim Edwards' mantle.[17] It is a sense of the heart, not imparting information like a sixth sense but as an empirical metaphor imparting appreciation, like a sense of beauty. The evaluation of the experience is flexible in allowing for variation of emotional and psychological personality. It counters spiritual confusion, though, by espousing an unashamedly rigorous pattern of testing. As God is the source of true experience, experience of him will bear certain characteristics. There need be orthodoxy to the doctrine and moral similitude to the ethic of Scripture.

Thirdly, Edwards' epistemology counters what is called, perhaps by 'modernists,' relativism, or which may be termed non-pejoratively as a lack of affinity with absolute or universal truth. Nietzsche may have been one of the first philosophers to feel the dangers of modernistic nihilism and the lack of any 'God-hypothesis,' whether one believes that such dangers were his doctrine or his nemesis, but since him more have recognised the totalitarian potential of modernity and its nausea of meaningless. As a result alternative, 'postmodern' if you will, non-metaphysical, even non-epistemological, projects to the Enlightenment project have been advanced.

Edwards' epistemology counters these developments. On the one hand, he also criticised the Enlightenment. Reason was too exalted over emotions and the spiritual. Knowledge was too dualistic to the detriment of coherence. The picture of reality was too mechanical, leaving little room for plurality and beauty. Yet on the other hand, it was a criticism that led to a contrary reassessment to that of the postmodern. His reformed Enlightenment sought to envelop the discoveries of the new science within a framework that encouraged belief in the vital, present activity of the living God. There was plurality, but also universal or absolute truth, not relativism. Edwards epistemology counters relativism with an alternative alternative project to the Enlightenment project. One where the absolute is not a totalitarian metaphysical abstract, but the living God; where plurality does not lead to relativism but to beauty. Discordant relativism dances in concert to divine music.

Defence

How might this knowledge be defended?[18] Edwards defends his doctrines in various ways with many and complex arguments, some more persuasive than others, some more original than others. It is clear that Edwards thought defence of his beliefs to be important. It is my opinion that Edwards was in general, though not always in detail, successful with his defences. It is the structure within which he fits his plentiful arguments and reasons which is compelling. He gives a compelling framework for cognitive belief, and a compelling example of social reorientation to faith.

First, the framework within which Edwards argues is one which holds to the absolute rationality of Christian doctrine, yet believes that without revelation, without personal experience of God, the rationality will not be grasped. Natural theology, then, has a place in Edwards' framework. However, Edwards differs from some proponents of this kind of apologetics in that he does not believe that such arguments will convince. Revelation is necessary, scriptural and illuminative, which in Edwards' hands, the 'sense' of God, becomes a powerful apologetic itself for the reality of God.

Against this framework of Edwards, it may be argued he is really engaged in little more than an elaborate sleight of hand. At one moment in his sermons and notes and papers he seems to give all to reason and natural authority, at another he insists that though his arguments are fully convincing a listener will not be convinced unless the truth is revealed to them. One can not escape from such a tight circle. If you believe it is because the truth has been revealed to you, if you do not it is because it has not, and ne'er the twain shall meet. Though well expressed to avoid appearing to be a privatised knowledge, this does still in effect seem to be a kind of sanctified reason, a privileged knowledge of the elect. In effect, one might reply to Edwards' true light that it fails to meet the necessary criteria of a statement of truth, that it is potentially falsifiable.[19] If one can not disagree with the truth without showing that one is lacking the necessary ability to perceive the truth, then the 'truth' is indeed established, but so what? Surely this 'truth' is in danger of becoming little more than the play-thing of a supercilious minority of society, looking down their enlightened noses at all who disagree!

An answer to this kind of criticism might be on these lines. Edwards' doctrine is, after all, consistent on its own terms, and that such coherence is an adequate criteria of truth in certain cases. There may be something circular about Edwards' argument, but most arguments are in some degree or other circular; the question is not if it is circular, but whether it is viciously circular, making no contact or appeal with external factors. Edwards' arguments, in fact, are carefully constructed to make appeals and contact with external factors, arguing at length on the basis of common reason, and so seeming to escape the charge of vicious circularity. Yet having said this, it seems that at some point or other Edwards must inevitably come to the issue of revelation and in the end internal illumination. One might say that it comes down to privatised knowledge in the end. But an Edwardean might legitimately rejoin the fray with a similar exclamation as the above critique — so what? We accept that not all agree on any substantial matter at all. There is no such thing as universal acceptance of one universal truth. We are thus left with a choice. Given that at least some of those who disagree as to the nature of universal truth are sufficiently educated to have considered alternative positions, it seems that we can either conclude that there is no such thing as universal truth, that relativism in some shape or form must rule (if that is not an oxymoron),[20] or that there is universal truth but some people do not believe in it.[21] That is, some people are wrong and will be wrong however much they are educated, persuaded, or cajoled. It seems that if we are to accept the world as it evidently is, then we may either be relativists or believe that some are wrong.

If we take the latter view, the question remains why, all other things being equal, some are wrong. Various answers could perhaps be given, but the proposition of God's revelation seems by no means an unreasonable one. After all, if all other things are equal, education and experience and intelligence for example, then it may be that something outside of normal parameters of human cognition might be required to explain such divergence.

Secondly, Edwards offers a compelling example of social reorientation to faith. I am referring to the Great Awakening and to Edwards' theory and practice of revival. I list this as a prime and compelling defence of Edwards because it would be here that Edwards would point. God, for him, supernaturally broke into history to awaken people to his reality. Is this an irrelevance to secular society? Initially it may appear so, but it is not as open and shut a case as it seems. Eighteenth century New England, it is true, was a society where most at least publicly claimed allegiance to the historical events of Christianity.[22] A theology of revival has rather different resonances in a society where most make no such claim, where perhaps the Christian preacher need not so much revive the nominal as convert the 'pagan.' Yet, while for Edwards an 'awakening' was theologically distinguishable from regeneration, awakenings were the best opportunity for regeneration and therefore he looked for conversions from revival.[23] Furthermore, though these conversions were normally from nominalism and not paganism, it is instructive that the same 'awakening' language was used to describe Native American conversions as white Anglo-Saxon Protestant conversions.[24]

In fact, it may be argued that revival is the epistemological key to the heart of secular society as much as nominal Christian society. For such a dependence upon God for supernatural salvation in the present may help to encourage the belief that the gospel has reference outside the individual subject, and thus work for gospel objectivity. Revival does not bring things into the objective realm in the way that a mathematical proof does; but it counters privatisation as Mount Carmel countered the worshippers of Baal. Revival fire from heaven demonstrates the objectivity of religion in the sense that it brings religion from the private to the public realm.

FINAL WORD

It is not unusual to talk of Edwards in near messianic terms. To speak in hushed voice of his contribution to philosophy, to theology, to the church. Edwards, no doubt, had his failings, and his system of thought had its failings too. Yet, I do not feel that such language is wholly inappropriate. For concerning one thing at least his message is well worth hearing: the reformation of the Enlightenment. True enlightenment, for Edwards, could only begin with knowing the presence of God.

NOTES

1. Eulogy is the mark that mars these studies of Edwards. Works in praise of Edwards are not the sole possession of any particular school of scholarship and are far from rare. From Miller to Jensen, analysis of Edwards has attracted something of a messianic tone. Miller is infamous in the nether world of Edwards' scholarship for arguing for the 'modernity' of Jonathan Edwards, though to be fair he did recognise that Edwards "speaks from a primitive religious conception" before saying that he was "so much ahead of his time that our own can hardly be said to have caught up with him," (Perry Miller, *Jonathan Edwards*, [New York, 1949], xiii); Jensen's work exhibits scholarly restraint as well as affectionate enthusiasm, but he does not manage to avoid ending on a note of eulogy. (Robert W. Jensen, *America's Theologian: A Recommendation of Jonathan Edwards*, [New York, 1988], 195).

2. For discussion of the concept of the Enlightenment see the "Introduction."

3. Thomas H. Johnson, "Jonathan Edwards' Background of Reading," *The Publications of the Colonial Society of Massachusetts*, vol.xxviii, (1931), 193–222. Bebbington identifies the doctrine of assurance as the distinctive factor of the evangelical awakening, and believes that this greater soteriological confidence stems from the psychological confidence of Locke. It is in this sense that for Bebbington there is a, "palpably Enlightenment tone about Edwards' form of expression" as, "Edwards derived his confidence about salvation from the atmosphere of the English Enlightenment," (D.W. Bebbington, *Evangelicalism in Modern Britain*, [London, 1989], 48). Miller is the progenitor of a modernist interpretation of Edwards, (Perry Miller, *Jonathan Edwards*, [New York, 1949]).

4. Parrington saw Edwards as anachronistic, (V.L.Parrington, *Main currents of American thought*, [3 vols., New York, 1927, 1930]). Gay and Thomas argued that Edwards was medieval, (Peter Gay, *A Loss of Mastery: Puritan Historians in Colonial America*, [Berkeley, 1966]; Vincent Tomas, "The Modernity of Jonathan Edwards," *New England Quarterly*, 25, [1952], 60–84). Aldridge argued for a traditional Edwards, (Alfred Owen Aldridge, *Jonathan Edwards*, [New York, 1966]), and more recently there has been a move towards locating Edwards in his historical context. (Harry S. Stout and Nathan O. Hatch, eds., *Jonathan Edwards and the American Experience*, [Boston, 1981]).

5. Perry Miller, *The New England Mind*, (New York, 1954), 90.

6. Flower and Murphy, *A History of Philosophy in America*, (New York, 1977), 20, 21.

7. *Ibid.*, 74–76.

8. Michael J. McClymond, "God the Measure: Towards an Understanding of Jonathan Edwards' Theocentric Metaphysics," *Scottish journal of Theology*, vol.47, no.1, (Winter 1994), 44.

9. McClymond understands the difficulty of summarising Edwards, but offers 'theo-centricity' as the appropriate model, (*Ibid.*, 45); Cooey also sees the problem of characterising Edwards, but like McClymond resorts to 'theocentricity,' (Paula M. Cooey, *Jonathan Edwards on Nature and Destiny*, [Lewiston, 1985], 11&12); Lee holds to the importance of the priority of 'theo-activity' for Edwards, (Sang Hyun Lee, *The Philosophical Theology of Jonathan Edwards*, [Princeton, 1988], 14).

10. Wainwright feels that Edwards' 'heart' experience requires controls to be reliable, but these seem already present in Edwards' 'signs of experience,' (William J. Wainwright, *Reason and the Heart: A Prolegomenon to a Critique of Passional Reason*, [Ithaca, 1995]). Kenny argues for an epistemology that incorporates emotions, (Anthony Kenny, *Action, Emotion, and Will*, [Bristol, 1994]).

11. There has been an evident development in the employment of secularization theory, moving from a view of secular society as leading towards extinction of traditional religion, to one of secular society as creating privatised religions. For discussion of secularization see, Owen Chadwick, *The Secularization of the European Mind in the Nineteenth Century*, (Cambridge, 1975), D. Martin, *A General Theory of Secularization*, (Oxford, 1978), and Philip E. Hammond, ed., *The Sacred in a Secular Age*, (Los Angeles, 1985).

12. So Wilson argues that even if secular society does have religion, it will be of a privatised kind: "The inherited model of secularization does not predict the eventual total eclipse of all religion, however. In this private sphere, religion often continues, and even acquires new forms of expression, many of them much less related to other aspects of culture than were the religions of the past," (Bryan Wilson "Secularization: The Inherited Model," *The Sacred in a Secular Age*, ed., Philip E. Hammond, [Los Angeles, 1985], 20).

13. The exceptions are found in the phenomena of the numerical stability and perhaps growth of the conservative churches, and in the increasing involvement of religion in the public sphere. Casanova and Johnson discuss the latter, (José Casonova, *Public Religions in the Modern World*, [Chicago, 1994]; Benton Johnson, "Religion and Politics in America: The Last Twenty Years," *The Sacred in a Secular Age*, ed. Philip E. Hammond, [Los Angeles, 1985], 301–316) and since Kelly's work (Dean Kelly, *Why the Conservative Churches Are Growing?* [New York, 1977]), the former has been the subject of sociological analysis, (Philip E. Hammond, ed., *The Sacred in a Secular Age*, [Los Angeles, 1985]; Steve Bruce, "The Persistence of Religion: Conservative Protestantism in the United Kingdom," *The Sociological Review*, vol.31, [1983], 453–470).

14. Various patterns of historical cause and effect might be traced. A history of the effects of great philosophers might be described (tracing a pattern from Locke to Hume to Kant to Hegel to Nietzsche to the various proponents of existentialism and modernism and post-modernism), so might some history of the effects of economic development (tracing a Marxist pattern of religion as the opium of the people, increasing religious disillusionment may be identified with increasing wealth), a history of the results of natural science (the patent success of the empirical method of modern science traces a pattern that questions the relevance of supernatural factors), and also a history of the effects of the political distinction between church and state in

modern liberal democracies (tracing a pattern of the association of religion with the private realm in the polis encouraging religion to be without public reference but only personal allegiance). See José Casanova, *Public Religions in the Modern World*, (Chicago, 1994), P. Hammond ed., *The Sacred in a Secular Age*, (Los Angeles, 1985), D. Lyon, "Secularization: The Fate of Faith in Modern Society?" *Them*, vol.10, no.1, (1984), 14–22.

15. Profound reflections on the problem of squaring the God of the monotheistic traditions with the legacy of a secularism that guarantees pluralism of belief and freedom of conscience are found in, *New Perspectives Quarterly*, (Spring 1994).

16. José Casonova, *Public Religions in the Modern World*, (Chicago, 1994); Steve Bruce, "The Persistence of Religion: Conservative Protestantism in the United Kingdom," *The Sociological Review*, vol. 31, (1983), 453–470.

17. The terms 'non-charismatic evangelicalism' and 'charismatic evangelicalism' are used to loosely identify what may be taken to be the two opposing poles in contemporary western evangelicalism. A 'charismatic' is defined as someone who believes that the extraordinary gifts of the Spirit evident in the New Testament are operative today, a 'non-charismatic' as someone who believes that they are not. The word originates from the Greek 'charisma,' which means something like 'grace-gift.' Evangelicalism is defined with Bebbington as being crucicentric, biblicist, conversionist, and activist (D.W. Bebbington, *Evangelicalism in Modern Britain*, [London, 1989], 3), and therefore as potentially including both charismatics and non-charismatics. The word 'evangelicalism' originates from the Greek 'evangel' which means 'gospel' or 'good news,' deriving from the German use of the term to define reformed religion.

Edwards is clearly anti-'charisma' but not because of his epistemology. For him, all 'extraordinary' gifts have a high revelatory function, were intended to reveal the mind of God, and so ceased with the closing of the canon. Edwards' logic is that as "all the extraordinary Gifts & Influences of the Spirit implied immediate Revelation," meaning, "God's making known Some truth by immediate Suggestion of it to the mind without its being made known by Sense—Reason or by any former Revelation;" as this high kind of revelation is the same throughout Scripture, "So it was with all the extraordinary influences of the Spirit that were given of before there was any written word. . . . So it was with all the extraordinary Influences & Gifts of the Spirit we read of in the N.T.;" therefore, "we may learn That if it is not to be expected That any of these Gifts that imply divine Revelation should be loosened in These days," as, "The Words of the H[oly] SS[Scriptures] in the Conclusion of our Bibles do manifestly hold forth this much to us that now the canon of Scriptures is finished," (1 Corinthians 13:8–13, May 1748, "The extraordinary influences of the Spirit of God imparting immediate revelations to men designed only for a temporary continuance and never were intended to be steadily upheld in the Christian church," *MSS*, Beinecke). To Edwards, "they that leave the sure word of prophecy, that God has given us to be a light shining in a dark place, to follow such impressions and impulses, leave the guidance of the pole star, to follow a Jack-with-a-lanthorn," ("The Distinguishing Marks," *Yale Works*, iv, 282; *Yale Works*, viii, 351–365).

Nevertheless, Edwards has been widely used as a guide in recent unusual Charismatic manifestations, particularly those dubbed the 'Toronto Blessing.' By and large these popular interpretations fail to garner full benefit from Edwards because his more mature work on religious experience, "The Religious Affections," is ignored in favour of analysis of his more accessible and earlier works on revival in general, especially "The Distinguishing Marks." This is the reason for the misdirection of the otherwise thorough chapter on Edwards in Guy Chevreau's, "Catch the Fire," (London, 1994), 70–145. One can not purport to give a true picture of Edwards' doctrine of religious experience if no attempt is made to interact with "The Religious Affections." The same story can be told for the one reference to Edwards in the recent analysis of revival in *Prophecy Today*. The article is entitled "Why Revivals Don't Last," and the reference is found in Edwards' early, "Some Thoughts Concerning the Revival," (*Prophecy Today*, vol. 9, no. 6, November/December 1993). *The Evangelical Times* falls into this trap in the article by John Legg, "Jonathan Edwards On Revival," (*Evangelical Times*, September 1994), which, though giving a careful application of Edwards' refusal to draw conclusion from the presence or absence of physical manifestations, fails to use Edwardean doctrines drawn from outside of "The Distinguishing Marks." While *Christianity Today* has at least published a review which carefully considers "The Religious Affections" it does not analyse this as a maturation of Edwards' thinking, (Richard T. Lovelace, "The Surprising Works of God: Jonathan Edwards on Revival, Then and Now," *Christianity Today*, [September 11, 1995], 28–32). Those which made least play of the Edwards-Toronto Blessing link were the publications of the Anglicans and the Methodists. *The Church of England Newspaper* published a compilation article, incorporating three different opinions, none of which referred to Edwards specifically, though one made some analysis of the Great Awakening in general, ("Testing Toronto," *The Church of England Newspaper*, July 8 1994). *The Methodist Recorder* similarly published an assessment with no link to Edwards, ("Testing the Spirit," *The Methodist Recorder*, November 10 1994). The paper that made the most of attempted insightful analysis of the 'Toronto Blessing' and also the link to Edwards was *Evangelicals Now*, with no less than five major articles on the movement between October 1994 and June 1995, one entirely on Edwards and another making significant reference to him. The article that was entirely on Edwards, though otherwise balanced, unfortunately also failed to take any account of "The Religious Affections," (Gary Benfold, "Jonathan Edwards and Toronto," *Evangelicals Now*, October 1994); the article that referred to Edwards is, to my knowledge, the sole popular article that at least noted the importance of the development within Edwards' thought, culminating in "The Religious Affections," (Roy Clements, "Don't Tread on My Toron—toes," *Evangelicals Now*, June 1995). The lesson to be learned from this survey is that in the future if the Church is to make effective use of Edwards they must learn the importance of Edwards' 'sense of the heart,' of his 'affections;' if this is ignored Edwards becomes little more than a sop for any kind of religiosity.

18. Assertion is insufficient, Edwards' doctrines need be defended as true. For, as Hebblethwaite argues, truth is central to any approach to religion, (Brian Hebblethwaite, "Religious Truth and Dialogue," *The Scottish Journal of Religious Studies*, [Spring, 1984], 3–17).

19. Popper famously argued that this was a necessary criterion for a scientific theory, (Karl Popper, *The Logic of Scientific Discovery*, [New York, 1959]), 40–41.

20. Relativism is not further considered here for the sake of clarity and brevity. Otherwise, given that we are attempting to construct a basis for knowledge of universal truth it would seem appropriate at this place to consider the premise that such an attempt is unwarranted. The classic answer to total relativism is, of course, similar to that given in the following footnote to the assertion that there is universal truth but no one knows it. That is, that 'universal relativism' is an oxymoron: one can not seriously argue that there are absolutely no universals for that itself is a universal.

21. A third alternative might be to argue that there is universal truth and no one knows it, but if this is so there seems that there is nothing anyone can do about it, and, more to the point, that the proposition can not be formally true on its own terms. The proposition itself seems to be a universal truth and yet by its own definition I cannot know that it is so, therefore it is not true, therefore it is unassertable.

22. The Deist and Arminian backdrop to the Great Awakening is not the contemporary one. Penelhum avoids the anachronistic pitfall by attempting to relate Butler's apologetic stance to the deists to more modern concerns not by drawing a comparison between deism and later movements, but by suggesting how Butler's response to deism might operate in a different situation. (Terence Penelhum, *Butler*, [London, 1985], 106). Cragg argues that Deism is the root cause of many modern philosophical assumptions: "Its [Deism's] philosophic authority may have been shaken by Butler and Hume, but it still shapes the unexamined presuppositions which govern men's outlook, and those who make no allowance for its conclusions are at a loss to understand the modern mind." (G.R. Cragg, *From Puritanism to the Age of Reason*, [Cambridge, 1950], 92).

23. The full title of Edwards' "Faithful Narrative" reveals his attitude, "A Faithful Narrative of the Surprising Work of God in the Conversion of Many Hundred Souls in Northampton and the Neighbouring Towns and Villages of New Hampshire, in New England in a Letter to the Revd. Dr. Benjamin Colman of Boston." (*Yale Works*, iv, 128). It was the surprising work of God to produce so many conversions. See the chapter "True Salvation."

24. Edwards describes Brainerd as being the "instrument of a most remarkable awakening, and an exceeding wonderful and abiding alteration and moral transformation of such subjects who peculiarly render the charge rare and astonishing." (*Yale Works*, vii, 90). Brainerd writes in his diary on Friday June 28th 1745: "My soul rejoiced to find that God enabled me to be faithful, and that he was pleased to awaken these poor Indians by my means. O, how heart-reviving and soul-refreshing is it to me to see the fruit of my labours!" ("Brainerd's Life and Diary," *Yale Works*, vii, 301). And later he describes how it was that, "the truths of God's word seemed, at times, to be attended with some power upon the hearts and consciences of the Indians. And especially this appeared evident in a few instances, who were awakened to some sense of their miserable estate by nature, and appeared solicitous for deliverance from it. Several of them came, of their own accord, to discourse with me about their souls' concerns; and some with tears, inquired 'what they should do to be saved?'" ("A Brief Account of the Endeavours Used by the Missionaries," *Banner Works*, ii, 433).

Bibliography

COLLECTED WORKS

The Works of Jonathan Edwards, 14 vols., General Editor Harry S. Stout (New Haven, Conn., 1957–). Cited in text as *Yale Works*. Publication continuing.
The Works of Jonathan Edwards, 2 vols., ed. Edward Hickman, (London, 1834). Cited in text as *Banner Works*.
The Works of President Edwards, 10 vols., ed. Sereno E. Dwight, (New York, 1829–1830).
A Jonathan Edwards Reader, ed. John E. Smith, (New Haven, Conn., 1995).

EDWARDS MANUSCRIPTS

Cited in text as MSS.

Beinecke Rare Book and Manuscript Library, Yale University, New Haven.
Princeton Library, Princeton University, Princeton, New Jersey.
Edwards' Manuscripts described by:
Rice, Howard C. Jr., "Jonathan Edwards at Princeton: With a Survey of Edwards Materials in the Princeton University Library," *Princeton University Library Chronicle*, vol. xv, (1953–1954), 69–89.
Schafer, Thomas A., "Manuscript Problems in the Yale Edition of Jonathan Edwards," *Early American Literature*, vol. 3, (1968–69), 159–71.

Sermons

Listed in canonical order, with date, where known, and doctrine.

Genesis 1:27, August 1751: "That God has given men reason and understanding . . . man being made in God's image . . . made holy . . ."

Genesis 3:4, December 1740: "One principle means that the Devil makes to persuade men to sin is to persuade 'em that they shall escape punishment."

Genesis 3:11, February 1738, four sermons: "The act of our first father in eating the forbidden fruit was a very heinous act."

Genesis 3:17–19, fragment: concerning the circumstances of the fall.

Genesis 3:24, not dated: "When man fell, God drove him away from all his former blessedness."

Genesis 32:26–29, not dated: "The way to obtain the blessing of God is not to let God go except he bless us."

Deuteronomy 5:27–29, November 1743: "Godliness consists not in an heart to purpose to do the will of God, but in an heart to do it."

Deuteronomy 15:16–17, April 1742: "When persons love God they have a principle that will make 'em willing to serve God forever."

Exodus 16:20, October 1741: "For person to lay up past experiences to live upon them . . ."

Psalm 14:1(a), not dated: "A principle of Atheism possesses the hearts of all ungodly men."

Psalm 14:1(b), December 1752: "There certainly is a God."

Psalm 18:35, not dated, only application remaining: "In the doctrinal handling of these words I shewed 1. how they are become great and 2. how 'tis God's gentleness that hath made them so."

Psalm 19:12, September 1739: " 'Tis an exceeding hard thing for men to be sensible of those things in themselves that are sinful and offensive to God."

Psalm 55:12–14, September 1741: "Men are not sufficient positively to determine the state of the souls of others that are of Gods visible people."

Psalm 119:60, September 1751: "Man is made to differ from all the brute creatures in that respect, that he is capable of knowing God and knowing his will."

Psalm 139:7–10, not dated: "That God is everywhere present."

Proverbs 24:20, October 1737: "I shall not raise a doctrine in any other words but shall insist on the words of the text and shall shew . . . wherein the candle of the wicked is put out."

Isaiah 6:5, July 1734: "There is nothing like seeing what God is, to make men sensible what they are."

Matthew 5:8, 1753, not dated: "1. Prop. that it is a thing truly happifying to the soul of man to see God. 2. Prop. That having a pure heart is the certain and only way to come to the blessedness of seeing God."

Matthew 5:15–16, December 1746: "That holy thing that is in the saints is a shining light."

Matthew 7:14 (a), not dated: "That the entrance into eternal life is a straight and narrow passage."

Matthew 13:3–4, November 1740, April 1756: "Those that God sends forth to preach the gospel are fitly compared to an husbandman that goes forth to sow his seed."

Matthew 13:3–4, 1756: "I would shew how that there are some kinds of hearers of the word preached whose hearts are like the wayside."

Matthew 13:4, January 1752: "1. How there are some sorts of men who hear the word preached that are like the path that men travel in. 2. How the devil immediately catches away that which such men hear in the preaching of the word."

Matthew 13:5–6, 1740, 1756: "There are many of the hearers of the word whose hearts are like a rock with a thin covering of earth."

Matthew 13:5–[6], November 1740: "Sudden Conversions are very often false."

Matthew 13:5–6: "That religion that arises only from superficial impressions is wont to whither away for want of root when it comes to be tried by the difficulties of religion."

Matthew 13:5–6, February 1753: "The preaching of the word of God to some men is like sowing seed on a rock where there is but a thin covering of earth."

Matthew 13:7, 1740, 1756: "1. That the hearts of some of the hearers of the word are so carnal and worldly that they appear to be a ground that was never plowed and so is overgrown with thorns."

Matthew 13:7, March 1752: "Some that have the word preached have their hearts so carnal and worldly that they appear to be a ground that was never plowed, all over run with thorns."

Matthew 13:8, March 1752: "Doc. 1. There are some men that hear the word of God whose hearts are like good ground fitted to receive the seed sown. Doc 2. Good men have such an understanding of the word of God as wicked men never have."

Matthew 13:22, not dated: "That the cares of this life are what often hinders any saving effect of the word of God."

Matthew 13:22, April 1733: "The world is commonly a great snare to the souls of men."

Matthew 13:23, June 1757: "That which distinguishes the profitable hearers of God's word from all others is that they understand it and bring forth the fruit of it."

Luke 6:45, August 1753: "1. A good man has a great treasure in his heart . . ."

Luke 11:13, November 1740: "Of the more excellent nature any blessing is that we stand in need of the more ready God is to bestow it in answer to prayer."

Luke 19:40, March 1736: "Those persons unaffected with the great and glorious things of the gospel have hearts harder than the very stones."

Luke 19:42, June 1741: "1. If ever those that are in a special manner far from conversion are converted, 'tis most likely to be at a time when X[Christ] is extraordinarily present."

Luke 24:32, June 1736; October 1755: " 'Tis a common [thing] with the saints that their hearts do burn within them while divine things are represented to them."

Romans 1:20, 1743, 1756: "The being and attributes of God are clearly to be seen by the works of creation."

Romans 12:4–8, August 19 1739: "The offices that Christ has appointed in his church do respect either the souls or bodies of men."

1 Corinthians 2:11–13, May 7 1740: "Ministers are not to preach those things which their own wisdom or reason suggests but the things that are already dictated to them by the Superior wisdom & knowledge of God."

1 Corinthians 6:11, March 1747; June 1755: "A work of Conversion as a great effect of God's power and grace in the heart is not a meer whim or fancy but a great and certain reality."

1 Corinthians 13:8–13, May 1748: "The extraordinary influences of the Spirit of God imparting immediate revelations to men were designed only for a temporary continuance and never were intended to be steadily upheld in the Christian church."
1 Corinthians 15:34, not dated: "It is matter of awful note and consideration that there are some men that have not the knowledge of God."
2 Corinthians 2:14, 1748, 1755: "The spiritual knowledge of Christ is as it were a sweet savour that the souls hath of Christ."
Ephesians 3:10, March 1733: "The wisdom appearing in the way of salvation by Jesus Christ is far above the wisdom of the angels."
Ephesians 4:29, July 1740: "Professing Christians when they meet together should avoid all corrupt discourse one with another and should practise that whereby they may promote the good of each other's souls."
James 2:19, 1746: "No such experiences as the devils in hell are the subjects of are any sure sign of grace."
2 Peter 1:16, not dated: "That seeing the glory of Christ is what tends to assure the heart of the truth of the gospel."
2 Peter 1:19, August 1737: "Divine revelation is like a light that shines in a dark place."
2 Peter 1:19, November 1737: "Divine revelation is like a light that shines in a dark place."
1 John 4:16, not dated: "The spirit of the true saints is a spirit of divine love."
1 John 5:1–4, July 1750: "1. Saving faith differs from all common faith in its nature, kind and essence. 2. All that are in a state of salvation obey God's commands not only from fear of hell but love to God, and do love him more than the world."
1 John 5:1–4, July 1750: "1. Saving faith differs from all common faith in its natuessence. 2. All that are in a state of salvation obey God's commands not only from fear of hell, but love to God, and do love him more than the world." [different sermon from above]
1 John 5:2, June 1736: "1. 'Tis commonly so with the saints, that some graces are more sensible in them than some others."
Jude 19, December 1750: "There was a sort of persons in the apostles' day who separated themselves from the steady ministers and churches that pretended to be very spiritual, but who really were carnal and had not the Spirit of God."
Revelation 2:17, December 1742: "The subject that I would now handle, viz. that white stone and the name written in it that no man knows but he that receives it."
Revelation 3:12, 1740, 1752: "1. I would shew that those that are, thorough Christians are properly decyphered by that, that they are they that overcome. 2. I would speak particularly of these three promises to such . . . viz. that Christ will write upon them."
Revelation 8:2–3, July 1742: "The prayers of saints is a great and principal means of carrying on the great designs of Christ's kingdom in the world."
Revelation 17:14, not dated: "1. Those that are of Christ's and belonging to him, 'tis of God that they are so. 2. They that belong to Jesus Christ, they are faithful to Christ."

Notebooks and Papers

Listed alphabetically.

"Efficacious Grace."
"Miscellanies," a-500 published, 501–1360 unpublished.
"Miscellaneous observations Concerning Faith."
"Miscellaneous Observations on the Holy Scriptures."
"Notes on conversion from various authorities."
"Notes on the scriptures."
"Of the Decrees of God."
Preface to the farewell sermon, two fragments.
"Profession of Faith."
"Q"[Questions on theological subjects].
"Signs of Godliness" [front page] or "Signs of Grace" [title at page 1].
"Subjects of Enquiry."
"Rough notes on the truth of the Christian religion."
"X'[Christ's] Example," untitled.

Letters

Listed Chronologically.

From: Jonathan Edwards. To: Joseph Bellamy, Stockbridge, not dated, concerning the education of Jonathan Edwards Jr.

From: Jonathan Edwards. To: Joseph Bellamy. Northampton, October 3 1736, concerning sheep.

From: Jonathan Edwards. To: Joseph Bellamy. Northampton, 1747, concerning sheep and Brainerd.

From: Jonathan Edwards. To: Joseph Bellamy. Northampton, April 4 1748, concerning sheep and death of Jerusha Edwards.

From: Jonathan Edwards. To: Rev. Mr Eleazar Wheelock. New Haven, September 14 1748, concerning Brainerd.

From: Jonathan Edwards. To: Joseph Bellamy. Northampton, December 6 1749, concerning communion controversy.

From: Peter Clark. To: Ebenezer Pomeroy. April 4 1750, transcript, concerning communion controversy.

From: Jonathan Edwards. To: Peter Clark. May 7 1750, Edwards' extract transcription, concerning communion controversy

From: Peter Clark. To: Jonathan Edwards. Salem, May 21 1750, concerning communion controversy in reply to May 7 letter.

From: Edward Billing. To: Jonathan Edwards. June 11th 1750, concerning communion controversy.

From: Samuel Davies. To: Jonathan Edwards. August 26 1750, concerning Davenport.

From: Jonathan Edwards. To: Colonel Elisha Williams. Stockbridge, August 18 1752, concerning controversy at Stockbridge.

From: Jonathan Edwards. To: Reverend John Erskine. Stockbridge, December 11 1755, concerning war and books recently received.

Published Manuscript Selections

Faust, Clarence, and Thomas H. Johnson, eds., *Jonathan Edwards: Representative Selections*, (New York, 1962).

Helm, Paul, ed., *Treatise on Grace and Other Posthumous Writings by Jonathan Edwards*, (Cambridge, 1971).

Grosart, Alexander, ed., *Selections from the Unpublished Writings of Jonathan Edwards*, (Ligonier, Pa., 1992).

Townsend, Harvey G., ed. *The Philosophy of Jonathan Edwards from his Private Notebooks*, (Eugene, 1955).

Williams, Stanley T., ed., "Six Letters of Jonathan Edwards to Joseph Bellamy," *New England Quarterly*, (1928), 226–242.

Winslow, Ola Elizabeth, ed., *Jonathan Edwards: Basic Writings*, (New York, 1966).

OTHER PRIMARY LITERATURE

Ames, William, *Medulla Theologica*, (London, 1642).

——, *Conscience and Cases Thereof*, (New Jersey, 1975).

Augustine, of Hippo, "Treatise on the Trinity," *Works*, vol. 7, (Edinburgh, 1873).

——, *Confessions*, ed. H. Chadwick, (Oxford, 1992).

Bacon, Francis, *Two Books of the Proficiencie and Advancement of Learning*, (London, 1808).

Baumer, Franklin Le Van, *Main Currents of Western Thought*, (New Haven, Conn., 1978).

Berkeley, George, *A Treatise Concerning the Principles of Human Knowledge*, (London, 1734); *Ibid.*, (New York, 1957).

——, *A New Theory of Vision*, (London, 1914).

Berlin, Isaiah, *The Age of Enlightenment: The Eighteenth-Century Philosophers*, (Oxford, 1979).

Brainerd, David, *The Gospel the Only True Reformer*, (New York, 1856),

Boyle, Robert, *The Life and Works of the Honourable Robert Boyle*, ed., Louis Trenchard More, (London, 1944).

Buffon, George-Louis Leclerc, *Histoire Naturelle*, (Paris, 1984).

Burke, Edmund, *Reflections on the Revolution in France*, (London, 1986).

Burr, Esther Edwards, *Journal, 1754–1757*, ed. Carol F. Karsen and Laurie Crumpacker, (Yale, 1984).

Bushman, Richard L., ed., *The Great Awakening: Documents on the Revival of Religion, 1740–1745*, (New York, 1970).

Butler, Joseph, *The Analogy of Religion, Natural and Revealed, to the Constitution and Course of Nature*, (New York, 1900).
British Reformers, 14 vols., (London, 1831).
Calvin, John, *Institutes*, 2 vols., (London, 1949).
Channing, William Ellery, "Baltimore Sermon," *Classics of Protestantism*, ed. Vergilia Fern, (London, 1959).
Chauncy, Charles, D.D., *Seasonable Thoughts on the State of Religion in New England* (New York, 1975).
Chubb, Thomas, *A Collection of Tracts on Various Subjects*, (London, 1730).
Clarke, Samuel, *The Scriptural Doctrine of the Trinity*, (London, 1719).
Coleridge, S.T., "Biographia Litereraria," "Aids to Reflection," *Works*, vols. 1&9, (London, 1962).
Collins, Anthony, *Discourse of Free Thinking*, (London, 1713; Stuttgart, 1965).
Cudworth, Ralph, *The True Intellectual System of The Universe*, (London, 1678).
Dante, Alighieri, *The Divine Comedy*, (London, 1994).
Descates, René, *A Discourse on Method*, (London, 1949).
———, "Rules for the direction of the mind," *The Essential Descartes*, ed. Margaret Wilson, (New York, 1969).
Diderot, Denis, *Supplement au Voyage de Bougainville*, (Paris, 1972).
———, *La Religieuse; Le Neveau de Rameau*, (Moscow, 1980).
Drury, John, *Critics of the Bible, 1724–1873*, (Cambridge, 1989).
Dummer, Jeremiah, "The List of Books Sent by Jeremiah Dummer," *Papers in honour of Andrew Keogh*, (New Haven, 1938), 432–492.
Dwight, Sereno E., *Life of President Edwards*, (New York, 1829), reprinted, "Memoirs of Jonathan Edwards," *Banner Works*, i.
Dwight, Timothy, *Travels in New England and New York*, 4 vols., (Cambridge, Mass., 1969).
Finney, Charles G., *Revival Lectures*, ed. W.G. McLoughlin, (Cambridge, Mass., 1960).
Flavel, John, *The Works of John Flavel*, 6 vols., (London, 1968).
Franklin, Benjamin, *The Autobiography of Benjamin Franklin*, (New Haven, Conn., 1964).
———, *A Dissertation on Liberty and Necessity, Pleasure and Pain*, (New York, 1930).
Frothingham, Ebenezer, *The Articles of Faith and Practice that is Confessed by the Separate Churches of Christ in General in this Land*, (Newport, 1750).
Gibbon, Edward, *The History of the Decline and Fall of the Roman Empire*, 7 vols., (London, 1912).
Graydon, Samuel, ed., *The American Trilogy*, (New York, 1939).
Helvetius, Claude Adrien, *De L'Esprit*, (Paris, 1988).
Henry, Matthew, *Commentary on the Whole Bible*, (London, 1960).
Hobbes, *Leviathan*, (London, 1963).
Holmes, Oliver Wendell, "Jonathan Edwards," *International Review*, vol. 9, (July 1880), 1–28; reprinted, *Critical Essays on Jonathan Edwards*, ed. William J. Scheick, (Boston, 1980).

Holbach, Baron d', *System of Nature*, (New York, 1970).
Hopkins, Samuel, "Life of Jonathan Edwards," (Boston, 1765); reprinted, *Jonathan Edwards: A Profile*, ed. David Levin, (New York, 1969).
Hume, David, *Dialogues Concerning Natural Religion*, (Edinburgh, 1947).
——, *A Treatise of Human Nature*, (London, 1970).
——, *Essays on Suicide, the Immortality of the Soul, and Miracles*, (London, 1821).
Hutchenson, Francis, *An Inquiry into the Original Ideas of Beauty and Virtue*, (London, 1726).
Kant, Immanuel, "What is Enlightenment?" *Berlinische Monatsschrift*, (1783), reprinted, *Immanuel Kant, Qu'est ce Que les Lumières*, Jean Mondot, ed.,(Paris, 1991), 71–86.
——, *Critique of Pure Reason*, (London, 1929).
——, *Prolegomena to Any Future Metaphysics*, (Manchester, 1953).
——, *Grounding for the Metaphysics of Morals*, (Indianapolis, 1985).
Lafitau, Joseph-Francois, *Moeurs des Sauvages Americains*, 2 vols., (Paris, 1983).
Law, William, *A Serious call to a Devout and Holy Life*, (London, 1898).
Leland, John, *A View of the Principal Deistical Writers*, (London, 1764).
Locke, John, *An Essay Concerning Human Understanding*, (London, 1706).
——, *Two Treatises of Government*, (London, 1943).
Lonsdale, Roger, ed., *The New Oxford Book of Eighteenth Century Verse*, (Oxford, 1992).
Luther, Martin, *Sermons of Martin Luther*, 4 vols., (Grand Rapids, 1983).
——, *Basic Theological Writings*, ed. Timothy F. Lull, (Minneapolis, 1994).
Malebranche, Nicholas, *The Search After Truth*, (Columbus, 1980).
Mandeville, Bernard, *The Fable of the Bees, or Private Vices, Publick Benefits*, (London, 1723).
Mather, Cotton, *Magnali Christi Americana*, 2 vols., (Edinburgh, 1979).
——, *The Christian Philosopher*, (London, 1721).
——, "The Diary of Cotton Mather," *Massachusetts Historical Society Collections*, 7th series, viii, (Boston 1919).
Miller, Perry and Alan Heimert, *The Great Awakening: Documents Illustrating the Crisis and its Consequences*, (New York, 1967).
Montesquieu, Baron de, *The Spirit of the Laws*, (Cambridge, 1989).
More, Henry, *The Immortality of the Soul*, (London, 1659).
——, *A Collection of Several Philosophical Writings*, (Ann Arbor, Mich., 1963).
Newton, Isaac, *The Mathematical Principles of Natural Philosophy*, (London, 1729).
——, *Opticks*, (New York, 1979).
Nissenbaum, Stephen, ed. *The Great Awakening at Yale College*, (Belmont, Calif., 1972).
Owen, John, *Works*, 16 vols., (Edinburgh, 1990).
Paley, William, "Natural Theology; or Evidences of the Existence and Attributes of the Deity, Collected from the Appearances of Nature," *The Works of William Paley*, vol. 4, *Natural Theology*, (Oxford, 1838).
Pascal, Blaise, *Pensées*, (London, 1966).
Perkins, William, *The Work of William Perkins*, ed. Ian Breward, (Appleford, 1970).
Pope, Alexander, *Essay on Man*, (London, 1984).

Preston, John, *The New Covenant, or the Saints Portion*, (London, 1629).
Prince, Thomas, *The Christian History*, (Boston 1743–5).
——, *An Account of the Revival of Religion in Boston in the Years 1740–3*, (Boston, 1823).
Reid, Thomas, *An Inquiry into the Human Mind*, (Bristol, 1990).
Robertson, *The Progress of Society in Europe*, (London, 1769).
Rousseau, Jean-Jacques, *A Discourse on Inequality*, (London, 1984).
——, *The Social Contract*, (London, 1968).
——, *Confessions*, (London, 1933).
Rutman, Darrett B., *The Great Awakening: Event and Exegesis*, (New York, 1970).
Shaftesbury, Anthony Ashley Cooper, Third Earl of, *Characteristics of Men, Manners*, (London, 1732).
Sherlock, Thomas, *The Tryal of the Witnesses of the Resurrection of Jesus*, (London, 1731).
Shishkina, T., ed., *The American Age of Reason*, (Moscow, 1977).
Sibbes, Richard, *Works*, 7 vols., (Edinburgh, 1983).
Smith, John, *Select Discourses*, (London, 1660).
Stoddard, Solomon, *The Safety of Appearing*, (Boston, 1687).
——, *The Sinner Guided to the Saviour*, (Edinburgh, 1848).
——, *Treatise Concerning Conversion*, (Boston, 1719).
Taylor, John, *The Scripture Doctrine of Original Sin Proposed to Free and Candid Examination*, (London, 1741).
Tillotson, John, *Works*, 3 vols., (London, 1752).
Tindal, Matthew, *Christianity as Old as Creation, or the Gospel a Republication of Nature*, (London 1732; Stuttgart, 1967).
Toland, John, *Christianity Not Mysterious*, (London, 1702).
Tracy, Joseph, *The Great Awakening*, (Edinburgh, 1989).
Venn, Henry, *The Complete Duty of Man*, (1763).
——, *The Letters of Henry Venn*, (Edinburgh, 1993).
Vico, Giambattista *Selected Writings*, ed., Leon Pompa, (Cambridge, 1982).
Voltaire, *Letters on England*, (London, 1988).
Watson, Thomas, *A Body of Divinity*, (London, 1890).
Wesley, John, *Works*, 18 vols., (Grand Rapids, 1958).
——, *Sermons on Several Occasions*, 3 vols., (London, 1865).
Whitby, Daniel, *Discourse on Five Points*, (London, 1710).
Whitefield, George, *Select Sermons of George Whitefield*, (Edinburgh, 1990).
——, *Sermons On Important Subjects*, (London, 1829).
——, *George Whitefield's Journals*, (Edinburgh, 1960).

SECONDARY LITERATURE

Aaron, Daniel, ed., *American Crisis*, (New York, 1952).
Adorno, Theodor and Horkheimer, Max, *Dialectic of Enlightenment*, (London, 1973).
Aldridge, Alfred Owen, "Jonathan Edwards and Hutchenson," *The Harvard Theological Review*, vol. 44, (1931), 35–53.

——, *Jonathan Edwards*, (New York, 1966).
——, *The Ibero-American Enlightenment*, (Urbana, 1971).
Alexander, H.G., ed., *The Leibniz-Clarke Correspondence*, (Manchester, 1965).
Allen, Alexander V.G., "Jonathan Edwards," (Boston, 1889), 281–99; reprinted, *Critical Essays on Jonathan Edwards*, ed. William J. Scheick, (Boston, 1980).
Anderson, Wallace E., "Immaterialism in Jonathan Edwards' Early Philosophical Notes," *Journal of the History of Ideas*, vol. 25, (1964), 181–200.
Angoff, Charles, ed., *Jonathan Edwards - His Life and Influence*, (Rutherford, 1975).
Bates, David, "The Epistemology of Error in Late Enlightenment France," *Eighteenth Century Studies*, vol. 29, no. 3, (Spring 1996), 307–327.
Bebbington, David W., *Patterns in History*, (Leicester, 1979).
——, *Evangelicalism in Modern Britain: A History From the 1730s to the 1980s*, (London, 1989).
——, Mark A. Noll, George A. Ranlyk, eds., *Evangelicalism*, (Oxford, 1994).
Becker, C.L., *The Heavenly City of the Eighteenth Century Philosophers*, (New Haven, Conn., 1932).
Beeke, Joel R., *Assurance of Faith: Calvin, English Puritanism, and the Dutch Second Reformation*, (New York, 1991).
Bercovitch, Sacvan, *The Puritan Origins of the American Self*, (New Haven, 1975).
——, *The American Jeremiad*, (Madison, Wisc., 1978).
Bizer, Ernst, "Reformed Orthodoxy and Cartesianism," *Journal for Theology and the Church*, vol. 2, (New York, 1965), 20–32.
Black, Jeremy, *Eighteenth Century Europe*, (London, 1990).
Bogue, Carl W., *Jonathan Edwards and The Covenant of Grace*, (New Jersey, 1975).
Boorstin, Daniel J., "The Myth of An American Enlightenment," *America and the Image of Europe*, (New York, 1960).
Brand, David C., *Profile of the Last Puritan: Jonathan Edwards*, (Atlanta, 1991).
Brantley, Richard E., "The Common Ground of Wesley and Edwards," *Harvard Theological Review*, vol. 83, no. 3, (1990), 271.
Bricke, John, "On the Interpretation of Hume's Dialogues," *Religious Studies*, vol. 11, (1975), 1–18.
Brown, John, *Pilgrim Fathers of New England and their Puritan Successors*, (London, 1895).
Bryant, M. Darrol, *Jonathan Edwards' Grammar of Time, Self and Society*, (Lewiston, 1993).
Burns, R.M., *The Great Debate on Miracles: From Joseph Glanville to David Hume*, (London, 1981).
Burke, Peter, ed., *New Perspectives on Historical Writing*, (Cambridge, 1991).
Bushman, Richard L., "Jonathan Edwards as Great Man: Identity, Conversion and Leadership in the Great Awakening," *Soundings*, vol. lii, (1969).
——, *From Puritan to Yankee: Character and the Social Order in Connecticut, 1690-1765*, (Cambridge, Mass. 1967).
——, "Jonathan Edwards and the Puritan Consciousness," *Journal for the Scientific Study of Religion*, vol. 5, (1966), 383–396.

Butler, Jon, "Enthusiasm Described and Decried: The Great Awakening as Interpretative Fiction," *Journal of American History*, vol. 69, (1982), 305–325.

Butts, Francis T., "The Myth of Perry Miller," *American Historical Review*, vol. 87, no. 3, (June 1982), 665–694.

Cady, Edwin H., "The Artistry of Jonathan Edwards," *New England Quarterly*, (March 1949), 61–72; reprinted, *Critical Essays on Jonathan Edwards*, ed., William J. Scheick, (Boston, 1980).

Cantor, Geoffrey, *The Discourse of Light from the Middle Ages to the Enlightenment*, (Los Angeles, 1970).

———, "The Eighteenth Century Problem," *History of Science*, vol. 20, (1982), 44–63.

Carpenter, Frederick I., "The Radicalism of Jonathan Edwards," *New England Quarterly*, vol. 4, (October 1931), 631–33.

Carse, James, *Jonathan Edwards and the Visibility of God*, (New York, 1967).

Cassirer, Ernst, *The Philosophy of the Enlightenment*, (Princeton, 1951).

Chadwick, Owen, *The Secularization of the European Mind in the Nineteenth Century*, (Cambridge, 1975).

Chamberlain, Ava, *Jonathan Edwards Against the Antinomians and the Arminians*, (Ph.D., Columbia University, 1990).

———, "Self-Deception as a Theological Problem in Jonathan Edwards's 'Treatise Concerning Religious Affections,'" *Church History*, vol. 63, no. 4, (December 1994), 541–556.

Charlton, D.G., *New Images of the Natural*, (Cambridge, 1984).

Chaunu, Pierre, *La Civilisation de L'Europe des Lumières*, (Paris, 1971).

Cherry, Conrad, *The Theology of Jonathan Edwards: A Reappraisal*, (New York, 1966).

———, "The Puritan Notion of the Covenant in Jonathan Edwards Doctrine of Faith," *Church History*, vol. 34, (1965), 329.

———, "Conversion: Nature and Grace," *Critical Essays on Jonathan Edwards*, ed. William J. Scheick, (Boston, 1980).

Clarke, J.C.D., "Reconceptualizing Eighteenth Century England," *British Journal for Eighteenth Century Studies*, vol. 15, no. 2, (Autumn 1992), 135–139.

Coalter, *Gilbert Tennent: Son of Thunder*, (New York, 1986).

Cobban, A., "The Enlightenment," *The New Cambridge Modern History*, vol. 7, (Cambridge, 1957), 85–112.

Coffman, Ralph J., *Solomon Stoddard*, (Boston, 1978).

Cohen, I.B., *The Newtonian Revolution*, (Cambridge, 1980).

Collingwood, R.G., *The Idea of History*, (Oxford, 1946).

Collinson, Patrick, "What is Religious History?" *What is History Today?* ed. Juliet Gardiner, (London, 1988).

Conforti, Joseph, *Jonathan Edwards, Religious Tradition, and American Culture from the Second Great Awakening to the Twentieth Century*, (Williamsburg, Va., 1995).

———, "Jonathan Edwards and American Studies," *American Quarterly*, vol. 4, no. 1, (March 1989).

———, *Samuel Hopkins and the New Divinity*, (Grand Rapids, 1981), 175–190.

Conkin, Paul, *Puritans and Pragmatists*, (New York, 1968).
Cooey, Paula M., *Jonathan Edwards on Nature and Destiny*, (Lewiston, 1985).
―――, "Eros and Intimacy in Edwards," *The Journal of Religion*, vol. 69, no 4, (October 1989), 484–501.
Cragg, G. R., *From Puritanism to the Age of Reason*, (Cambridge, 1950).
―――, *Reason and Authority in the Eighteenth Century*, (Cambridge, 1964).
Craig, William Lane, "The Historical Argument for the Resurrection of Jesus During the Deist Controversy," vol. 23, *Text and Studies in Religion*, (Lewiston, 1985).
Crocker, Lester G., *Nature and Culture: Ethical Thought in the French Enlightenment*, (Baltimore, 1963).
Curley, Edwin, "Calvin and Hobbes, or, Hobbes as an Orthodox Christian," *Journal of the History of Philosophy*, vol. xxxiv, no. 2, (April 1996), 257–272.
Daniel, Stephen H., *The Philosophy of Jonathan Edwards: A Study in Divine Semiotics*, (Bloomington, 1994).
Darnton, Robert, *Mesmerism and the End of the Enlightenment in France*, (Cambridge, Mass., 1968).
Davidson, Edward H., *Jonathan Edwards: The Narrative of a Puritan Mind*, (Cambridge, Mass., 1960).
Davies, Horton, *The Worship of the American Puritans, 1629–1730*, (New York, 1990).
Davies, Paul C., "The Debate on Eternal Punishment in Late Seventeenth Century and Eighteenth Century Literature," *Eighteenth Century Studies*, iv, (1970–71), 257–276.
Davies, R.E., *Jonathan Edwards and his Influence on the Development of the Missionary Movement from Britain*, (N.A.M.P. seminar, Cambridge University Divinity School, May 23 1996).
Delattre, Roland A., *Beauty and Sensibility in the Thought of Jonathan Edwards*, (New Haven, Conn., 1968).
―――, "Beauty and Theology: A Reappraisal of Jonathan Edwards," *Soundings*, (Spring 1968), 60–79.
―――, "The Theological Ethics of Jonathan Edwards: An Homage to Paul Ramsey," *The Journal of Religious Ethics*, vol. 19, no. 2, (Fall 1991), 71–102.
De Prospo, R.C., *Theism in the Discourse of Jonathan Edwards*, (Newark, 1985).
―――, "Review of Yale Works vol. 9 'History of the Work of redemption' & vol., 8 'Ethical Writings,'" *Modern Philology*, vol. 8, (November 1990), 204–209.
Dever, Mark, *Richard Sibbes and the Truly Evangelical Party of the Church of England*, (Ph.D., Cambridge University, 1992).
Dodd, Elizabeth D., *Marriage to a Difficult Man: The Uncommon Union of Jonathan and Sarah Edwards*, (Philadelphia, 1971).
Doyle, W., *The Old European Order, 1660–1800*, (Oxford, 1981).
Dreyer, F., "Faith and Experience in the Thought of John Wesley," *American Historical Review*, vol. 88, no. 2, (1983), 12–30.
Duff, Wm. Boyd, *Jonathan Edwards Then and Now: a Satirical Study in Predestination*, (Pennsylvania, 1959).
Edwards, Rem B., *The Return to Moral and Religious Philosophy in Early America*, (Washington, 1982).

Ehrard, Jean, *L'Idée de Nature en France*, 2 vols., (Paris, 1963).
Eliot, S. and Stern, Beverley, eds., *The Age of the Enlightenment*, 2 vols., (New York, 1979).
Elwood, Douglas E., *The Philosophical Theology of Jonathan Edwards*, (New York, 1960).
Erdt, Terrence, *Jonathan Edwards: Art and the Sense of the Heart*, (Amherst, Mass., 1980).
Faust, Clarence, and Thomas Johnson, "Introduction," eds. Faust and Johnson, *Jonathan Edwards*, (New York, 1962).
——, *Jonathan Edwards' View of Human Nature*, (Ph.D., Chicago University, 1935).
——, "Jonathan Edwards as a Scientist," *American Literature*, 1, (January 1930), 393–404, reprinted, *Jonathan Edwards and the Enlightenment*, ed. John Opie, (Lexington, Mass., 1969).
Fiering, Norman, "Will and Intellect in The New England Mind," *William and Mary Quarterly*, 3rd ser., vol. xxix, (1972), 515–558.
——, "Early American Philosophy," *Transactions of the Charles S. Pierce Society*, vol. xiii, (1977), 216–237.
——, *Jonathan Edwards' Moral Thought and its British Context*, (Williamsburg, Va., 1981).
——, "The First American Enlightenment: Tillotson, Leverett, and Philosophical Anglicanism," *New England Quarterly*, vol. 54, (1981), 307–344.
——, *Moral Philosophy at Seventeenth Century Harvard*, (Williamsburg, Va., 1981).
Flower, Elizabeth, and Murray G. Murphy, *A History of philosophy in America*, 2 vols. (New York, 1977).
Foote, Henry Wilder, *Three Centuries of American Hymnody*, (Cambridge, Mass., 1940).
Foster, Frank Hugh, *A Genetic History of the New England Theology*, (Chicago, 1907).
Frei, Hans W., *The Eclipse of Biblical Narrative: A Study in Eighteenth Century Hermeneutics*, (New Haven, 1974).
Galli, Mark, "In Praise of Foolish Lovers: Why Would Martin Luther and Jonathan Edwards Make Fools of Themselves Over the Return of Christ?" *Christianity Today*, vol. 34, no. 17, (November 19, 1990), 35–36.
Gaustad, Edwin Scott, *The Great Awakening in New England*, (New York, 1957).
——, *A Religious History of America*, (New York, 1966).
Gay, Peter, *A Loss of Mastery: Puritan Historians in Colonial America*, (Berkeley, 1966).
——, *The Enlightenment*, 2 vols., (New York, 1966, 1969).
Gerstner, John H., *Steps to Salvation: The Evangelistic Message of Jonathan Edwards*, (Philadelphia, 1976).
——, "The Apologetics of Jonathan Edwards," *Bibliotheca Sacra*, vol. 133 (January–March, 1976), 3–10; vol. 133, (April–June, 1976), 99–107; vol. 133, (July–September, 1976), 195–201; vol. 133, (October–December, 1976), 291–298.
——, "Edwardsean Preparation for Salvation," *The Westminster Theological Journal*, vol. xlii, no. 1, (Fall 1979), 5–71.

——, "Jonathan Edwards and the Bible," *Tenth, An Evangelical Quarterly*, (Fall 1979).
——, *Jonathan Edwards - A Mini Theology*, (Wheaton, Illinois, 1987).
——, *The Rational Biblical Theology of Jonathan Edwards*, 3 vols., (Powheton, Va. 1991–1993).
Gilson, E., *History of Christian Philosophy in the Middle Ages*, (London, 1955).
Glacken, C., *Traces on the Rhodian Shore*, (London, 1967).
Goen, C.C., "A New Departure in Eschatology," *Church History*, vol. xxviii, (1959), 25–40.
——, *Revivalism and Separatism in New England*, (New Haven, Conn., 1962).
Goldmann, Lucien, *The Philosophy of the Enlightenment*, (London, 1968).
Gomes, Peter, J., "Review of Michael G. Hall, 'The Last American Puritan: The Life of Increase Mather,'" *New England Quarterly*, (1989), 116–120.
Griffin, Edward M., "Jonathan Edwards: A New Departure in Eschatology," *Church History*, vol. xxviii, no. 1, (1959), 25–40.
——, *Old Brick: Charles Chauncy of Boston, 1705–1787*, (Minnesota, 1980)
Griffin, Martin I.J., Jr., "Latitudinarianism in the Seventeenth Century Church of England," *Brill's Studies in Intellectual History*, ed. Lila Freeman, vol. 32, (Leiden, 1992).
Guelzo, Allen C., *Edwards on the Will: A Century of American Theological Debate*, (Middletown, Conn., 1989).
Hall, Basil, "Calvin Against the Calvinists," *John Calvin*, ed. G.E.Duffield, (Abingdon, 1966).
Hall, David, "The Uses of Literacy in New England, 1600–1850," *Printing and Society in Early America*, ed. W.L. Joyce, 1–47.Hall, Richard A.S., *The Neglected Northampton Texts: Edwards on Society and Politics*, (Lewiston, 1990).
Haller, William, *The Rise of Puritanism*, (New York, 1957).
Harlan, David, *The Clergy and the Great Awakening in New England*, (Ann Arbor, Mich., 1980)
Haroutunian, Joseph G., *Piety Versus Moralism: The Passing of New England Theology*, (New York, 1932).
Harvey, David, "Explaining Salem: Calvinist Psychology and the Diagnosis of Possession," *American Historical Review*, vol. 101, no. 2, (April 1996), 307–330.
Hazard, P., *The European Mind*, (Cleveland, 1963).
——, *European Thought in the Eighteenth Century*, (Cleveland, 1963).
Heimert, Alan, *Religion and the American mind*, (Cambridge, Mass., 1966).
——, *Puritans in America*, (Cambridge, Mass., 1985).
Helm, Paul, "John Locke and Jonathan Edwards: A Reconstruction," *Journal of the History of Philosophy*, vol. 7, (January 1969), 51–61.
Hemming, T.D., ed., *The Secular City: Studies in the Enlightenment*, (Cambridge, 1994).
Hill, Christopher, "Science in Seventeenth Century England," *The Listener*, vol. 7, (June 1962).
Hof, Im, *The Enlightenment*, (Oxford, 1994).
Höffding, Harold, *A History of Modern Philosophy: A Sketch of the History of Modern Philosophy from the Close of the Renaissance to Our Own Day*, (New York, 1950).

Hofstadter, Richard and Wilson Smith, eds., *American Higher Education: A Documentary History*, (Chicago, 1961).
Holbrook, Clyde A., *Jonathan Edwards, the Valley and Nature: An Interpretative Essay*, (New York, 1987), 45–63.
———, *The Ethics of Jonathan Edwards*, (Ann Arbor, Mich., 1973).
———, "Jonathan Edwards on Self-Identity and Original Sin," *The Eighteenth Century: Theory and Interpretation*, vol. 25, no. 1, (1984).
———, "Jonathan Edwards and His Detractors," *Theology Today*, vol. 10, (October, 1953), 384–96.
Hoopes, James, *Consciousness in New England: From Puritanism and Ideas to Psychoanalysis and Semiotic*, (Baltimore, 1989).
———, "Jonathan Edward's Religious Psychology," *Journal of American History*, vol. 69, (1982–3), 849–865.
Hooykas, R., *Humanisme, Science et Réforme: Pierre de la Ramée*, (Leyde, 1958).
Howard, Leon, '*The Mind' of Jonathan Edwards: A Reconstructed Text*, (Berkeley, 1963).
Howe, Daniel Walker, "The Cambridge Platonists of Old England and the Cambridge Platonists of New England," *Church History*, vol. 57, (1988), 470–486.
———, *The Making of the American Self: Jonathan Edwards to Abraham Lincoln*, (Cambridge, Mass., 1997).
Hudson, Winthrop S., *Religion in America*, (New York, 1981).
Hurley, Edwin, "Calvin and Hobbes, or, Hobbes as an Orthodox Christian," *Journal of the History of Philosophy*, vol. xxxiv, no. 2, (April 1996), 257–272.
Iggers, G.G., *The Theory and Practices of History*, (New York, 1973).
Jacob, Margaret C., *The Radical Enlightenment*, (London, 1981).
Jamieson, John F., "Jonathan Edwards's Change of Position on Stoddardeanism," *Harvard Theological Review*, vol. 74, (1981), 79–99.
Jenson, Robert W., *America's Theologian: A Recommendation of Jonathan Edwards*, (New York, 1988).
Jinkins, Michael, "'The Being of Beings:' Jonathan Edwards' Understanding of God as Reflected in his Final Treatises," *Scottish Journal of Theology*, vol. 46, no. 2, (June 1993), 161–191.
Johnson, Thomas H., "Jonathan Edwards' Background of Reading," *Colonial Society of Massachusetts Publications*, vol. xxviii, (1931), 193–222.
Keating, Ann-Louise, "The Implication of Edwards' Theory of the Will on Ahab's Pursuit of Moby Dick," *English Literature Notes*, vol. 28, no. 3, (March 1991).
Keats, John, "Letter to Benjamin Bailey (Saturday 22 November 1817)," *The Letters of John Keats*, ed. Robert Gittings, (Oxford, 1970).
Kendall, R.T., *Calvin and English Calvinism to 1649*, (Oxford, 1979).
Kimnach, Wilson H., "Jonathan Edwards' Sermon Mill," *Early American Literature*, vol. 10, (1975–76), 167–176.
———, "The Brazen Trumpet: Jonathan Edwards' Concept of the Sermon," *Critical Essays on Jonathan Edwards*, ed. William J. Scheick, (Boston, 1980).
———, *Three Essays in the Honor of the Publication of David Brainerd*, (New Haven, Conn., 1985).

Knight, Janice, "Learning the Language of God: Jonathan Edwards and the Typology of Nature," *The William and Mary Quarterly,* vol. 48, no. 4, (October 1991), 531–551.
——, *Orthodoxy in Massachusetts,* (Cambridge, Mass., 1994).
Lankevich, George J., ed., *Boston: A Chronological and Documentary History, 1602–1970,* (New York, 1974).
Lesser, M. X., *Jonathan Edwards,* (Boston, 1988).
Levin, David, ed., *The Puritan in the Enlightenment: Franklin and Edwards,* (Chicago 1963).
——, *Jonathan Edwards: A Profile,* (New York, 1969).
——, "Edwards, Franklin and Cotton Mather: A Meditation on Character and Reputation," *Jonathan Edwards and the American Experience,* ed. Harry S. Stout and Nathan O. Hatch, (Boston, 1981).
Lewis, Paul Allen, *Rethinking Emotions and the Moral Life in Light of Thomas Aquinas and Jonathan Edwards,* (Ph.D., Duke University, 1991).
Lowance, Mason I., Jr., "Typology, Millennial Eschatology, and Jonathan Edwards," *Critical Essays on Jonathan Edwards,* ed. William J. Scheick, (Boston, 1980).
——, *The Language of Canaan: Metaphor and Symbol in New England From the Puritans to the Transcendalists,* (Cambridge, Mass., 1980).
Lawrence, D.H., *Studies in Classic American Literature,* (New York, 1923).
Lee, Sang Hyun, *Philosophical Theology of Jonathan Edwards,* (Princeton, 1988).
Lesser, Wayne, "Textuality and the Language of Man," *Critical Essays on Jonathan Edwards,* ed. William J. Scheick, (Boston, 1980).
Loeb, Louis E., *From Descartes to Hume: Continental Metaphysics and the Development of Modern Philosophy,* (Ithaco, 1981).
Lowell, D.O.S., "The Descendents of Jonathan Edwards," *Munsey's Magazine,* vol. 35, (1906), 263–273.
Lucas, Paul R., *Valley of Discord,* (Hanover, N.H., 1976).
Manuel, Frank, *The Eighteenth Century Confronts the Gods,* (Cambridge, Mass., 1959).
Marsden, George M., "Perry Miller's Rehabilitation of the Puritans: A Critique," *Church History,* (March 1970), 91–105.
Marley, Robert, "Robert Boyle In and Out of His Time," *The Eighteenth Century,* vol. 35, no. 3, (Autumn 1994), 280–286.
Martinich, A.P., *The Two Gods of Leviathan,* (Cambridge, 1992).
Maurer, Armand A., "Jonathan Edwards," *The Encyclopedia of Philosophy,* vol. 2, (New York, 1967), 460–462.
May, H.F., *The Enlightenment in America,* (New York, 1976).
McAdoo, H., *The Spirit of Anglicanism,* (London, 1965).
McClymond, Michael J., "God the Measure: Towards an Understanding of Jonathan Edwards' Theocentric Metaphysics," *Scottish Journal of Theology,* vol. 47, no. 1, (Winter 1994), 43–59.
McDermott, Gerald R., "Jonathan Edwards, the City on a Hill, and the Redeemer Nation: A Reappraisal," *Journal of Presbyterian History,* (Spring 1991).
——, *One Holy and Happy Society: The Public Theology of Jonathan Edwards,* (Pennsylvania, 1992).

——, "What Jonathan Edwards Can Teach Us About Politics," *Christianity Today*, vol. 38, no. 8, (July 18 1994), 32–35.

——, "The Deist Connection: Jonathan Edwards and Islam," *Jonathan Edwards's Writings*, ed. Stephen J. Stein, (Bloomington, 1996).

——, *Jonathan Edwards and the Deists*, (Seminar, Vanderbilt Divinity School, April 26, 1997).

McDonald, H.D., *Ideas of Revelation: An Historical Study, 1700–1860*, (London, 1959).

——, *Theories of Revelation: An Historical Study, 1860–1960*, (London 1963).

McLoughlin, William G. Jr., *Modern Revivalism: Charles Grandison Finney to Billy Graham*, (New York, 1974).

Miller, Perry, *Jonathan Edwards*, (New York, 1949).

——, "Edwards, Locke, and the Rhetoric of Sensation," *Critical Essays on Jonathan Edwards*, ed. William J. Scheick, (Boston, 1980).

——, "Jonathan Edwards on the Sense of the Heart," *The Harvard Theological Review*, vol. 41, (1948), 123–145.

——, *The New England Mind: The Seventeenth Century*, (Cambridge, Mass., 1954).

——, *The New England Mind: From Colony to Province*, (Cambridge, Mass., 1953).

——, *Errand Into the Wilderness*, (Cambridge, Mass., 1956).

Mitchell, Louis Joseph, *The Experience of Beauty in the Thought of Jonathan Edwards*, (Ph.D., Harvard University, 1995).

Mondot, Jean, ed., *Immanuel Kant, Qu'est ce Que les Lumières*, (Paris, 1991).

Moore, Robert L., "Justification Without Joy: Psychological Reflections on John Wesley's Childhood and Conversion," *History of Childhood Quarterly*, vol. ii, (1974), 31–52.

Morgan, Campbell Ian, ed., *Meditations, Prayers and Poems by George Matheson*, (London, 1990).

Morimoto, Anri, *Jonathan Edwards and the Catholic Vision of Salvation*, (Pennsylvania, 1995)

Morison, Samuel Elliot, "[Note On] the Library of George Alcock, Medical Student 1676," *Transactions of the Colonial Society of Massachusetts*, vol. xxviii, (1935), 350–357.

——, *The Tercentennial History of Harvard College*, 5 vols., (Boston, Mass., 1935).

——, *Harvard College in the Seventeenth Century*, (Cambridge, Mass., 1936).

Morris, George Perry, "The Human Side of Jonathan Edwards," *Congregationalist and Christian World*, vol. 88, (October 3 1903), 454.

Morris, William Sparks, *The Young Jonathan Edwards: A Reconstruction*, (Ph.D., 1955, Brooklyn, N.Y., 1991).

——, "The Reappraisal of Edwards," *New England Quarterly*, vol. xxx, (1957), 515–525.

Murray, Iain H., *Jonathan Edwards*, (Edinburgh, 1987).

——, *Revival and Revivalism*, (Edinburgh, 1994).

Nagy, Paul J., "The Beloved Community of Jonathan Edwards," *Transactions of the Charles S. Pierce Society*, vol. vii, no. 2 (1971), 93–104.

Neil, Stephen, *A History of Christian Missions*, (London, 1990).

Niebuhr, H. Richard, *The Kingdom of God in America*, (New York, 1937).
Noll, Mark A., "Moses Mather (Old Calvinist) and the Evolution of Edwardeanism," *Church History*, vol. 49, (1980), 273–285.
——, "God At the Centre: Jonathan Edwards on True Virtue," *The Christian Century*, vol. 110, no. 25, (September 8 1993), 854–858.
Norton, Arthur O., "Harvard Text-Books and Reference Books of the Seventeenth Century," *Transactions of the Colonial Society of Massachusetts*, vol. xxviii, (1935), 361–438.
Null, John Ashley, *Thomas Cranmer's Doctrine of Repentance*, (Ph.D., Cambridge University, 1994).
Nuttall, Geoffrey F., *Visible Saints: The Congregational Way*, (Oxford, 1957).
Ong, Walter J., *Ramus, Method and the Decay of Dialogue*, (Cambridge, Mass., 1958).
Opie, John, ed., *Jonathan Edwards and the Enlightenment*, (Lexington Mass., 1969).
Orme, William, *Memoirs of the Life of John Owen*, (London, 1820).
Orr, James, "Jonathan Edwards: His Influence in Scotland," *Congregationalist and Christian World*, vol. 88, (October 3 1903), 467–469.
Oviatt, Edwin, *The Beginnings of Yale, 1701–1726*, (New Haven, Conn., 1916).
Pagden, Anthony, *European Encounters With the New World*, (New Haven, Conn., 1993).
Parker, Kim Ian, "John Locke and the Enlightenment Metanarrative: A Biblical Corrective to a Reasoned World," *Scottish Journal of Theology*, vol. 49, no. 1, (1996), 57–73.
Parkes, Henry Bamford, *Jonathan Edwards: The Fiery Puritan*, (New York, 1930).
Parrington, V.L., *Main Currents of American Thought*, 3 vols., (New York, 1927, 1930).
Peacock, Virginia, *Problems in the Interpretation of Jonathan Edwards' 'True Virtue'*, (Lewiston, 1990).
Penelhum, Terence, *Butler*, (London, 1985).
Pettit, Norman, *The Heart Prepared*, (New Haven, Conn., 1966).
Pfisterer, Karl Dietrich, *The prism of Scripture: Studies on History and Historicity in the Work of Jonathan Edwards*, (Frankfurt, 1975).
Pierce, David C., "Jonathan Edwards and the New Sense of Glory," *The New England Quarterly*, vol. 41, (1968), 82–91.
Plongeron, Bernard, "Recherches sur L'Aufklärung Catholique en Europe Occidentale," *Revue d'Histoire Moderne et Contemporaine*, vol. 16, (1969), 555–605.
Pierson, George W., *The Founding of Yale: The Legend of the Forty Folios*, (New Haven, Conn., 1988).
Pocock, J.G.A., "Enlightenment and Revolution: the Case of English-Speaking North America," *Transactions of the Seventh International Congress on the Enlightenment*, (Oxford, Voltaire Foundation, 1989) 249–261.
Pope, R.G., *The Half Way Covenant*, (Princeton, 1969).
Post, Stephen G., *Christian Love and Self Denial: An Historical and Normative Study of Jonathan Edwards, Samuel Hopkins and American Theological Ethics*, (Lanham, 1987).

Potter, Alfred C., "Catalogue of John Harvard's Library," *Transactions of the Colonial Society of Massachusetts*, vol. xxi, (1919), 190–230.
Prince, Michael B., "Hume and the End of Religious Dialogue," *Eighteenth Century Studies*, vol. 25, no. 3, (Spring 1992), 283–308.
Proudfoot, Wayne, "From Theology to a Science of Religions: Jonathan Edwards and William James on Religious Affections," *Harvard Theological Review*, vol. 82, no. 2, (April 1989), 149–168.
Randall, John Herman Jr., *The Making of the Modern Mind*, (Cambridge, Mass., 1926).
———, *The Career of Philosophy*, 3 vols., (New York, 1964, 1965, 1977).
Raposa, Michael L., "Jonathan Edwards Twelfth Sign," *International Philosophical Quarterly*, vol. 33, no. 2, (June 1993), 153–162.
Redwood, J., *Reason, Ridicule and Religion: the Age of Enlightenment in England, 1660–1750*, (London, 1976).
Reedy, Gerard S.J., *The Bible and Reason: Anglicans and Scripture in Late Seventeenth Century England*, (Philadelphia, 1985).
Reventlow, Henning Graf, *The Authority of the Bible and the Rise of the Modern World*, (London, 1984).
Riley, Woodbridge I., *American Philosophy: The Early Schools*, (New York, 1958).
Rivers, Isabel, *Reason, Grace and Sentiment: A Study of the Language of Religion and Ethics in England, 1600–1780. Volume 1: Whichcote to Wesley*, (New York, 1992).
Ross, Sydney, "Scientist: The Story of a Word," *Annals of Science*, vol. 18, (1962), 65–86.
Rupp, George, "The Idealism of Jonathan Edwards," *Harvard Theological Review*, vol. 62, (April 1969), 209–226.
Schafer, Thomas A., "Jonathan Edwards's Conception of the Church," *Church History*, vol. 24, (1950), 51–66.
Schafer, Simon, "Natural Philosophy," *The Ferment of Knowledge*, ed. G.S Rousseau and Roy Porter, (Cambridge, 1980).
Scheick, William J., ed., *The Writings of Jonathan Edwards: Theme, Motif, and Style*, (Texas, 1975).
———, *Critical Essays on Jonathan Edwards*, (Boston, 1980).
———, ed., *Two Mather Biographies*, (New York, 1989)
Scott, Donald M., *From Office to Profession: The New England Ministry 1750–1850*, (Chapel, Philadelphia, 1978).
Sell, Alan, *The Great Debate: Calvinism, Arminianism and Salvation*, (Worthing, 1982).
Shapiro, Gary, "The Man of Letters and the Author of Nature: Hume on Philosophical Discourse," *Eighteenth Century*, vol. 26, (1985), 115–137.
Shipton, Clifford K., *Sibley's Harvard Graduates*, (Cambridge, Mass., 1942)
Shea, Daniel B., "Jonathan Edwards: The First 200 years," *Journal of American Studies*, vol. 14, (1980), 181–197.
———, "The Art and Instruction of Jonathan Edwards," *Critical Essays on Jonathan Edwards*, ed. William J. Scheick, (Boston, 1980).

Shuffleton, Frank, *Thomas Hooker 1586–1647*, (Princeton, 1977).
Simpson, Harold P., *Jonathan Edwards: Theologian of the Heart*, (Grand Rapids, 1974).
Smalley, Beryl, *The Study of the Bible in the Middle Ages*, (Oxford, 1941).
Smith, Claude A., "Jonathan Edwards and the 'Way of Ideas,'" *Harvard Theological Review*, vol. lix, (1966), 153–173.
Smith, John E., *Jonathan Edwards, Puritan Preacher and Philosopher*, (London, 1992).
———, *Jonathan Edwards*, (London, 1992).
———, "Jonathan Edwards as Philosophical Theologian," *The Review of Metaphysics*, vol. xxx, no. 2, (1976), 306–324.
———, "Jonathan Edwards: Piety and Practice in the American Character," *The Journal of Religion*, vol. liv, no. 2, (1974), 166–180.
Spiegel, James S., "The Theological Orthodoxy of Berkeley's Immaterialism," *Faith and Philosophy*, vol. 13, no. 2, (April 1996), 216–235.
Spellman, W.M., *The Latitudinarians of the Church of England, 1660–1700*, (Athens, Ga., 1993).
Stead, Christopher, *Divine Substance*, (Oxford, 1977).
Steele, Richard B., *Gracious Affection and True Virtue According to John Wesley and Jonathan Edwards*, (London, 1994).
Stein, Spehen J., "Jonathan Edwards and the Rainbow: Biblical Exegesis and Poetic Imagination," *New England Quarterly*, vol. 47, (1974), 440–456.
———, "The Quest for the Spiritual Sense: The Biblical Hermeneutics of Jonathan Edwards," *Harvard Theological Review*, vol. 70, (1977), 99–113.
———, "A Notebook on the Apocalypse by Jonathan Edwards," (Ph.D., 1970), reprinted, *Critical Essays on Jonathan Edwards*, ed. William J. Scheick, (Boston, 1980).
———, "Review of R.C. De Prospo, 'Theism in the discourse of Jonathan Edwards,'" *Journal of American History*, vol. 73, (1986), 454.
———, "Jonathan Edwards," *Encyclopedia of Religion*, vol. 5, (New York, 1987), 32–36.
———, ed., *Jonathan Edwards's Writings*, (Bloomington, 1996).
Stephen, Leslie, "Jonathan Edwards," *Critical Essays on Jonathan Edwards*, ed. William J. Scheick, (Boston, 1980).
———, *History of English Thought in Eighteenth Century*, (Bristol, 1991).
Stoever, William K.B., *A Faire and Easie Way to Heaven*, (Middletown, Conn., 1978)
Stout, Harry S., Kenneth Minkema, John E. Smith, eds., *A Jonathan Edwards Reader*, (New Haven, Conn., 1995).
———, *Benjamin Franklin, Jonathan Edwards and the Representation of American Culture*, (New York, 1993)
———, *The New England Soul: Preaching and Religious Culture in Colonial New England*, (New York, 1986).
———, and Nathan O. Hatch, *Jonathan Edwards and the American Experience*, (Boston, 1981).
———, "Religion, Communication and the Career of George Whitefield," *Communication and Change in American Religious History*, (Grand Rapids, 1993).

———, *The Divine Dramatist: George Whitefield and the Rise of Modern Evangelicalism*, (Grand Rapids, 1991).
Stripes Watts, Emily, *Jonathan Edwards and the Cambridge Platonists*, (Ph.D., University of Illinois, 1963).
———, "The Neoplatonic Basis of Jonathan Edwards' 'True Virtue,'" *Early American Literature*, vol. 10, (1975-1976), 179-189.
Stuart, Robert Lee, " 'Mr Stoddard's Way:' Church & Sacraments in Northampton," *American Quarterly*, vol. 24, (1972), 243-253.
Sullivan, R.E., *John Toland and the Deist Controversy: A Study in Adaptations*, (Cambridge, Mass., 1982).
Sweeney, Kevin, *River Gods and Related Minor Deities*, (Ph.D., Yale University, 1986).
Sweet, William Warren, *Religion in Colonial America*, (New York, 1947).
Tanselle, G.T., "Some Statistics on American Printing, 1764-1783," *The Press and the American Revolution*, B. Bailyn and W.B. Herch, eds., (Boston, 1981), 315-364.
Tomas, Vincent, "The modernity of Jonathan Edwards," *New England Quarterly*, vol. 25, (1952), 60-84.
Tracy, P.J., *Jonathan Edwards, Pastor*, (New York, 1980).
Trevor-Roper, Hugh, *Religion, the Reformation and Social Change*, (London, 1967).
Turner, James, *Without God Without Creed: The Origins of Unbelief in America*, (Baltimore, 1985).
Vailati, Ezio, "Leibniz and Clarke on Miracles," *Journal of the History of Philosophy*, vol. xxxiii, no. 4, (October 1995), 543-562.
Valeri, Mark, "The New Divinity and the Revolution," *William and Mary Quarterly*, 3rd ser., vol. xlvi, (October 1989), 741-769.
———, "The Economic Thought of Jonathan Edwards," *Church History*, vol. 60, no. 1, (March 1991), 37-54.
Van Doren, *Jonathan Edwards and Benjamin Franklin*, (New York, 1920).
Venturini, Franco, *Utopia and Reform in the Enlightenment*, (Cambridge, 1971).
Veto, Miklos, *Pensée de Jonathan Edwards Avec Une Concordance*, (Les Éditions du Cerf, 1987).
Wade, Ira O., *The Intellectual Origins of the French Enlightenment*, (Princeton, 1971).
Wainwright, William J., "Jonathan Edwards and the Sense of the Heart," *Faith and Philosophy*, vol. 7, no. 1, (January 1990), 43-63.
———, *Reason and the Heart: A Prolegomenon to a Critique of Passional Reason*, (Ithaca, 1995).
Walker, Williston, *Creeds and Platforms of Congregationalism*, (New York, 1893).
Walters, Kerry S., *The America Deists: Voices of Reason and Dissent in the Early Republic*, (Kansas, 1992).
Warch, Richard, *School of the Prophets: Yale College, 1701-1740*, (New Haven, Conn., 1973).
Ward, W.R., *The Protestant Evangelical Awakening*, (Cambridge, 1992).
Warfield, B.B., "Edwards and New England Theology," *Encyclopedia of Religion and Ethics*, ed., James Hastings, (Edinburgh, 1912).

——, and John Murray, *The Imputation of Adam's Sin*, (Grand Rapids, 1959), 54.
Watts, Emily Stipes, *Jonathan Edwards and the Cambridge Platonists*, (Ph.D., Illinois University, 1963).
——, "The Neoplatonic Basis of Jonathan Edwards 'True Virtue,'" *Early American Literature*, vol. 10, (1975–76), 179–189.
Webber, Donald, "The Figure of Jonathan Edwards," *American Quarterly*, vol. 35, (1983), 157–60.
Westfall, Richard S., *Science and Religion in Seventeenth Century England*, (New Haven, Conn., 1958).
Westra, Helen Porter, "Jonathan Edwards and What Reason Teaches," *Journal of Evangelical Theological Society*, vol. 34, (1991), 495–503.
Westron, Helen, *Ministers Task and Calling in the Sermons of Jonathan Edwards*, (Lewiston, 1986).
White, Morton, *Science and Sentiment in America: Philosophical Thought from Jonathan Edwards to John Dewey*, (New York, 1972).
Whittemore, Robert E., "Jonathan Edwards and the Theology of the Sixth Way," *Church History*, vol. 35, (March, 1966), 60–75.
Wieand, Jeffrey, "Pamphilus in Hume's Dialogues," *Journal of Religion*, vol. 65, (1986), 33–45.
Williams, David R., *Wilderness Lost: The Religious Origins of the American Mind*, (New Jersey, 1987).
Wilson, David Schofield, "The Flying Spider," *Critical Essays on Jonathan Edwards*, ed. William J. Scheick, (Boston, 1980).
Wilson, John F., "Jonathan Edwards as Historian," *Church History*, vol. 46, (1977), 5–18.
Winship, Michael P., "Prodigies, Puritanism, and the Perils of Natural Philosophy: The Example of Cotton Mather," *William and Mary Quarterly*, vol. li, no. 1, (January 1994), 92–105.
Winslow, Ola Elizabeth, *Jonathan Edwards*, (New York, 1940).
——, "Foreword," *Jonathan Edwards: Basic Writings*, (New York, 1966), vii-xxviii.
Witherspoon, John, "An Account of the Life of John Witherspoon," *The Works of John Witherspoon*, vol. 1, (Edinburgh, 1804), 17.
Wolf, A., *A History of Science, Technology, and Philosophy in the Sixteenth and Seventeenth Centuries*, (London, 1950).
Yale University, The 250th Anniversary of: Speeches and Documents of the Year of Celebration, 1951–2, (New Haven, Conn., 1952).
Yolton, John W., ed., *The Blackwell Companion to the Enlightenment*, (Oxford, 1995).
Yong, Peter Y. de, *The Covenant Idea in New England Theology*, (Grand Rapids, 1945).
Zemsky, Robert, *Merchants, Farmers, and River Gods*, (Boston, 1971).

Modern Theology and Philosophy

Abbott, W.M., ed., *The Documents of Vatican II*, (London, 1966).
Abhihshiktananda, *Hindu-Christian Meeting Point*, (Delhi, 1976).

Bibliography

Abraham, William J., *The Divine Inspiration of Holy Scripture*, (Oxford, 1981).
Allison, Joel, "Recent Empirical Studies Religious Conversion Experiences," *Pastoral Psychology*, vol. xvii, (1966), 21–34.
Alston, William, "Religious Experience and Religious Belief," *Nous*, vol. xvi, (1982).
——, *Perceiving God: The Epistemology of Religious Experience*, (London, 1991).
Ayer, A.J., *Language, Truth, and Logic*, (London, 1946).
——, *The Problem of Knowledge*, (Harmondsworth, 1966).
——, *The Central Questions of Philosophy* (London, 1973).
Barr, J.E., *The Bible in the Modern World*, (London, 1973).
Barth, Karl, *The Word of God and the Word of Man*, (London, 1928).
——, *Church Dogmatics*, 4, (Edinburgh, 1956–8).
——, and E. Brunner, *Natural Theology*, (London, 1964).
——, *Protestant Theology in the Nineteenth Century*, (London, 1972).
Beardsworth, Timothy, *A Sense of Presence*, (The Religious Experience Research Unit, Manchester College, Oxford, 1977).
Benjamin, Andrew, ed., *The Lyotard Reader*, (Cambridge, Mass., 1989).
Bennington, G., *Lyotard, Writing the Event*, (Manchester, 1988).
Berkouwer, G.C., *A Half Century of Theology*, (Grand Rapids, 1977).
Beversluis, John, "Reforming the 'Reformed' Objection to Natural Theology," *Faith and Philosophy*, vol. 12, m, (April 1995), 189–206.
Bowker, John, *The Sense of God*, (Oxford, 1973).
Bradley, F.H., *Essays on Truth and Reality*, (Oxford, 1914).
Blanshard, Brand, *Reason and Belief*, (London, 1974).
Bruce, Steve, "The Persistence of Religion: Conservative Protestantism in the United Kingdom," *Sociological Review*, vol. 31, (1983), 453–470.
Bultmann, R., *Theology of the New Testament*, vols. 1–2, (London, 1952–55).
Camus, Albert, *L'Etranger*, (London, 1958).
——, *The Essential Writings*, ed. Robert E. Meagher, (New York, 1979).
Casanova, José, *Public Religions in the Modern World*, (Chicago, 1994).
Chevreau, Guy, *Catch the Fire*, (London, 1994).
Chisholm, Roderick M., *Theory of Knowledge*, (London, 1989).
Clifford, W.K., "The Ethics of Belief," *Lectures and Essays*, (London, 1879).
Cupitt, Don, *The Sea of Faith*, (London, 1984).
——, *The Time Being*, (London, 1992).
Davies, Brian, *Introduction to the Philosophy of Religion*, (Oxford, 1993).
Derrida, Jacques, *Dissemination*, (London, 1981).
Donovan, Peter, *Interpreting Religious Experience*, (London, 1979).
Dumett, Michael, *Truth and Other Enigmas*, (London, 1978)
Einstein, Albert, "The Meaning of Relativity," *Stafford Little Lectures 1921*, (Princeton, 1974).
Eribon, Didier, *Michel Foucault*, (London, 1993).
Epp, Eldon Jay, *The New Testament and its Modern Interpreters*, (Philadelphia, 1990).
Feldman, Richard, "An Alleged Defect in Gettier Counter-Examples," *The Australasian Journal of Philosophy*, vol. 52, no. 1, (1974), 68–69.

Flew, Antony, *The Presumption of Atheism*, (London, 1976).
Ford, David F., ed., *Essentials of Christian Community: Essays for Daniel W. Hardy*, (Edinburgh, 1996).
Foucault, Michel, *Mental Illness and Psychology*, (New York, 1976).
——, *Power/Knowledge: Selected Interviews and Other Writings, 1972–1977*, ed., Colin Gordon, (Brighton, 1980).
——, *This is Not a Pipe*, (London, 1983).
——, *The Foucault Reader*, ed. Paul Rabinow, (London, 1984).
——, *The Archaeology of Knowledge*, (London, 1994).
Freud, S., *Totem and Taboo*, (Harmondsworth, 1940).
——, *Early Psychoanalytic Writings*, ed. Philip Rieff, (New York, 1963).
Gettier, Edmund, "Is Justified True Belief Knowledge?" *Analysis*, vol. 23, no. 6, (1963), 121–123.
Hammond, Philip E., ed., *The Sacred in a Secular Age*, (Los Angeles, 1985).
Hardy, Daniel W., and Ford, David, *Jubilate: Theology in Praise*, (London, 1984).
——, ed., *The Weight of Glory*, (Edinburgh, 1991).
——, *God's Way With the World: Thinking and Practising Christian Faith*, (Edinburgh, 1996).
Hawking, Stephen, *A Brief History of Time*, (London, 1988).
Hebblethwaite, Brian, *Evil, Suffering and Religion*, (London, 1976).
——, *The Problems of Theology*, (Cambridge, 1980).
——, *The Christian Hope: An Introduction to Christian Doctrine*, (Basingstoke, 1984).
——, "Religious Truth and Dialogue," *The Scottish Journal of Religious Studies*, (Spring, 1984), 3–17.
——, "On Experience of God," *Preaching Through the Year*, (Oxford, 1985).
——, *Ethics and Religion in a Pluralistic Age*, (Edinburgh, 1997).
Hegel, Georg Wilhelm Friedrich, *Hegel: The Essential Writings*, ed., Frederick G. Weiss, (New York, 1974).
Hick, John, *An Interpretation of Religion*, (Basingstoke, 1989).
——, *Philosophy of Religion* (New Jersey, 1990).
——, *A John Hick Reader*, ed., Paul Badham, (London, 1990).
Hodge, Charles, *Systematic Theology*, 3 vols., (Grand Rapids, 1952).
Hoitenga, Dewey Jr., *Faith and Reason From Plato to Plantinga: An Introduction To Reformed Epistemology*, (New York, 1991).
Huxley, T.H., *Man's Place in Nature*, (London, 1927).
James, William, *The Will to Believe*, (London, 1897).
——, *Pragmatism, a New Name for Some Old Ways of Thinking*, (London, 1907).
——, "The Varieties of Religious Experience," *Works*, vol. 13, (Cambridge, Mass., 1985).
Katz, Stephen "Language, Epistemology and Mysticism," *Mysticism and Philosophical Analysis*, ed. Katz, (London, 1978).
Kelly, Dean, *Why the Conservative Churches Are Growing?* (New York, 1977).
Kenny, Anthony, *Action, Emotion and Will*, (Bristol, 1994).
Kierkegaard, Søren, "Concluding Unscientific Postscript," *Classics of Protestantism*, ed. Vergilia Fern, (London 1959).

———, *The Sickness Unto Death*, (London, 1989).
Kuhn, Thomas, *The Structure of Scientific Revolutions*, (Chicago, 1962).
Kvanig, John V., "Review of William Alston, Perceiving God: The Epistemology of Religious Experience, (London, 1991)," *Faith and Philosophy*, (April 1994), 311–321.
Losee, John, *A Historical Introduction to the Philosophy of Science*, (Oxford, 1993).
Lyon, D., "Secularization: The Fate of Faith in Modern Society?" *Them*, vol. 10, no. 1, (1984), 14–22.
Lyotard, Francois, *The Postmodern Condition: A Report on Knowledge*, (Manchester, 1984).
Martin, D., *A General Theory of Secularization*, (Oxford, 1978).
Marx, Karl, and F. Engels, *Capital*, (Moscow, 1954).
———, *The Communist Manifesto*, (London, 1967).
Moltmann, J., *Theology of Hope*, (London, 1967).
———, *Experiences of God*, (London, 1980).
———, *God in Creation: an Ecological Doctrine of Creation*, (London, 1985).
———, *The Way of Jesus Christ*, (London, 1990).
Morris, Thomas V., *God and the Philosophers*, (New York, 1994).
Moser, Paul K., and Arnold Vander Nat, *Human Knowledge: Classical and Contemporary Approaches*, (Oxford, 1987).
Nietzsche, Friedrich, *The Use and Abuse of History*, (New York, 1957).
———, *Thus Spoke Zarathustra*, (Harmondsworth, 1968).
———, *Beyond Good and Evil*, (Harmondsworth, 1977).
Plantinga, Alvin, *The Ontological Argument, From St. Anselm to Contemporary Philosophers*, (New York, 1965).
———, "Is Belief in God Properly Basic?", *Nous*, xv, (1981), 41–51.
———, and Nicholas Wolterstorff, *Faith and Rationality*, (London, 1983).
———, *Christian Theism and the Problems of Philosophy*, ed. Michael D. Beaty, (Notre Dame, 1990).
———, *Warrant: The Current Debate*, (Oxford, 1993)
———, *Warrant and Proper Function* (Oxford, 1993).
Popper, Karl, *The Logic of Scientific Discovery*, (New York, 1959).
Powell, Mark Allan, ed., *The Bible and Modern Literary Criticism: A Critical Assessment and Annotated Bibliography*, (London 1992).
Rahner, K., *Foundations of Christian Faith: An Introduction to the Idea of Christianity*, (London, 1978).
Rorty, Richard, *Philosophy and the Mirror of Nature*, (Oxford, 1980).
Rothberg, Donald, "Contemporary Epistemology and the Study of Mysticism," ed. Robert K.C. Forman *The Problem of Pure Consciousness: Mysticism and Philosophy*, (New York, 1990), 163–210.
Rumscheidt, Martin, H., ed., *Revelation and Theology: An Analysis of the Barth-Harnack Correspondence of 1923*, (Cambridge, 1972).
Russell, Bertrand, *Free Thought and Official Propaganda*, (London, 1922).
———, *Why I am not a Christian*, (New York, 1957).
———, *The Problems of Philosophy*, (London, 1982).

———, *A History of Western Philosophy*, (London, 1989).
Salzman, Leon, "The Psychology of Religious and Ideological Conversion," *Psychiatry*, vol. xvi, (1953).
Sanneh, Lamin, *Encountering the West: Christianity and the Global Cultural Process*, (London, 1993).
Sartre, Jean-Paul, *The Age of Reason*, (New York, 1968).
Sellars, Wilfrid, "Empiricism and the Philosophy of the Mind," *Science, Perception and Reality*, (London 1963).
Spurgeon, Charles H., "The Warrant of Faith," *Metropolitan Tabernacle Pulpit*, Sermon 531, (1863).
Tillich, Paul, *Systematic Theology*, vols. 1–2, (London, 1951, 1957).
Warfield, B.B., *Biblical Doctrines*, (Edinburgh, 1988).
Weber, Max, *The Protestant Ethic and the Spirit of Capitalism*, (London, 1930).
———, *Economy and Society*, (New York, 1968).
Wisdom, John, "Gods," reprinted in *Logic and Language*, ed. Antony Flew (Oxford, 1951).
Wolterstorff, Nicholas, *Reason Within the Bounds of Religion*, (Grand Rapids, 1976).
———, ed., *Rationality in the Calvinian Tradition*, (London, 1983).
———, "The Migration of the Theistic Arguments: From Natural Theology to Evidentialist Apologetics," *Rationality, Religious Belief, and Moral Commitment*, ed. Robert Audi and William J. Wainwright, (Ithaca, 1986), 38–81.
———, *Rationality and Relativity: The Quest for Objective Knowledge*, (Avebury, 1989).
———, *Divine Discourse: Philosophical Reflections on the Claim that God Speaks*, (Cambridge, 1995).
———, *John Locke and the Ethics of Belief*, (Cambridge, 1996).
Yung, C.G., *Modern Man in Search of a Soul*, (New York, 1933).

Popular Articles Relating to Edwards

Prophecy Today, vol. 9, no. 6, "Why Revivals Don't Last," (November/December 1993).
Church of England Newspaper, "Testing Toronto," (July 8th 1994).
Evangelical Times, John Legg, "Jonathan Edwards on Revival," (September 1994).
Evangelicals Now, Gary Benfold, "Jonathan Edwards and Toronto," (October 1994).
———, Roy Clements, "Don't Tread on My Toron-toes," (June 1995).
Methodist Recorder, "Testing the Spirit," (November 10 1994).
Christianity Today, Richard T. Lovelace, "The Surprising Works of God: Jonathan Edwards on Revival, Then and Now," (September 11 1995).

Reference Works

Emerson, Everett H., "Jonathan Edwards," *Fifteen American Authors before 1900: Bibliographical Essays on Research and Criticism*, ed. Robert A. Rees and Earl N. Harbert, (Madison, 1971), 169–184.

Faust, Clarence H. and Thomas H. Johnson, *Jonathan Edwards: Representative Selections*, (New York, 1962).
Fiering, Norman, "Bibliographical Note," *Jonathan Edwards' Moral Thought and its British Context*, (Williamsburg, Va., 1981), 372–379.
Johnson, Thomas H., *The Printed Writings of Jonathan Edwards 1703–1758: A Bibliography*, (New Jersey, 1940).
Lesser, M.X., *Jonathan Edwards: A Reference Guide*, (Boston, Mass., 1981).
Manspeaker, Nancy, *Jonathan Edwards: Bibliographical Synopses*, (New York, 1981).
Sliwoski, Richard S., "PhDs on Jonathan Edwards," *Early American Literature*, vol. 14, (1979–80).
Trent, William Peterfield, ed., *The Cambridge History of American Literature*, vol. 1, (New York, 1917), 432–438.

Index

The Age of Reason. *See* Enlightenment
Alston, William: arguments for existence of God, 74–75; Kvanig's criticism of, 93n174; mystical perception, 74–75, 93n168, 93n170; "Perceiving God: The Epistemology of Religious Belief," 74–75
American Pragmatism, 72
Antinomianism, 84n77, 87n107
Aristotle, 120, 139n3, 156
Arminianism: backdrop to Great Awakening, 167n22; concept of salvation, 17–20, 43n4, 51n130; Edwards' disagreement with, 22, 32–35, 38, 42n1, 43n4, 46n52; Enlightenment influence, 37–38; social church, 37; *See also* Deism; *See also* Predestination; *See also* Stoddard
Atheism, 15n42, 126, 144n60; Edwards' argument against, 157n183, 128–129; *See also* The Bible, Psalm 14:1
awakening: genuine spiritual, 18, 21, 23, 27–28, 42, 58n189, 82n63, 84n77, 153n146, 162, 163n3; *See also* Brainerd; *See also* George Whitefield; *See also* Great Awakening

Awakening of 1735, 21–22, 44n26, 46n59

baptism, 34–35, 38, 54n149
Barth, Karl: historical Jesus, 153n149; rational arguments for Christianity, 153n153; view of the Enlightenment, 11n5, 12n26, 15n44
Baxter, Richard, 39, 55n170
Beauty: spiritual understanding, 61–63, 71–72, 74–7105, 81n47, 134, 159; Edwards' discussions of, 79n33, 81n47, 103–106, 89n132, 160; Enlightenment influence, 105, 160; objectivity of, 104–6; of Christ, 58, 62, 106; of God, 63, 71–72, 74, 75, 103–104, 108; of humanity, 89n132; of nature, 82n55, 106; subjectivity of, 105–106
Berkeley, George: comparison to Edwards, 96–97, 111n24, 111n25; Enlightenment, 3, 11n12; immaterialism, 94; opposition to Deism, 144n60; philosophy of true existence, 96–97, 111n23, 114n79, 115n103
The Bible, select passages listed in canonical order: Genesis 1:27, 31, 50n119; Genesis 3:17–19, 149n105;

Genesis 3:24, 50n122, 149n105; Genesis 19:14, 25; Genesis 32:26–29, 27; Exodus 16:20, 42; Psalm 14:1, 56n183, 127–129, 148n88; Psalm 32:3–4, 77n20; Psalm 55:12–14, 83n65; Psalm 139:7–10, 117n137; Isaiah 1:18–20, 131; Matthew 5:8, 124, 137, 143n55; Matthew 13 (Sower series), 23–26; Luke 11:13, 28; Luke 19:42, 21; Luke 24:32, 81n49; John 1:9, 65, 82n62; Acts 16, 77n20; Romans 1:20, 127–128, 147n86; Romans 2:29, 86n92; Romans 9:3, 87n119; Romans 10, 42; 1 Corinthians 1:20, 77n23; 1 Corinthians 6:11, 63, 80n42; 1 Corinthians 13:8–13, 165; Ephesians 3:10, 151n133; Ephesians 4:29, 28, 48n89; James 2:19, 81n47; 2 Peter 1:16, 135–136, 151n130; 2 Peter 1:19 136–7, 150n120; 1 John 4:16, 87n118; 1 John 5:1–4, 37, 144n60; 1 John 5:2, 37; Jude 19, 133, 54n150, 150n120; Revelation 13:18, 110n17; Revelation 17:14, 30; 2 Thessalonians 2:10, 37

Brainerd, David: missions, 41–42, 57n185, 167n24

Bushman, Richard L., 18, 79n30, 87n118, 88n132, 89

Calvinism: *See* Reformed Theology

Cambridge Platonists, 3, 12n24, 49n95, 94–95, 109n12

Channing, William Ellery, 98, 112n50

Chauncy, Charles: early work, 39; education, 39; Great Awakening, 40, 44n25; liberalism, 40, 122; ministry of, 39; rationalism of, 122; salvation theology, 40–41, 56n177, 56n178; similarity to Baxter, 55n170; slander of Davenport, 56n173; theological differences from Edwards, 14n39, 39–40, 44n25, 55n164, 56n178, 56n179, 122; Unitarianism, 39–40; *See also* Edwards; *See also* Separatists

Christ, Jesus: beauty of, 62; centrality of, 41–2; character of in the Christian, 71; come to, 33; crucified, 41–42; experience of, 134–5; faith in, 36, 38; heart for, 69; Jews believed on, 32; knowledge of, 69; love of, 24; mediation of, 36; presence during conversion, 21–24, 30, 39; "A Sinner is not Justified . . . Except Through the Righteousness of Christ. . . ," 38; union with, 29; *See also* The Bible; *See also* Sermons; *See also* Trinity

Clarke, Samuel, 107, 108n3, 144n63, 153n148; *See also* Leibniz

Communion: Controversy, 31–38, 46n60, 51n134, 52n135, 54n144, 54n150; Edwards' position, 31–38, 52n135, 54n144, 54n150

Copernicus, 107

Covenant Theology, 17, 29–39, 43n6, 49n107, 50n113, 51n134, 151n129

D'Alembert, 119

Davenport, James, 39–40, 56n173

Deism, 19, 37–38; *See also* Deists; *See also* Enlightenment

Deists, 8, 37, 124, 144n60, 144n62, 144n63, 167n22

Edwards, Jonathan: concept of existence, 97–102; *See also* epistemology; concept of 'visible saints,' 53n138; evangelist, 19; gospel message, 29, 38; Lockean philosophy, 11n16; prayer, 48n87; principle of Biblical interpretation, 77n20; works: *The Distinguishing Marks*, 65–68, 76n16, 77n20, 78n25, 83n68, 84n71, 84n74, 86n94, 121, 141n19, 165n17; —, *A Divine and Supernatural Light . . .* , 43n5, 50n114, 65, 75, 134; —, *The End for which God Created the World*, 56n182;—, *A Faithful Narrative of the Surprising Work of God*, 167n23;—, *Freedom of the Will*, 56n182, 46n38, 95, 109n6, 109n10, 126–127;—, *God Glorified in Man's Dependence*, 29, 78n23;—, *A History and the Work of Redemption*, 20, 45n35, 56n182;—, *An Humble Inquiry*, 53n138;—, *Justification by Faith Alone*, 22, 43n5, 49n101;—, *The Nature of True Virtue*, 46n43, 56n182, 79n30, 85n89, 109n12, 148n95;—, "Observations Concerning Faith," 36;—, *Original Sin*, 56n182;—, *The Religious Affections*, 46n43, 59, 65–70, 76n16, 78n25, 79n35, 80n43, 81n52, 82n59, 83n69, 84n70, 85n77, 85n87, 85n89, 86n96, 87n104, 87n106, 87n115, 87n116, 87n119, 88n120, 88n130, 165n17;—, *Righteousness of Christ Obtained by Faith*, 37–38;—, *A Sinner is not Justified in the Sight of God Except . . . Righteousness of Christ . . .* 37;—, *Sower Series*, 23–26; See also Covenant Theology; See also epistemology; See also Great Awakening; See also reason; See also Reformed Theology; See also Revival; See also Theology

Eliot, John: Ministry to Native Americans, 57n186

Enlightenment, 1–9, 17, 120–121; American, 100; Bacon, Francis, 4, 139n3, 154n154; Bayle, Pierre, 4; concept of nature, 139n1; debate of true understanding of God, Descartes, Rene, 4, 72, 91n151, 91n152, 156, 158; Edwards' against, 38–39; Gassendi, Pierre, 4; Hobbes, Thomas, 4, 8, 93, 95, 100–102, 109n6, 156;legacy of rational enquiry, 7; Leibniz, Gottfried Wilhelm von, 4–5, 107, 108n3, 153n148; "light," 5, 140n6; Locke, 2–4, 6–7; See also Lockean philosophy; Malebranche, Nicholas, 3–4, 12n24, 109n12, 130, 148n94, 148n95; Montaigne, Michel de, 4; Newton, Isaac, 2, 4, 6–7, 95–96, 100,-101, 107, 109n11, 116n106, 119, 139n1, 140n6, 156; Edwards' citation of, 110n17, 116n106;—, Newtonian physics, 95–96, 100–101, 107, 110, 116n106, 156; treatment of the Bible, 120–121; use of relativism, 113n73; Voltaire, Francois-Marie Arouet, 113n73; See also Jonathan Edwards; See also epistemology; See also reason

epistemology: centrality in Enlightenment, 8, 72–73, 90n146, 118n138, 157–160; contemporary, 72, 92n155; of Edwards, vii, 22, 102, 106–108, 115n97, 156–160; of light, 120; of reality, 97–98, 108; of satanic influence, 24; of salvation, 40–41; of signs, 84n76; of spiritual experience, 8, 22, 60, 64, 72; "Perceiving God: The Epistemology of Religious Belief," 74–75, 93n168, 93n169, 93n170; reformed, 153n153, 156–160; response to Enlightenment, 8, 157; See also Foundationalism; See also William Alston

evangelical: movement in contemporary West, 165n17; discussion of revival, 19–20; modern discomfort with preparation theology, 33; understanding of gospel, 17

evangelism, 19–20, 31, 41, 52n134; See also evangelist

Evangelist, Edwards the, 17

Existentialism, 9n2, 164n14

faith: Edwards' concept of, 30–39, 49n101, 50n101, 123; See also Edwards;—, See also justification by faith; factual foundation of Christian faith, 123

fall of man, 31, 128, 130–131, 137, 139, 149n105
fear: of God, 87n118, 129, 152n146; of hell, 25–26, 77n20, 82n63, 172
Finney, Charles, G., 20, 26
Foucault, Michel, 10n4, 154n156
Foundationalism, 90n145
France: Enlightenment in, 4, 6, 140n5
Francke, August, 4
free will, see Edwards, *Freedom of the Will*
Freudian: analysis of revival, 18–19
Frothingham, Ebenezer, 54n150, 56n180
fundamentalism, 156

Gassendi, Pierre, 4
Gaunilo, 145n70
Gaustad, Edwin S., 18
Gerstner, John H., 31, 51n127, 51n132, 145n71
Gettier, Edmund, 73, 92n156; *See also* epistemology
gifts: of the Spirit, 38, 70, 165n17; revival as, 48n84
glory: of God, 21, 143n55; of Christ, 134–5
godliness, 8, 38, 48n89, 54n149, 68, 87–8n119
gospel, centrality of Christ to, 41–2; Edwards' propagation of, 17, 29ff; four Gospels reconciled by Edwards, 123; "good news," 165n17; heart of, 17; truth of, 134–5, 138; Whitefield's dramatizing of, 18–19; *See also* evangelism
grace: covenant of, 30, 34, 38; distinct from miracles, 87n116; of God, 17, 24; in holiness, 32; newness of life, 87n115; in prayer, 27; Puritan view of, 46n38; signs of, 69; spiritual effect of, 67; in spiritual 'preparation,' 30–33
Great Awakening: 22, 23, 27–28, 40, 42, 134, 162; Edwards' disillusionment with, 21, 78n25; Edwards' interpretation of, *see also* Jonathan Edwards; as international revival, 19; controversies associated with, 40, 78n25, 83n67, 84n70; psychological makeup of, 19; socioeconomic significance of, 18–19; theological interpretations of, 18–19; *See also* Northampton; *See also* Second Great Awakening
Gulliver's Travels. *See* Jonathan Swift

Hume, David, 72, 107
Half-Way Covenant, 33, 38, 52
Hall, David, 34
Harvard College, 8, 39, 140n8
Hebblethwaite, Brian, 73–74, 166n18
Heimert, Alan, 18
hell, reality of, 25–26
hell-fire preaching, Edwards' reputation for, 3, 104
Hick, John, 74
Hobbes, Thomas: See Enlightenment
holiness, 31–32, 65, 130; and beauty, 104, 106; and modern scholarship, 19; as consequence of revival, 21; Edwards' conception of, 67–72; of God, 101
Hume, David, 156
humility, 59, 62, 71, 89

Islam, 125, 136

Jacob: wrestling, 27
James, William, 19, 69, 91n153, 153
Jubilee, year of, 21
judgement, of God, 63, 74, 81n47, 104, 134, 138
Jung, C.G., 19
justification by faith, 17, 22, 29, 36, 38; *See also* Edwards; *See also* Reformed Theology

Kant, Immanuel, 5, 72, 111n23, 115n91, 115n96, 119, 122, 164n14

Kvanig, Jonathan: *See* Alston

Latitudinarianism, 14–15, n52
Leibniz, Gottfried von 4, 5, 107
light, 9, 132–134, 158; Edwards' views on, 62, 65, 75, 82n59, 82n62, 87n118, 119–122, 124–125, 129–139, 161; eighteenth-century usage of, 119–120, 124–125, 131–132, 140n6; Separatists doctrine of, 150n120
Locke, John: See Enlightenment; See Lockean Philosophy
Lockean Philosophy, 103; Edwards' use of, 11n16, 29, 49n102, 63, 80n46, 94, 97, 101, 110n16, 156; *See also* Enlightenment

Marxism, 18, 164n14
Materialism, 8, 80n46, 94–95, 100, 107, 108n1, 108n3, 109n5, 109n11
Mather, Cotton, 5, 8, 57n186, 156; "The Christian Philosopher", 107
Mather, Increase, 52n134
Mechanism 84, 108n1
Metaphysics, 14, 95, 99, 102–103, 110n21, 112n45, 114n80, 115n99, 117n137, 119, 159–160
Miller, Perry, 10n14, 11n16–17, 13n38, 30, 32, 45n35, 46n59, 49n102, 49n107, 51n133, 78n23, 79n35, 80n46, 112n49, 142n31, 163n1
Modernity, 9, 18, 45n35, 91n151, 94, 121, 138, 156–157, 160, 163n1, 164n14
Mysticism, 29, 49n95, 93n166; Mystical Perception, 74–75, 93n168, 93n170

Native Americans, 30, 50n119, 57n183, 57n189, 162; Ministry to, 41–42, 57n186, 148n88, 167n24
Natural Theology, 125–128, 138, 145n65, 153n153, 160

Neonomianism, 38; *See also* Antinomianism; *See also* Arminianism
New Lights, 83n70, 84n77, 87n107; *See also* Antinomianism
Newton, Isaac, 2, 4, 6–7, 111n17, 119, 139n1; God and, 107, 140n6; Newtonian atomism, 94–96; Newtonian Physics, 100, 107, 116n106, 156
Niebuhr, Richard H., 18
Northampton, 4, 23–24, 27–30, 41, 46n59–60, 48n90–91, 51n133, 52n134; Revival in, 56n183, 78n89, 85n89, 167n23; *See also* Preaching, 127, 148n88

Old Lights, 83n70
original sin, 100

Paley, William, 107
Parrington, V.L., 11n16, 18, 163n4
Pascal, Blaise, 4
Postmodernism, 1, 9n2, 15n51, 94, 157, 160
prayer, 137, 139; Edwards' views on, 26–30, 48n87, 49n92, 55n167, 152n142; Practice, relation to, 23, 28–29, 42, 49n93, 59; Puritan notions of, 27
preaching, 22–24, 29, 34, 42, 57n189; Edwards', 8–9, 17, 22–26, 38, 41–42, 46n58, 48n89, 56n183, 117n137, 133, 156; Puritan, 17n66, 121, 51n132; Sower series, 23–25; Spurgeon, 51n132; See also Chauncy
"Preparation", spiritual: of the sinner, 26, 31, 50n122, 51n132, 117n137, 152n146; *See also* salvation; *See also* sin
Preston, John, 30, 50, 141n10; works, 50n113; *See also* Puritanism
Privatisation, 138, 159, 162

"The Progress of Society in Europe", 45n36; See Robertson, William
proto-Gnostic background to 2 Peter, 134
Puritanism, 3, 14n39, 17–18, 27, 29–30, 36, 39–40, 46n38, 49n95, 50n113–114, 55n154, 76n2, 80n46, 82n55, 85n77, 101, 107, 108n2, 110n16, 155–157; agreement with Bacon, 154n154; agreement with Hobbes, 109n10; concept of evil, 153n147; evangelism, 42; federal theology, 50n113; light, 132, 152n146; reason and knowledge, 120–122, 139, 154n154, 156; works, 50n113, 50n114
Puritans: See Puritanism; See John Preston

"Q", 28–29; See also Prayer

Rationalism, 6–9, 18, 109n12, 122–123, 126, 158; See also Rationalists
Rationalists, 72, 84n70, 130, 217
Reason, 1–2, 6, 31, 40, 142n37, 144n63–64, 148n87, 154n156; Edwards' use of to defend Biblical revelation, 60–62, 65, 102, 120–124, 146n72, 146n75, 157–161, 165n17
Redemption: work of, 20, 45n35; See also salvation
Reformed Theology: doctrine of assurance, 31, 36, 55n154, 89, 95; Edwards' identification with, 46n38; "light," 131–132; —, theological framework, 22, 30–31, 46n38, 89, 95–96, 98, 108n1, 109n10, 155, 157; —, view of revival, 45n27; epistemology, 153n153; gospel doctrine, 29; See also Edwards; See also justification by faith
Relativism, 74–5, 93n173, 94–6, 100, 105–6, 110n21, 114n73, 158, 160–1, 167n20

Remonstrance of 1610, The, 17; See also Arminianism
Revival, 8, 18–30, 42, 83n70, 162; causes, 18–19, 21–27, 48n84, 152n146; Edwards' Interpretation of, 19–21, 23–27, 42, 78n25; longevity of, 165n17; novelty vs. tradition, 22; various interpretations of, 18–22; prayer and, 26–27, 48n87; psychological aspects, 22, 26, 40; results, 21, 28, 85n89, 166n17; See also Great Awakening
Robertson, William, 20; "The Progress of Society in Europe", 45n36
Rousseau, 4, 119

Salvation, 17, 21–24, 37–39, 42, 50n116, 130–131; preparation for, 24–26, 30–33; revival and, 20–21; spiritual reality and, 24–26; See also Arminianism; See also Deism; See also Halfway Covenant; See also Separatists; See also Neonomianism
Second Great Awakening, 20
Secularism, 18–19, 44n21, 44n24, 95, 159, 162, 164n11, 164n12, 165n15; See also Spiritual Reality
Sermons: See The Bible; See Bibliography; See Jonathan Edwards
Separatists, 36, 40–41, 53n136, 53n138, 54n150, 83n65, 133, 150n120; See also Frothingham
Sin, 23, 27; Edwards' views on, 22–25, 31, 37–38, 49n89, 70–71, 100–101, 128–129, 138, 151n132
Soteriological, 17, 130–131, 163n3
Spurgeon, Charles, 51n132
Spiritual Reality, 23, 25–26, 29, 39–42; Edwards' preaching of, 22–26
Stockbridge, 23, 30, 41, 127; See also Native Americans
Stoddard, Solomon, 8, 31–32, 34–35, 51n134, 53n137, 79n30, 86n95; Stoddardeanism, 34, 51n130, 52n135

Stout, Harry S., 18, 48n84
Swift, Jonathan, *Gulliver's Travels*, 113n73

Theology: Covenant, 17, 29–31, 50n113, 51n130; Edwards and, 32–33, 38–39, 43n6; Natural, 125–128, 136–138, 139n3, 145n65, 148n87, 153n153, 160–161; Puritan, 13n39, 27, 31, 40–41, 50n113–114, 55n154, 80n46, 120–121, 132, 152n146, 156; Revealed, 121, 128–129, 132, 136–137, 148n87, 161; Stoddard, 31–34, 51n130, 51n134, 52n135, 53n137, 79n30, 86n95, 130; *See also* Chauncy; *See also* Puritanism; *See also* Reformed Theology
Tindal, 124, 140n5, 143n59, 144n62; *See also* Deism
Trinity, 101–102

Unitarianism, 39–40; *See also*, Chauncy
United States of America, 136; Puritans in, 41; *See also* Native Americans; *See also* American Pragmatism

Voltaire. *See* Enlightenment

Ward, W.R., 19, 83n67
Weber, Max, 18
Wesley, John, 46n43, 59, 76n11, 80n38, 85n89
Whitefield, George, 18–19, 28, 152n146; *See also* Great Awakening
Wittgenstein, "Philosophical Investigations", 74
Wutternberg, 4

Yale College, 141n9; *Lux et Veritas*, 119–120, 140n8